transforming schools

D0421270

Also available from Bloomsbury

Creative Educational Leadership Jacquie Turnbull

Effective Teaching and Learning in Practice Don Skinner

Exploring the School Leadership Landscape Peter Earley

transforming schools

creativity, critical reflection, communication, collaboration

Miranda Jefferson and Michael Anderson

Bloomsbury Academic
An imprint of Bloomsbury Publishing Plc

BLOOMSBURY
LONDON · OXFORD · NEW YORK · NEW DELHI · SYDNEY

Bloomsbury Academic

An imprint of Bloomsbury Publishing Plc

50 Bedford Square	1385 Broadway
London	New York
WC1B 3DP	NY 10018
UK	USA

www.bloomsbury.com

BLOOMSBURY and the Diana logo are trademarks of Bloomsbury Publishing Plc

First published 2017

© Miranda Jefferson and Michael Anderson, 2017

Miranda Jefferson and Michael Anderson have asserted their right under the Copyright, Designs and Patents Act, 1988, to be identified as Authors of this work.

All rights reserved. No part of this publication may be reproduced or transmitted in any form or by any means, electronic or mechanical, including photocopying, recording, or any information storage or retrieval system, without prior permission in writing from the publishers.

No responsibility for loss caused to any individual or organization acting on or refraining from action as a result of the material in this publication can be accepted by Bloomsbury or the author.

British Library Cataloguing-in-Publication Data

A catalogue record for this book is available from the British Library.

ISBN:	HB:	978-1-4742-3263-0
	PB:	978-1-4742-3262-3
	ePDF:	978-1-4742-3261-6
	ePub:	978-1-4742-3260-9

Library of Congress Cataloging-in-Publication Data

Names: Jefferson, Miranda, author. | Anderson, Michael, 1969- author.
Title: Transforming schools : creativity, critical reflection, communication
and collaboration / Miranda Jefferson and Michael Anderson.
Description: London, UK ; New York, NY : Bloomsbury Academic, an imprint of
Bloomsbury Publishing, Plc, [2017] | Includes bibliographical references.
Identifiers: LCCN 2016028767 (print) | LCCN 2016030900 (ebook) | ISBN
9781474232630 (hardback) | ISBN 9781474232623 (pbk.) | ISBN 9781474232616
(epdf) | ISBN 9781474232609 (epub)
Subjects: LCSH: Transformative learning. | Critical pedagogy. | School
improvement programs.
Classification: LCC LC1100 .J44 2017 (print) | LCC LC1100 (ebook) | DDC
371.2/07—dc23
LC record available at https://lccn.loc.gov/2016028767

Cover image © Noelle Smith / Getty Images

Typeset by RefineCatch Limited, Bungay, Suffolk
Printed and bound in India

Transforming Schools *is dedicated to all the students, teachers and school leaders who have helped us learn the real meaning of transformation through their creativity, critical reflection, communication and collaboration.*

Contents

Figures and tables

Figures

Tables

Foreword

And did the Countenance Divine,
Shine forth upon our clouded hills?
And was Jerusalem builded here,
Among these dark Satanic Mills?

William Blake

The dark satanic mills that William Blake writes about in his famous poem *Jerusalem* are often thought of as the factories that were beginning to not only blot the English landscape but were to sell millions into the servitude of the industrial age. Yet there was another factory designed at the same time: The school. Schools were built on the same premise as factories. They had top-down management systems, centralized planning, standardized testing and clearly defined outcomes; their value determined by the quality of their product. The product in mind is still a ready, compliant and willing consumer of goods. By understanding that schooling was originally designed on the factory model, and built on the thinking of another century's engagement with a now out-dated technology, we can recognize the importance of transforming schools for different times.

Perhaps, however, the greatest tragedy facing schooling at present is that schools are being rapidly transformed, back to the dated factory model of the 1800s. The promise of the transformative progressive ideas of John Dewey and others has been attacked by what Pasi Sahlberg describes as the Global Education Reform Movement (The GERM). He argues that, like a virulent virus, global elites are deliberately undermining the significant and important progressive reforms of the twentieth century so as to plunge education back to Dickensian factory conditions. Education in almost every country in the world is subject to the grip of education 'reform', which is diminishing public schooling, promoting privatization and destroying teacher unionism. It aims to produce the worker who is only smart enough to read instructions but not critical enough to challenge them.

And nowhere has that more dramatically happened than on Blake's green and pleasant land. Public education has been systematically, ruthlessly and thoroughly dismantled in England. It is in the process of being academized to death. Rich, broad curriculum designed to create critical, creative citizens has been deliberately replaced by mechanistic functionalist outcomes. Nick Gibb, the English Minister of Education, admonished teachers this year for their lack of the teaching of facts. His predecessor, Michael Gove, had already called for a return to rote learning, and the supremacy of external examinations.

Blake might have lamented

And all the Arts of Life they changed into the Arts of Death in Albion

As global education companies realize obscene profits from their international testing regimes, the notion of schools as factories is replaced by the idea of schools as competing small businesses. Students become merely units of potential capital, commodities to be traded, bought and sold over the international education market.

The purposes of these reforms are deliberate and coincide with the rapid growth of inequality and the emergence of the super rich, who increasingly want to transform schools for their own ideological agendas. They have hijacked education reform and transformation to meet the needs and desires of global capital. The threat to schooling by these overly rich reformers is dire. The gloss of technology to be found in many classrooms doesn't hide the newly deadened curriculum and the global push for unthinking consumer citizens to be fed and lulled to sleep on a diet of reality television and celebrity culture. It is imperative that educators embrace the possibilities of other ways of conceptualizing education.

So this book, which talks about transforming schools, should be treated with great suspicion. At a time when schools are already transforming, losing at an accelerating rate all the saving graces of the progressive reforms of the mid to late twentieth century, another book about school transformation should invite enduring scepticism. Fortunately this is not another meta-analysis that proves the superhero teacher can fix the failings of the capitalist system, or enjoins teachers to be more effective. Thankfully it is a book that can be seen as part of an antidote to the GERM.

What this book offers is a compelling argument for continued belief and hope for schooling. The authors offer a counter reformation, another way of conceiving education that doesn't merely return us to what we have lost in the recent reforms but might move schools finally beyond being a factory. Their offering of creativity, critical reflection, communication and collaboration is a breath of fresh air in comparison with the four Cs of the GERM: choice, capitalism, conformity and consumerism.

Miranda and Michael remind us of the central importance of critical reflection, not just in schools but in life itself. In that spirit of critical reflection I would suggest that there is one C that makes sense of the four Cs they offer as necessary to bring about transformation. I refer to compassion. The world we live in now sees the displacement and misery of human beings as a result of conflict at a level unknown in human history. We live at a time of growing radicalization and extremism of young people attracted to dehumanizing ideologies. It is a time of growing entropy and hopelessness in the face of an all-powerful global capitalist system that does everything in its power to maintain a feudal grip on the poor and disenfranchised.

Critical reflection, creativity, communication and collaboration are vital in the politics of school transformation. But they must be fed by compassion and a commitment to social action. Paulo Freire reminds us that the purpose of education is to make us more fully human. Critical pedagogy compels a commitment to social justice. The end purpose of the transformation of schools cannot be about improving test scores and international test ranking, or producing better equipped and more compliant workers, the end goal must be a more socially just world.

This book powerfully reminds us that the transformation of schools must also be about how we transform the crisis that is our world. It is about recognizing schooling as a political activity that can either sustain the criminal injustices of current life or is part of the great counter-revolution needed to allow all humans to live lives of dignity.

Peter O'Connor, The University of Auckland, New Zealand
May 2016

Acknowledgements

We would like to acknowledge all of our friends, family and colleagues that have assisted us in the creation of this book. We would also like to thank the staff at Bloomsbury for supporting this idea to fruition.

The authors would like to acknowledge that the following figures remain the property of 4C Transformative Learning and are reproduced here with their permission:

Figure 3.2 The Learning Prism

Figure 3.3 The Learning Disposition Wheel

Figure 3.4 The Transformative Spinning Wheel

Figure 4.1 The pedagogy diagram

Figure 7.2 A model for collaborative communication pedagogy

Figure 9.1 Leading transformations in the 4Cs approach

The designs of the creativity cascade, critical reflection crucible, communication crystal and collaboration circle.

Some parts from Chapter 1 have been adapted from:

Anderson, M. (2014). The challenge of post-normality to drama education and applied theatre. *Research in Drama Education*, 19(1), 110–120.

Introduction

It is probably a widespread fault of authors to think that they live in critical times of change. The opening pages of books on education (and this book is no exception) talk of 'waves of change' that are about to crash on humanity. Heraclitus famously said, around 500 BCE, 'there is nothing permanent except change'. So, in a sense, there is nothing new about us claiming that we are in a state of change. We think we have reached a critical point of disconnect between the way communities are changing and the way schools are largely not changing. We are calling here for realignment between changes we see in the world around us, and the way schools need to respond to meet the challenge of this change. Ironically, the changes we are calling for in this book are not necessarily new. Educators such as Paulo Freire, Michael Apple, John Dewey and Maxine Greene have been promoting creativity, critical reflection, communication and collaboration (the 4Cs) for at least a century. Yet change to the ways schooling works is slow.

We have called this book *Transforming Schools* because we feel a feature of education currently is the relative intransigence of large and cumbersome school systems to make the required changes. The current political climate seems to make systems so risk averse that changes are most likely at the school rather than system level.

Many educators before us have called for the 4Cs to be more centrally embedded in schools and learning. There is, however, a gap between the aspirations reflected in these discussions and what actually happens at a school, teacher and student level. This book aims to close that gap. Our intention is to demonstrate the change we need can only take place if we recalibrate, reorientate and reconnect learning in schools with the 4Cs. We think this will become possible when schools have clear and practical strategies that can be applied to classrooms across the curriculum.

The coherence makers that we discuss throughout this book (Creativity Cascade, Critical Reflection Crucible, Communication Crystal and Collaboration Circle) are our approach to closing that particular gap. The structures are products of research and practical application in real schools from early childhood to secondary education. The learning approaches contained in these pages emerge from the continuous transformation process in several schools that we have worked in. The strategies contained here are designed to provide a simple yet rich way to reconceptualize learning. Following are some caveats and notes that may assist you as you navigate this book.

We come from arts education backgrounds. This experience will become clear throughout the book. Both of us have also been involved in the last decade in translating strategies and approaches from arts education into other areas. We have worked in teacher education, business education, early childhood, science education and mathematics education. This work has forced us to think broadly about the strategies and approaches we understand and to apply them with integrity to new contexts. This book is a product of our experience applying teaching strategies across the curiculum.

Even though the book has the rather grand title of *Transforming Schools*, it cannot cover everything that relates to school learning. In this sense it is better understood as the beginning of a conversation rather than an encyclopaedic treatment of learning. This book is written for those in education who have become weary or frustrated with learning and teaching in schools that does not meet the needs of twenty-first-century learners. This book will provide evidence and inspiration for doing schooling differently. As we have discussed, the strategies and approaches we have mentioned here emerge from work in real schools. We have made several references throughout this book to examples of practice that we have been part of in schools. Sometimes we have changed the details of the examples we use to preserve the anonymity of students, teachers and schools. At times we have used a *bricolage*[1] of schools and experiences to make our point and for the sake of brevity. These situations are however all based in our experiences of schools, teachers and education. While we have changed some of the details, the substantive features of the cases remain the same.

There are several ways to read this book. It is designed to be read in chapter sequence but can be revisited chapter by chapter as you focus on collaboration or leadership (for instance). It should be understood, however, that the 4Cs are an approach to holistic learning. In our view schools will not transform if this approach to school change is approached in a piecemeal way. All of the 4Cs are mutually dependant on one another. In other words you cannot teach and learn creativity without critical reflection, communication and collaboration.

Transforming Schools is structured so that the initial chapters set up the rationale and frameworks for the 4Cs learning approach (Chapters 1–4). Chapters 5–8 outline our approach to creativity, critical reflection, communication and collaboration in depth, including details of the coherence makers that frame that learning. Chapters 9 and 10 extend some of these discussions to explain how 4Cs learning can be implemented in schools for transformation.

You will notice that in most of the chapters throughout this book we have provided a section with the term 'road map' in the heading. These sections are designed to provide a series of suggestions for the way forward for schools interested in implementing the 4Cs. For some reason it is very difficult for humans to imagine a future in ways other than how it is at the moment. For instance our ancestors thought human mechanized flight unlikely or unwise and even in a more banal way we find it difficult to imagine it raining if we are in the middle of bright sunshine, even if the forecasts predict a storm. This difficulty is also prevalent when educators consider schools and schooling. Part of the reason we have articulated in these road maps a way of navigating forward is to differentiate ourselves from those who say 'something' needs to be done without any suggestion how 'something' might occur. These road maps are more like a 'mud map' (a mud map is a sketchy indication) rather than a detailed cartographic representation of the way ahead. We have deliberately set out broad parameters for our road maps to allow for the inclusion of diverse local contexts.

You may also notice throughout this book that we use personal stories of our experiences in education to illustrate or introduce our arguments. As this is a co-authored book we will make clear who is speaking by referring to ourselves in the first instance in the third person (e.g. 'Miranda') and then for the rest of the story in the first person (e.g. 'I' or 'my').

We have provided here a précis of the chapters so you can see at a glance the way the book is organized.

Chapter 1: Transforming schools: A model for twenty-first-century learners and schools

This chapter sets out the issues that our society currently faces: chaos, contradiction and complexity (Sardar, 2010). In this chapter we make a case for creativity, critical reflection, communication and collaboration being crucial to remaking our schools and helping our students proactively respond to postnormal times. This chapter argues for a revolutionary transition of schooling that moves them from places of knowledge transmission and/or acquisition to places in which co-creativity, ingenuity and imagination are central to learning.

Chapter 2: Freeing learning for transformation

In this chapter we discuss the ideas of critical pedagogy as an underpinning for school transformation. Transformation is the notion that to change we have to transform mindsets and habits of mind (Mezirow, 2009). Transformative learning requires being critically reflective of our assumptions and the assumptions of others, and to take action on our transformed perspective. True to the precepts of critical pedagogy, this transformational work is informed and sustained by praxis, that is, both theory and practice. We explore aspects of critical pedagogy and transformative learning and how they inform our understanding of the 4Cs and the 4Cs approach.

Chapter 3: Understanding learning in the 4Cs approach

In the 4Cs approach we introduce coherence makers to illuminate and harmonize the complexity of learning and the 4C capabilities: creativity, critical reflection, communication and collaboration. The coherence makers are designed to harness and guide student and teacher imaginings, questionings and discoveries about learning processes and the 4C capabilities and interconnections. This chapter includes the Learning Disposition Wheel, which focuses on and synthesizes what we need to develop to be a learner.

Chapter 4: Pedagogy and the 4Cs

In Chapter 4 we explore how the 4Cs approach to pedagogy is critical to empowered learners and human agency. We examine how pedagogy to develop the 4Cs means:

- really understanding and knowing learners and their needs,
- treating teaching and learning as a creative process,
- really understanding how learning is generated,
- developing self-regulated, self-directed autonomous learners.

Chapter 5: Creativity

In this chapter we imagine creativity as a standard expectation of schooling. To do this we discuss the problems that persist with creative learning that prevent its widespread adoption, explore some of the evidence for creative learning being critical to schooling and present a coherence maker for creativity learning in schools: 'The Creativity Cascade'. We argue that a full understanding of creativity in schools is critical because we see it as a game changer in the lives of young people and as critical to aligning schools with the expectations of the twenty-first century. As with the other three Cs, creativity overlaps, interacts and is dependent upon critical reflection, communication and collaboration.

Chapter 6: Critical reflection

Fundamentally, critical reflection relies on a deep and broad analysis that makes transparent each learner's presuppositions and assumptions about knowledge and power. The chapter begins by considering the role of social and emotional learning as the foundation of critical reflection and then explores the implications for schooling. This chapter considers how schools can become places of critical reflection that generate productive action. As a way of demonstrating how this can work in practice we introduce 'The Critical Reflection Crucible' coherence maker.

Chapter 7: Communication

Communication begins with the body and the voice and extends to representations and technologies that are written, visual, aural, tactile and multimodal. Communication is linked to identity formation, relationships, power, culture and agency. This chapter argues that communication is intrinsic to human thought, self-concept and development. We introduce the 'Communication Crystal' coherence maker that scaffolds an approach to understanding and developing communication skills. A 'crystal' prism with its many surfaces and angles is used to describe communication because, like a crystal, communication is multifaceted, and refracts and reflects messaging in myriad ways.

Chapter 8: Collaboration

A premise of the 4Cs approach is that through collaboration humans become their fuller selves. Through the mutuality of true collaboration we expand who we are. To achieve such beneficial mutuality however requires the navigation of complex dynamics in communication and relationships. The chapter examines the dynamics of effective student collaborative learning, teacher capacity building, and staff and leadership collaborations to transform schools for the future. We have synthesized collaborative processes into a coherence maker: 'Collaboration Circles'. It is a supporting structure or scaffold to frame how collaboration can be learnt and facilitated.

Chapter 9: Transformative leadership for twenty-first-century schools

This chapter explores leading transformation thorough the 4Cs. It presents a model for transformational change that integrates and enacts the 4Cs and makes school change achievable. The research and our experience suggests that while leadership is critical, leaders alone cannot achieve systematic and sustainable change in schools. Nonetheless, leaders and leadership teams are critical to making change happen in schools through the application of the 4Cs. This chapter also discusses the role of vision, culture, structure, strategy and integration, partnerships, research and evaluation in transformative leadership.

Chapter 10: Freeing learning: Implications for transforming schools through the 4Cs

The final chapter will bring together all of the theoretical and practical arguments of the book to make a case for why change is required to transform schools and to free learning. It examines the implications for transforming schools through the 4Cs. This chapter will argue that this change is not only a theoretical possibility; it is essential for the growth of a democratic, critical and just society.

Conclusion

When we began this book we understood that it was an ambitious undertaking. The current climate of risk aversion and system intransigence has left us with many schools that will not meet the needs of young people as our society changes. We may be ambitious in writing here about school change but the courage to make change a reality sits squarely with school leaders, teachers and others in school systems. We never claim any of these changes are easy (quite the opposite). We have, however, in our discussions with teachers and school leaders noticed a readiness for a different way – a way that connects with the radical hope that inspired many of us to become teachers in the first place. We are experiencing critical changes in our society and our communities. We hope this book makes a contribution to developing schools relevant to those changes. But beyond relevance we hope this book makes some small contribution to making our communities more democratic, tolerant and engaged through putting creativity, critical reflection, communication and collaboration at the centre of learning.

Note

1 A *bricolage* is a pieced together or composite picture.

Transforming schools

A model for twenty-first-century learners and schools

1

Michael had a chance encounter the other day with one of the teachers who taught him at high school:

He was a terrific teacher. In a school that was declining at the time he taught with excitement, compassion and joy. He shocked the students in his senior English class by reading the particularly sensuous bits of Thomas Hardy's *Tess of the D'Urbervilles* so we would sense the imagery and the beauty of the language. He got us to build trenches out of desks to understand the physicality of Wilfred Owen's poetry detailing the horrors of World War I. He taught me early on in his career, and he was an inspiration. He encouraged me to think about teaching as a serious career choice.

I saw Peter Wentworth again the other day on a cold Saturday in the Blue Mountains near Sydney as he was shopping. We talked, as you do, about what we had been up to (he is now a member of the senior executive at a large school) and then I asked the question 'Do you miss the classroom?' There was no pause. 'No! I am sick of all the box ticking and all the form filling – I think we have lost the art of teaching.' I said goodbye and went on my way wondering how we could regain the art of teaching. How we could renew, reinvent and rediscover schooling for the twenty-first century. Of course I have often wondered about this, but my casual chat with Peter Wentworth crystallized the problem for me. This chance encounter clarified the question that is at the heart of this book:

How can we regain the art of teaching and in so doing transform our curriculum, student learning and ultimately our society?

Engaging with the 'big picture'

This chapter sets out the big picture as we (and others) currently see it. While the big picture may not seem relevant to some individual schools, teachers or even leaders, we think the crosswinds of change in society, economics, media, technology and other sectors are changing the way we live and that has direct relevance for each school (and each individual teacher, student and leader in each of those schools). Schools (individually) and schooling can choose to be part of that change or to become sidelined, irrelevant and ultimately marginalized. The alternative we outline in this book is to engage and transform to meet the challenges of the new reality head on. Our response to this challenge is to concentrate on explicitly teaching those skills, understandings and knowledge that will directly build social capital for our students and prepare them for the challenges of the twenty-first century. In this chapter (and in the remainder of this book) we argue that creativity, critical reflection, communication and collaboration are crucial to reframing, reimagining and remaking our schools and helping our students proactively respond to postnormal times. This chapter argues for a revolutionary transition of schooling that moves schools from places of knowledge transmission and/or acquisition to places in which co-creativity, ingenuity and imagination are at the beating heart of learning. So what is the case for change?

Renewing schooling: The case for change

There is much that we feel needs to change about schools and schooling. It feels to us like we have been investing over and over in an institution (schools and schooling) and we are terrified to change that investment for fear of confronting the reality that we have squandered so much in the past – this is known in economics as 'the sunk investment' hypothesis. Of course not all of this investment is lost. Schools and schooling continue to grow, change and evolve. Yet the demands of the twenty-first century make the changes seem more urgent, more imminent. As Keating (2009) argues, our society's wellbeing depends on our schools' ability to change and to imagine a future, 'but in doing so it depends upon the past. It [education] has a role in advancing the economic future of the society, but it cannot do this unless it also underpins the social fabric of the society' (p. 4).

For many teachers and students the persistence of high stakes testing, standardized curriculum and corporate management models (Sahlberg, 2014, p.174) removes the potential for deep learning (or in Peter Wentworth's terms 'box ticking'). Our world has seen massive changes in the last three decades. The advent of globalization and the technological revolution have presented opportunities as well as the disruption and fragmentation of communities. To some extent these changes have destabilized the 'old certainties' our institutions (including schools) used to rely upon.

The problem with schooling today

We would like to begin by identifying some of the issues we currently see in our schools. We want to acknowledge however, that schools are the most likely sites for societal change. They have been the primary site for community cohesion and creative productivity and still remain perhaps the most positive force in our society. Schools are storehouses of compassion and hope. In our experience, teachers are overwhelmingly passionate, engaged and professional and want to see schools changing to meet the needs of the twenty-first century. There are substantial resources of commitment and energy in schools generally, and teachers specifically, that make the changes we imagine achievable. We all need to work to change the outmoded structures of schools and replace them with new ways of doing school that are a 'fit' for these times. These new structures will allow students to face the challenges of the twenty-first century with confidence. We have the resources in organizations, we just require the will to make the transformations in response to shifting conditions in our communities and our societies. So what are the prevailing conditions (the big picture) in our society that demand change in our schools?

The challenge of postnormality

The Western world is moving uneasily from one uncertainty to the next. In our nations the ravages of the Global Financial Crisis have brought into sharp focus the disparities between the rich and the poor. Additionally the issues of poverty and disease that many in the world face seems to lack effective global leadership to address the massive inequity in resources might be reimagined. The overwhelming greed of bankers and corporations has led to 'austerity', which means for citizens of Greece, Ireland, Spain and many other countries, poverty. At the same time those responsible for these corporate crimes have remained largely untouched, untarnished and in many cases rewarded. While there is nothing new about corporate greed, contemporary capitalism and hyperactive market economies have created globalized and networked economic misery. This crisis of confidence and crisis of trust has developed in the midst of other crises: the crisis of climate change, the crisis of food security and the crisis of mass refugee movements as a result of conflicts of various kinds. The rapid exchange of information that technology facilitates has created a maelstrom of crises that are complex, contradictory and confusing. As Marshall and Picou suggest: 'The critical question is not how do we reduce uncertainty, but rather how do we make better decisions in a world of irreducible uncertainties?' (2008, p. 230). For educators the question becomes how do we manage learning and teaching in a context that has moved beyond the certainties of normality?

Beyond 'normality'

The normality paradigm is an inadequate and to a large extent discredited starting point for education and schools. Education needs to take account of the prevailing conditions of postnormality (chaos, complexity and contradiction) to equip young people for their rapidly changing future. Yet schools are almost universally focused on assumptions that arise from normality: hierarchy, testing, standardization (Sahlberg, 2014), cause and effect, economic growth, industrial prosperity (Darling-Hammond, 2004). The testing and reporting regimes imposed on schools by governments in western economies such as Australia and the United Kingdom have created a market-driven schooling system that is much more about training for rapidly disappearing types of work than it is about imagined futures. In these systems economic gaps and skill shortages provide the impetus for change and yet they remain short and narrow sighted. Thomson, Lingard and Wrigley (2012) suggest that governments and education bureaucracies are driven by making students in schools more efficient in the new globalized economy; not by an 'imaginary of a better and more socially just future for all, but of a more competitive economy, powered by improved human capital and better skills' (p. 1).

The old models of schooling are at best inadequate and, at worst, failing. Postnormality presents challenges to all participants in education to reconsider the old 'normalities'. It provides an opportunity for us to re-imagine what schooling could be in a 'post-fact' world (Manjoo, 2011) where students require the skills and understandings to confront the contradictions, chaos and complexities of the future.

A postnormal tomorrow?

If we are moving into a state of contradictions, chaos and complexity there are profound implications for schools and schooling. Before we examine these implications in depth we would like to explore exactly what postnormality looks like in practice. According to Ziauddin Sardar (2010) the postnormal age is: 'characterised by uncertainty, rapid change, realignment of power, upheaval and chaotic behaviour' (p. 435). This is a moment of transition where the old ways seem outmoded and new ways seem unreliable, unimaginable or impossible. Sardar argues that the combination of complexity, confusion and contradiction has fuelled a shift from normality to postnormality, sweeping away the institutions and understandings society has clung to for thousands of years and replacing them with uncertainty. Sardar argues that this condition is different from other shifts in history as the combination of ubiquitous networked systems facilitates rapid and chaotic change. This is seen in the interaction between several sectors of society. As Ringland (2010) argues, economic models have been in decline long before the GFC struck: 'concerns about energy, environmental and security issues, food price increases, growing economic and financial imbalances and asset price inflation should have suggested that all was not well with this model' (p. 633).

While financial crises are not new, the rebalancing of labour and resource economics from the West to the East means that the business as usual model has become vulnerable. Ringland (2010) argues that we are in for some difficult times as we adjust to postnormality: 'Global systems issues – such as environmental change, but also international law and finance, access to raw materials and the management of intellectual property – all require the rich nations to sacrifice some of their power. This combination of power rebalancing and an institutional vacuum implies that the next decade will be a turbulent one' (p. 634).

While science and technology has driven economic growth in many economies, there has been a less welcome rise in the side effects of these technologies. As Marshall and Picou (2008) argue: 'these same advances tend to manufacture environmental problems that are increasingly complex, large-scale, and destructive' (p. 243). There is a paradoxical bind here. Society has become reliant on the network and market economies but the combined fruits of both of these are often poisonous (e.g. pollution, deforestation, climate change, global financial crises). The certainties of 'facts' and 'normality' have been replaced by societal conditions that Sardar nominates in a postnormal world: complexity, contradiction and chaos. The first condition of postnormality that Sardar identifies is complexity.

Complexity

One of the most compelling demonstrations of postnormal complexity are the ongoing 'wars' on 'terrorism', whether they are state sanctioned or initiated by organizations such as Hamas or ISIS. These conflicts are often in response to an abhorrent act such as a terror strike or a chemical weapons attack on civilian populations. There are however complex forces at work as the networked international community assesses the cost of action and/or non-action on the global community. Morality in these cases is shaped and driven at least in part by energy security and the economic pressures that higher oil prices bring to bear on local economies. The networking and linking of these geopolitical and economic factors integrated with the rapid delivery of news coverage brings new urgency and complexities to bear on decision-makers and creates tensions for political leaders.

In one of the main theatres of the war on terror, Afghanistan, the Eisenhower Study Group (2011) records the civilian death toll as 210,000 in addition to the 2,996 who were killed in the 9/11 attacks (Plumer, 2013). These wars on terror with their theatres in Orlando, New York, London, Bali, Afghanistan and Iraq have taken an enormous toll in human life and human hope. They are complex, confusing and chaotic conflicts. In the face of these postnormal conflicts how can individuals and communities untangle the issues and make clear and wise decisions? The attacks of 9/11 remain abhorrent but do they justify the torture and civilian deaths that have been the legacy of the West's war on terror? This 'war' seems in some ways more complex than many others from our past. And perhaps this complexity is a contributing factor to Sardar's next C, chaos.

Chaos

A new brand of chaos has become more prevalent in our mostly civil societies. In 2005 in Australia we saw the largest ever race riot being coordinated on mobile phones (Goggin, 2006). Racist anarchy reigned, the peaceful seaside Australian suburb of Cronulla exploded in the most extreme and chaotic racist violence seen in years. In 2011 in the UK in Hackney, Brixton, Chingford, Bristol, Manchester, Birmingham and Liverpool, chaotic riots also stained the landscape (Baker, 2009) and then again in the USA in Baltimore in 2015. Social media propelled the suddenness and ferocity of the chaos. As Stephanie Baker points out, riots in the UK are not novel but 'New social media played a key role in organising the recent riots with smart phones giving those with access to these technologies the power to network socially and to incite collective disorder' (2012, p. 45). Violent protest in the postnormal world is organized, coordinated and delivered through digitally networked crowds for the insatiable screen-based audience. The complexity and chaos invariably produce regular contradictions in the postnormal world.

Contradictions

Sardar's third C is contradictions. As he says, we now live in: 'A complex, networked world, with countless competing interests and ideologies, designs and desires, behaving chaotically, can do little more than throw up contradictions. . . . It is the natural product of numerous antagonistic social and cultural networks jostling for dominance' (2010, p. 439). A vivid example of this contradictory state is the mismatch between research evidence and public policy. This is particularly prevalent in the education sector and acute in teacher education policy. We know of the importance of sustained, supported teacher preparation (Darling-Hammond, 2004) that is grounded in robust theory that relates directly to practice. Yet we see governments in the UK, Australia and the US delivering programmes where six weeks' training makes you 'ready to teach'. Even though the evidence indicates these programmes have high attrition rates and are not necessarily effective (Rice, Volkoff and Dulfer, 2015), governments continue to invest in these schemes.

Another example of the contradiction of our times in education is the large-scale testing regimes that have become prevalent. We know from the overwhelming weight of research that large and frequent testing does not sustainably enhance student learning. Yet testing regimes persist in schools, which effectively makes the goal of learning, testing. As Thomson and colleagues argue: 'In stark contrast to this imaginary of a socially just world, and often driven by PISA[1] envy, educational policymakers mobilise various forms of audit and intervention designed to produce measurable increases in "performance" at system, school and student levels' (Thomson and colleagues, 2012, p. 2).

In these cases, fundamentally contradictory pieces of evidence become policy and practice. These contradictions have become so entrenched that often the practices go on largely unchallenged. Contradictory policy is allowed to stand because in postnormal times society seems to have lost its ability to discern or trust 'normal' sources of evidence.

So Sardar's postnormal conditions (complexity, chaos and contradiction) provide a dramatic context for the changes that face our society and our schools. It begs the question of educators: What needs to change to help young people interpret these issues authentically? And what skills will need to be promoted to allow young people to respond? Beyond the general context of postnormality there are pressing issues that relate directly to the way Western education systems are currently doing schooling and they relate to:

- schooling and the future of work,
- the needs of young people in the twenty-first century, and
- testing and the diversity of learning.

Understanding these issues and how they have shaped the schooling system we have today will help us rethink and redesign our schools for twenty-first-century learning.

Schooling and the future of work

In 2013 a team from Oxford University headed up by Karl Frey and Michael Osborne undertook a study called: 'The future of employment: how susceptible are jobs to computerisation?' (2013a). In this research study they investigated 702 different occupations to see how technology would change the kinds of jobs we do now. They also examined the workforce impact of technology such as cloud computing, automation and big data mining. They made some fascinating findings. They found that 47 per cent of workers in the US are currently at risk. In 2015 a report by the Committee for Economic Development Australia found a similar trend (CEDA, 2015). Critically jobs that do not require social interaction and that have low levels of creativity are more likely to be displaced by automation (Frey and Osborne, 2013b, p. 44).

So what can schools do to rethink how we prepare students for the world of work? Frey and Osborne make this finding: 'For workers to win the race, however, they will have to acquire *creative* and *social skills* [our emphasis] (Frey and Osborne, 2013b, p. 44). Labour market economists in at least two separate research studies find that almost half the jobs that currently exist are likely to be eliminated within a decade or so. By the time a child who is 5 years old in school today turns 16 half of the jobs we are preparing her for won't be there according to this growing body of research.

So maybe this is a massive wake-up call. This is a call to action that doesn't only encourage, but demands we rethink what we do at school. If one of the purposes of learning is to prepare young people to be economically literate and independent these studies alone show change is upon us and we need to act swiftly.

Changing schools

In our view the education system already has raw materials for change: skilled teachers, effective leaders and talented students. All that is required is the political will to make change a reality in our schools. In this book we want to bridge the gap between aspiration and classroom reality. We will describe pedagogical frameworks that can make transformation a reality. In all subjects and at all stages of schooling there are teachers and/or leaders who understand the power of creativity, critical reflection, communication and collaboration (the 4Cs) for learning. We need, however, to communicate clearly and coherently to our colleagues, school leaders and policy makers why the 4Cs are so critical and foundational to transforming schools.

We need to persuade our colleagues and communities about the need to reconfigure schools around the 4Cs and communicate what 'achievement' looks like in a twenty-first-century world. We need to transform our schooling system from a predominantly test-driven transmission model of learning to a place where creativity, collaboration, communication and critical reflection are central to learning. These are the capacities that Sardar (2010), Frey and Osborne (2013b) and others argue will be crucial to surviving and thriving in the mid to late twenty-first century.

Although critical, schooling is not only about 'training' young people for economic sustainability; the skills that contribute to young people engaging with the world of work are the same skills that will help them live life to the full as twenty-first-century citizens. Wyn (2015) argues that education can shift to recognize this necessity and to help young people 'be' and 'know' the realities and challenges of a twenty-first-century world. It is to assist them to build: 'capacities to navigate complexity and to contribute to a sustainable society. Education is about the production of ways of being and knowing – not just about sets of skills and areas of knowledge' (Wyn, 2015, p. 20). One critical feature of this transformation is to make schools places that are relevant to the students who pass through them.

Schools and the needs of young people

Schools are places where most young people spend most of their youth in economically developed countries. On average a student will spend 12,000 hours (Nakhid, 2014) of their life in schooling. So as a community we have a profound responsibility to ensure this massive human and financial investment is not wasted. Given the time and effort invested in schooling you might think that schools are focused squarely on the needs of young people above all other priorities. You might also be forgiven for thinking that the future economic needs of young people, their needs as future adult citizens, the ways young people learn and the interests of young people would be critical in the ways we design and deliver schooling. You would, however, for the most part, be mistaken. As Johanna Wyn argues (2015), schooling can be an experience that takes little account of the diversity and agency of young people: 'Positioning young people in a passive decision-making role with regard to learning, having an inflexible approach to age, and failing to tailor education to the diversity of young people do not make a good fit with the demands of living in late modernity' (p. 21).

The way some schools approach and position knowledge is a marker of how much change is required. Students have the opportunity to access knowledge from multiple sources in ways that would have been incomprehensible only one or two generations ago. So how has schooling responded to this explosion of access? Have schools also changed in response to the ways knowledge is accessed? In some ways the answer to this is yes and no. Teachers individually have attempted, often without informed systemic support, to make changes to their teaching but the systems they work within, for the most part, remain resolutely stuck in fixed forms of curriculum and learning that downplay choice and still privilege the transmission of knowledge to students who have little say (at least in the junior years of schooling) about what they are being taught. While there may be a strong interest from individual teachers and school leaders in changing learning, many of the structures in schooling strongly militate against transformation.

Change, whether we like it or not, is upon us and perhaps provides an opportunity to make learning more suited to the needs of young people. As Wyn (2015) argues, the opportunity is inherent as:

> [the] shifts in the nature and experience of youth compel educationalists to respond to social change with new and innovative approaches to learning, based on an understanding of who the learner is. In other words, the reality of social change encourages educationalists to recognise the diversity of youth and to understand and respond to the impact of different social environments and cultures on learning. (p. 15)

One way that learners can be re-engaged with schooling is to consider how the education system's current obsession with testing and teaching for the test might be overcome.

Testing has lost connection with the complexity and diversity of learning

Whatever your answer to the question 'what is school for?', it is probably not 'testing'. Yet in many modern education systems testing has become the central event around which learning and teaching has become organized: 'instead of fostering creativity and ingenuity, more and more school systems have become obsessed with imposing and micromanaging curriculum uniformity. In place of ambitious missions of compassion and community, schools and teachers have been squeezed into the tunnel vision of test scores, achievement targets and league tables of accountability' (Hargreaves, 2003, p. 1).

The great ambition of schooling to be a place where young people can be engaged and equipped to face the challenges that lie ahead has become swamped with the need to measure everything as if the act of measurement will magically improve and motivate students. In a classic case of 'cart before horse' thinking, testing has been allowed to dictate the curriculum and learning and teaching approaches. As Dorothy Bottrell (2015) argues, 'neoliberal educational policy, despite including broad democratic and inclusive goals, has increasingly taken a narrow focus on learning as basic skills of literacy and numeracy and these in the narrow form of performance on standardised tests' (p. 30). These paper and pen high stakes tests are ultimately summative assessment tools as they take little account of the development, growth, individual factors and prevailing conditions for a student on any given test day.

Governments routinely use these testing programmes to decide which schools are to be funded and defunded. Parents decide which schools their children will attend based on the outcomes of these tests. Of course we are not the first to raise concerns about this kind of testing (Wyn, 2015). There have been over the last decade many educators who have identified the problematic nature of 'high stakes testing'. Most of these concerns relate to the arbitrary nature of the assessment and the inability of the test to examine complex connected knowledge. As Bottrell (2015, p. 38) argues: 'Nation-wide administered achievement tests such as NAPLAN of necessity only partially reflect what has been taught in any specific school; such tests need to be short, and hence to include only a small sample of what has been taught.' Our concern with this kind of testing focuses on its inability to measure in any meaningful way some of the key capabilities required for the twenty-first century. These tests take little if no account of students' capacity to create, critically reflect, communicate or collaborate. While many argue that literacy testing measures communication skills, there is an apparent bias towards the kinds of skills that can be captured in a test (mostly written language and comprehension).

Another related issue is the tendency for high stakes testing to silo knowledge in ways that take no account of connectedness and complexity. As we discussed earlier in this chapter, many of the real-world issues that face our community are complex problems that require creativity, critical reflection, communication and collaboration. High stakes testing tends to separate out skills such as literacy and numeracy and assess them as disconnected. However, questions such as global warming, food security, refugee policy and democratic citizenship require learning and therefore assessment (and testing) that is interconnected and interdependent. While The Programme for International Student Assessment (PISA) style testing provides the basis for international comparison it does not genuinely support high-quality learning about complex and connected problems.

We are not arguing for the removal of assessment or testing. In our view assessment is critical for analysis of the quality and rate of each student's learning. We believe that instead of relying on narrow paper and pen tests, we need to develop strategies for analysing student learning in twenty-first-century skills such as the 4Cs. This is achievable when we draw on the wisdom and skills of experienced teachers to measure student achievement in a holistic, connected and relevant way. This is not beyond us. There are many examples of assessment practices that assess communication, collaboration, creativity and criticality in many fields of learning. We think that these examples of practice can be shared to help support educators devise assessment: Assessment that is meaningful, authentic and meets the needs of twenty-first-century learners leading to the development of social capital.

Schooling and social capital

Social capital relates to 'resources grounded in the durable exchange-based networks of persons' (Reid, 2015, p. 93) or in other words the capacities people require to navigate their way in society. In this view schools from low socioeconomic areas are filled with children who 'lack' rather than have contributions emerging from their family of origin. As Hayes (2016) argues,

> In such accounts, the value of the capital possessed by marginalized families invariably counts for less than that of less marginalized families. . . . Within a 'culture of poverty' framework, marginalized families are engaged in an unequal exchange since they are always positioned as receivers not givers; as listeners, not speakers; and, perhaps most perversely, as dysfunctional and unable to operate without the assistance and intervention of outside expertise and support that provides remediation and supplementation. (p. 215)

In Hayes' view, and that of other sociologists, the term can imprison people in pre-determined class structures from which they are unlikely to escape.

We think social capital can be reconceptualized as a series of culturally derived understandings and skills. In this way 'capital' can support learning and, like Thomson and Hall's virtual school bag (2008), these capacities need to be built upon and complemented as part of schooling rather than identified as deficits. They argue: 'children come to school with virtual school bags of knowledges, experiences and dispositions. However, school only draws on the contents of some children's school bags, those whose resources match those required in the game of education' (Thomson and Hall, 2008, p. 89). This creates two classes of students: those who have the 'right' social capital and those whose school bag is never 'unpacked' by schools because their capital is not considered valuable. For instance in some schools the ability to perform hip-hop is not as valued as classical ballet because each of these forms connotes a certain social standing. We want to reposition social capital not as a variable and culturally derived phenomenon but as a universal social entitlement. As such we believe that social capital and the skills that flow from that capital must be taught in a complementary way, building from the virtual school bag students bring with them. The 4Cs are a rich source of social capital that builds and draws upon the capitals (or virtual school bag) that students bring with them to school.

If as a community we want our schools to provide an education that equips students to live in the twenty-first century we need to explicitly teach social capital from a complementary rather than a deficit perspective. This is not an implausible dream. As Jean Anyon argues, this kind of change has happened before and with the passion and commitment of educators can happen again: 'Critical educators are involved in a . . . process of reimagining schools and classrooms as social justice building spaces. This work is incredibly difficult but, I would argue, not any more impossible than the reimagining of economic relations, the church and culture that black Americans undertook to achieve the victories of the civil rights movement' (2011, p. 99).

Where to now? Transforming learning through the 4Cs

The chance conversation with Peter Wentworth that opened this chapter uncovers a much deeper set of concerns about where education currently is and where it needs to be to meet the pressing challenges of the twenty-first century. The interconnectedness of the modern postnormal world with its 3Cs of complexity, chaos and contradiction demands new approaches to new (ish) problems. We have identified just a few of the societal and school system issues that we believe form a compelling case for change.

We need transformation for our schools, our teachers, our learners, our universities and ultimately our societies. And by transformation we do not mean small or trivial change. We are arguing here for schools to change in ways that make them unrecognizable from the old factory models where knowledge was transmitted and students were positioned as passive receivers. We are imagining new leadership, pedagogies and learning strategies that put the 4Cs, creativity, critical reflection, communication and collaboration, at the centre of learning. What we imagine is what we glimpse in the transformations we see in our work in schools on a daily basis. We believe this change is not only possible but that it is essential to make schools relevant to the needs of a changing and sometimes insecure world.

In the next chapter we explore some of the ideas underpinning the 4Cs. Chapter 2 discusses critical pedagogy and transformative learning and their role in shaping change in learning and teaching.

Note

1 PISA is the Programme for International Student Assessment run by the Organisation for Economic Co-operation and Development (OECD).

Freeing learning for transformation

Freeing learning is a dramatic metaphor, but it comes to mind when transforming schools. Freeing learning suggests emancipation from constraints. For us it conjures up the image of Gulliver in Lilliput tied to the ground on his back gazing skyward without understanding what is restraining him.

> I attempted to rise, but was not able to stir: For as I happened to lie on my Back, I found my Arms and Legs were strongly fastened on each side to the Ground; and my Hair, which was long and thick, tied down in the same manner. I likewise felt several slender Ligatures across my Body, from my Armpits to my Thighs. I could only look upwards, the Sun began to grow hot, and the Light offended mine Eyes. I heard a confused Noise about me, but in the posture I lay, could see nothing except the Sky. (Swift, 1726/2001, p. 23)

To free learning we have to break the 'slender ligatures' that are tying us down in schools. Like Gulliver, to break the ligatures is to recognize what the constrictions of the status quo really are, and how they can be broken. It is hard to break restraints if you don't know what they are, and they are hard to break if you know don't how to break them. But breaking the ligatures in schools is possible and, like Gulliver, the capacity to do so begins with us as individuals and communities.

To 'free and transform learning' is not a phrase we use lightly. Enormous expectations come with these words. They are aspirations informed by ideas from critical pedagogy and transformative learning. Twenty years ago we used to teach the theatre techniques of practitioner Augusto Boal and the critical pedagogy ideas of Paulo Freire. At the time we were engaged with their work, but the urgent need for Boal's *Theatre of the Oppressed* (1979/2000) and Freire's *Pedagogy of the Oppressed* (1970/2006) was not immediately apparent. We didn't see much oppression teaching in an affluent and democratic Australia. But now in the work we are doing in schools we do sense oppression and we are committed to freeing and transforming learning.

This chapter explores how critical pedagogy and transformative learning inform our understanding of the 4Cs and their implementation in schools. Critical pedagogy underpins the 4Cs as enablers of human agency and empowerment. Transformative learning informs our belief that to change we have to transform mindsets and habits of mind. We examine the following aspects of critical pedagogy and transformative learning as key to our ideas and practices in the 4Cs. They are:

- Change begins with imagination, reflection and action and engagement with community.
- Emancipation is through problem-posing, dialogue and interrogating the status quo.
- Transformation is sustained through praxis and collaboration.

Exploring these concepts help in understanding our perspective and processes for 4C school transformation. We begin by engaging with these ideas by considering critical pedagogy as a philosophy.

Critical pedagogy

In the late twentieth century, critical pedagogy for education evolved from critical social theory. Critical pedagogy critiques the politics and power of dominant ideologies in education. As a discourse it has given shape and coherence to the development of progressive and radical views and practices in emancipatory education. The work of Paulo Freire, Henry Giroux, Michael Apple, Maxine Greene, Peter McLaren and bell hooks, amongst many others has revitalized educational debate in transformative social action in schools. Critical pedagogy positions education as a social structure that transforms, by breaking the bonds that prevent the democratic engagement and participation of all.

Education as a social structure can also be constraining in creating the bonds that prevent democratic participation (see discussion of social capital in Chapter 1). Critical pedagogy critiques education by looking at the social structures that shape it. In the twenty-first century, it leads us to ask questions of education such as, 'How do schools reflect or subvert democratic practices and the larger culture of democracy? How do schools operate to validate or challenge the power dynamics of race, class, gender, sexuality, religion, indigenous/aboriginal issues, physical ability-related concerns etc? How do such processes play out in diverse classrooms located in differing social, cultural, and economic domains?' (Kincheloe, 2007, p. 130).

Critical pedagogy is not only about critiquing the social, political and cultural forces that impact on the functioning of classrooms, it also provides a language of hope and possibility. The possibility is for students and teachers being critical and responsible agents of personal and social change. Critical pedagogy provides the conditions for students to use knowledge for self-determination. 'Critical pedagogy is about more than a struggle over assigned meanings, official knowledge, and established modes of authority; it is also about encouraging students to take risks, act on their sense of responsibility, and engage the world as an object of both critical analysis and hopeful transformation' (Giroux, 2011, p. 14).

When there is no hope and possibility for self-determination and transformation in education, it can be described as 'oppressive'. When we hear school leaders say 'we haven't got time for creativity' or 'we haven't got time for critical reflection and collaboration', or teachers say 'I'm not creative', or system bureaucrats say 'we can't have you choose your own adventure schooling', we sense an oppression in schools. But we also hear the language of possibility when we hear teachers say, 'I can't believe what the students are able to do, I didn't know they could do that' or students say 'our teachers are learning with us too!' And we also hear 'this 4C pedagogy is really hard, it hurts my brain'. With possibility there is also struggle. To transform schools is to encourage teachers and students to take risks, have high expectations, and responsibly engage with the world as critical agents. In our experience with schools this only begins through processes in reflection and action.

Change begins with reflection and action

Empowerment and agency means taking responsibility, being self-directed and taking action with others. Theory or books or systems do not bring transformation. Transformation is achieved through people collaborating for change. The capacity to transform is in the *reflection and action* of people. To free and transform learning and schools is not to have someone else break the ligatures constraining them. Schools themselves have to free learning from its constraints, and schools themselves have to imagine an alternative way of doing and being.

The constraints to learning and possibility can be imagined as residing in a 'box'. The box may be constructed and shaped by things such as institutional culture, ideology, experience, habit, busyness, fear or a blind sense of compliance. To free learning from the box means first we have to be aware of the box and its constraints, and then imagine there are possibilities outside the box. This is reminiscent of the existential box moment in the play *Rosencrantz and Guildenstern Are Dead* (Stoppard, 1967), when Rosencrantz muses what it means to be dead lying in a box:

> Rosencrantz: It's silly to be depressed by it. I mean one thinks of it like being alive in a box, one keeps forgetting to take into account the fact that one is dead . . . which should make all the difference . . . shouldn't it? I mean, you'd never know you were in the box, would you? It would be just like being asleep in a box. Not that I'd like to sleep in a box, mind you, not without any air – you'd wake up dead, for a start, and then where would you be? Apart from inside a box. (p. 52)

It is only through asking questions, posing problems and critical reflection that we begin to see ourselves in the world beyond the box and to imagine what is possible. Too often in schools and organizations there is little or no time and opportunity for leaders, teachers and students to reflect on their actions and decide future action outside the oppressive, static reality of the box. In schools there must be time, processes and organizational structures for leaders, teachers and students to facilitate the opening of a space for reflection, awareness and action. Through mindful, Socratic questioning, leaders, teachers and students can be 'midwives', assisting the birth of each other's reflections, ideas and action. In the schools we mentor in, we frame our discussions with, what have you noticed or identified? Why do you think it is that way? Really, why? What are the possibilities we could explore? Change through reflection and action is also a feature of Mezirow's transformative learning as well as critical pedagogy.

Transformative learning

Paulo Freire and Jürgen Habermas, among others, inspired Jack Mezirow's work in transformative learning. Learning is transformational when it is a comprehensive shift in how we see ourselves; it involves a recalibration of personality and identity. Transformational learning is the result of challenges or a crisis-like situation that makes it necessary to change to get any further. It is 'both profound and extensive, it demands a lot of mental energy and when accomplished it can often be experienced physically, typically as a feeling of relief or relaxation' (Illeris, 2009, p. 14).

We know this is the experience of many leaders, teachers and students in schools who are experiencing recalibration through transformation. Transformation in the 4C approach is charged emotionally and cognitively because it involves a complete change in a person's 'frame of reference'. Frames of reference are preconceptions that define our life view and they become our habitual line of action unless we reflect critically on our own and others' assumptions. When ideas fail to fit our preconceptions we have a strong inclination to reject them and label them as irrelevant, undoable, fanciful, nonsense or mistaken (Mezirow, 1997). For example, when we discuss the possibilities of integrated curricula, collaborative teaching and creative learning in schools we sometimes hear the preconceived responses, 'we tried that in the 1970s', or 'the final school exams don't allow us to do that', or 'we won't get through the required content if we do that', or 'at this stage this might be a bridge too far'.

Instead, transformative learners move towards a frame of reference that is more inclusive, discriminating, self-reflective and integrative of experience and take action on their transformed perspective (Mezirow, 1997). They acquire a disposition to become more critically reflective of their own assumptions and those of others, and to follow through on decisions to act upon their transformed insights (Mezirow, 2009). Recently a teacher commented perceptively, 'it's all very well to think critically, but if you don't put it into action, what's the point? You have to be open to possibility to learn more, and do more'.

Leaders, teachers and students in schools involved in 4C transformation are aware that mindsets are crucial to sustaining real change. Eva, a principal who is implementing the 4C approach at her school, is making time and space to support teacher critical reflection as everyday practice. As they discuss and develop their 4C ideas and actions, she can see a change in mindset in the teachers. The mindset change is not one of acceptance, but one of openness and inquiry, and continuing critical reflection. At this school, the staff needed courage to imagine teaching and learning in new ways. Confidence has been nurtured by the principal and leadership team by their being involved in developing and leading the pedagogy with other teachers in the learning spaces. The gradual success achieved in those strategic interventions by the leadership team has generated interest and excitement throughout the rest of the staff. Critical reflection and action are intertwined with developing confidence to build capacity to imagine new ideas.

Change begins with the imagination

Being able to imagine is a state of mind absolutely necessary to create what may be possible in education (Greene, 1995). Exploring the arts in learning for example develops skills and understandings that arouse and release imaginative processes to explore possibility. Emily Dickinson's poem (1924) captures the human courage and power of imagining.

> The gleam of an heroic act
> Such strange illumination
> The Possible's slow fuse is lit
> By the Imagination

In the work we are undertaking with the 4Cs approach and school transformation, we notice that comfort zones, fear, apathy and indifference can only be stirred and challenged by a belief and capacity in imagining. The imagination is a space of freedom where humans are initiators and agents of an alternative reality (Greene, 1995). The imagination allows us to break from what we take for granted and to set aside the familiar.

For people to imagine, they have to learn *how* to imagine and dwell in an environment that allows for creative possibilities. Constructivist psychologist, Lev Vygotsky (1931/1998), argues that people with a less developed creative imagination cannot transform themselves from their immediate environment. Vygotsky describes the 'zero point of the imagination' as when 'the individual is in a state where he is unable to abstract himself from the concrete situation, unable to change it creatively, to regroup signs to free one's self from under its influence' (1931/1998, p. 152). To move from one concrete towards the possibility of a new concrete occurs as we engage with the abstract thinking of the imagination (see discussion of imagination and creativity in Chapter 5).

To imagine is to see something new but it is also to see other perspectives and points of view. Imagining takes us from viewing the world from our eyes, to seeing the world through others' eyes. In this way, imagining is key to humane relationships; it is an awakening to see possibility in others and to constructing a real connectedness with others. In our work with transformation in schools, we realize the importance of nurturing and challenging people through trusting relationships that allow and develop their 'imagining of possibility'. In turn, humane and compassionate relationships between leaders, teachers, students and communities are developed through the action of imagining and collaborating together.

Change begins with community

We have witnessed in schools the power of collaborative and co-constructed transformative action and learnt that the relationships created through these actions result in a sense of community and social cohesion. Community in this sense is not defined by coexistence and inhabiting the same space together. A sense of community is discovered through people feeling empowered in coming together in the pursuit of shared meaning. 'Community is not a question of which social contracts are the most reasonable for individuals to enter. It is a question of what might contribute to the pursuit of shared goods: what ways of being together, of attaining mutuality, of reaching toward some common world' (Greene, 1995, p. 39).

A sense of community is significant within schools and beyond schools and can develop in many ways. In a primary school (for students of 5–12 years of age), for instance, a connection with the parent community occurred when student learning at school impacted on family life at home. The driving question for the students' learning was, 'Is the sacrifice of sustaining a global future worth it?' As part of their learning the students had to put into action whether they could make sacrifices, and whether their families could make sacrifices to reduce their carbon footprint. Could they reduce air-conditioning, showers, lighting, technology use and waste? This immediately involved and challenged the school families as a community to be involved in the learning.

A central feature of critical pedagogy as a transformative pedagogy is the construction of identity through democratic-building relationships among individuals. It is the responding to others through the creation of community that develops both social consciousness and individual agency (Kincheloe, 2007). Relational connections of community are intrinsic to establishing the fabric of a democratic society and also support the social processes of learning. These ideas underpin the creation of community in and around 4C schools. We believe transformation in schools is achieved through collaborative leadership and collaborative communities, and emancipation through problem-posing and dialogue.

Emancipation through problem-posing and dialogue

Freire (1970/2006) describes a disempowered relationship between teachers and students as a banking transaction: there are the depositors and the depositories.

Students are depositories that are open (or closed) recipients of knowledge deposited by teachers. It's a one-way transaction that establishes student dependency on teachers as the providers of learning and knowledge. It creates a mindset that learners cannot invest in learning themselves or that teachers can learn from their students.

In critical pedagogy the two-way investment practice between teacher and students is achieved through the discourse of dialogue and problem-posing. As a two-way transaction, teachers learn from students, students learn from teachers, students from students, leaders learn from colleagues, colleagues from leaders. Dialogue and problem-posing are an ongoing co-construction of coming to know together what is possible in the world. In contrast to the 'banking model' of education, nothing is docile, passive or compliant about critical pedagogy and the 4Cs approach. Problem-posing and dialogue are active and reflective states that develop agency in learners and teachers. In the 4C approach to pedagogy we see dialogic communication and problem-posing as instrumental to self-directed and transformative learning. Dialogue (communication) and problem-posing (critical reflection) ultimately stimulate the emergence of consciousness and empowerment of critical intervention and creative power in the world (Freire, 1970/2006). Critical intervention and creative power in the world can seem an insurmountable challenge. This is particularly the case when 'reality' feels like an entrenched status quo impenetrable to change.

Emancipation by interrogating the status quo

The status quo in schools and education is there because of certain ideologies or hegemony that keep it that way. These ideologies are like 'dark matter' in the universe. Dark matter, according to a theory based on cosmological observations, makes up 27 per cent of the universe. The rest of the universe is 68 per cent dark energy and 5 per cent normal matter. Dark matter is dark because it is not in the form of stars and planets that we can see. In many ways the status quo in education is held up by ideology that we cannot necessarily see. Behind curriculums and institutions in education is the unseen dark matter that may be embedded deep within social structures.

Ideology as unseen dark matter produces and represents the ideas, values and beliefs that shape the way we do things. These social rituals become accepted as norms and 'common sense' practice. The frameworks provided by ideology help us make sense of the world, but critical pedagogy points out that some ideology can have a negative effect, and privilege certain social groups over others. McLaren (2015) explains how dark matter (which he refers to as the hidden curriculum) works in education: 'by legitimizing the school system as just and meritocratic, as giving everyone the same opportunity for success, the dominant culture hides the truth of the hidden curriculum – the fact that those whom schooling helps most are those who come from the most affluent families' (p. 142).

Critical pedagogy is a starting point for asking questions about ideology embedded in the hidden curriculum. Critiquing ideology and hegemony help in understanding the context of the status quo and in recognizing the dominant cultural assumptions and practices that may thwart possibility and empowerment. Critical pedagogy is primarily concerned with interrogating the relationship between power and knowledge. It asks fundamental questions such as:

- To what extent do traditional pedagogies legitimize the role of the teacher as the gatekeeper and controller of what and how students will gain knowledge?
- To what extent do traditional pedagogies empower the student?

Pedagogy for empowerment allows students, teachers and leaders to understand and engage with the world around them and exercise the courage to challenge and change what is taken for granted and assumed. Empowerment begins with self-recognition and self-confirmation through the gaining of knowledge and social relations that dignify the history, language and cultural traditions of one's own social group. From self-confirmation, empowerment is 'the process by which students learn to question and selectively appropriate those aspects of the dominant culture that will provide them with the basis for defining and transforming, rather than merely serving the wider social order' (McLaren, 2015, p. 149).

Self-confirmation and empowerment for transformation are especially significant to Indigenous or first peoples communities. In 2016 Australia, as Aboriginal and Torres Strait Islanders fight for recognition in the constitution, eminent Indigenous leader, Pat Dodson, asks 'If you are going to recognize Aboriginal people, what is the substance of it? The substance we are seeing at the moment is this: "We're going to close down communities, force you into assimilation kind of activities, deny your right to have sites protected, and reject your cultural base to exist"' (Gordon, 2015). Pedagogy for empowerment in 4C transformative education has a potentially powerful role in self-determination, recognizing cultural traditions and transforming rather than serving the wider social order.

The common beliefs or doxa of the wider social order and the status quo in education powerfully perpetuates itself. It is legitimized through government policy, curriculum documents, school funding models, students' socioeconomic status, parental expectations, system and teacher expectations, high stakes testing and compliance. Critical pedagogy critiques the inequalities of dominant orthodoxies in education through the political lens of gender, race, class and cultural capital.

Even with the capacity to critique, imagine and generate new ideas, it takes courage to question the privilege of the status quo and take action to transform. Courage and determination cannot be underestimated in the quest to free learning. Often those with radical ideas of the possible are pushed to the margins, stripped of their transformative intent and weakened into a more palatable form by the dominant culture. Those who question the established structures remain non-mainstream because they are not valued or legitimized by the mainstream. It takes courage and critical reflection to interrogate the status quo of our school institutions, and in that reflective discourse the tool of *praxis* illuminates our understandings and sustains transformation.

Transformation is sustained through praxis

The Large Hadron Collider, the world's largest and most powerful accelerator, allows nuclear physicists to experiment and test theories about the existence and nature of dark matter. The Higgs boson particle was imagined and theorized 60 years ago and in 2012 the Large Hadron Collider led to pinpointing the existence of the elusive sub-atomic particle. Practice, in the form of experiments, together with theory, interrogate and inform our understanding of the cosmos. Similarly, practice and theory illuminate our understanding of the 'dark matter' in education. They also critique and support our endeavours with the 4Cs in schools. In critical pedagogy, the alliance of theory and practice as 'praxis' encourages the ongoing interaction of reflection, dialogue and practice to question orthodoxies and advance new creative ideas and wisdom.

Knowledge is a human activity that is both a product for understanding the world and a force for shaping the world. This is a dialectical view of knowledge that inextricably links theory and practice to understanding and taking action in the world. Practice needs theory to illuminate understandings of an experience, and theory is affected by the practice and context of experience. Through praxis, 'theory cannot be reduced to being perceived as the mistress of experience, empowered to provide recipes for pedagogical practice. Its real value lies in its ability to establish possibilities for reflexive thought and practice on the part of those who use it; in the case of teachers, it becomes invaluable as an instrument of critique and understanding' (Giroux, 2003, p. 38).

Without practice, theory is an abstraction of empty words. Without theory, practice is blind and ungrounded in thinking. For instance, principal Eva is constantly cycling through praxis at her school. She relates to her staff how theory, research and critical reflection in the 4Cs effects her practice, and how her practice as action illuminates her conceptual understandings of the 4Cs. 'It's all about deeper learning for us as teachers and taking us forward to transform our school,' she says. In our 4Cs work with schools and organizations we use the dynamic of engaging with theory and practice, action and reflection as an ongoing dialogue and motion for students, teachers and leaders to affirm the gradual changes they make, their successes and their failures, and everything in between.

Without the tension of theory and practice, there is no meaning given to change. The constant application of praxis nurtures and sustains the transformative process. Critical pedagogy is a pedagogy of hope that claims that, through praxis, human beings look ahead and move forward (Freire, 1994). As we work in schools we have encountered elements of fear, apathy, distrust; a lack of resilience or an unwillingness to be empowered, to look ahead and imagine possibilities. It is in the collaboration of others that people are encouraged and emancipated to move forward.

Transformation is sustained through collaboration

The lone Gulliver in Lilliput does not free himself. Similarly, it is through the collective consciousness and creativity of a community that transformation of our context is possible. In our mentoring in school transformation we acknowledge that deep and respectful creative collaboration has been central to the empowerment of those involved. Collective change and creativity is why there has been success in making change, and 'recovering a lost spontaneity' in participants (Greene, 2001, p. 181). A very experienced school leader, Diana, new to the 4C approach, sighed as she said, 'It is exhausting, it is hard, but it has saved me. It has re-energized me.' In schools and organizations, imagination, creativity and innovation will thrive in a collaborative environment. And collaboration and community are forged in the process of discovering it.

Equal collaborators are more likely to encourage each other to take risks and, in doing so, find solutions in a wider social context (John-Steiner, 2000). Shared creativity is described by Moran and John-Steiner (2003) as an 'affair of the mind' where emotions transform people and their work. Creative collaboration and community are however often associated with like-minded people coming together. Critical pedagogy acknowledges the necessity and challenge to recognize diversity and pluralism in collaborative communities: 'All too often we think of community in terms of being with folks like ourselves: the same class, same race, same ethnicity, same social standing and the like. . . . I think we need to be wary: we need to work against the danger of evoking something that we don't challenge ourselves to actually practice' (hooks, 2003, p. 163).

The fear of diversity relates directly to established ideologies shaping the comfort zones and status quo of the 'gated communities' that people think they feel safe within. This is another bind that ties us down from freeing learning and transforming schools. To be open to diversity and plurality isn't necessarily easy, but it is through these difficulties that we become more tolerant and value difference and multiple perspectives. As we overcome the comfort of sameness and the fear of diversity, and share values, authentic community is created. 'Dominator culture has tried to keep us all afraid, to make us choose safety instead of risk, sameness instead of diversity. Moving through that fear, finding out what connects us, reveling in our differences; this is the process that brings us closer, that gives us a world of shared values, of meaningful community' (hooks, 2003, p. 197).

The ideals of critical pedagogy are predicated on the principles of equality, equity and freedom. It is with these beliefs that individuals and communities can move through fear, and take risks to create a shared meaning in possibility. These are the ideals that inform our understanding of the 4Cs approach to free learning and transform schools.

A road map for transforming schools

Ultimately, why does critical pedagogy matter in education? It only matters if you believe that human life is not predetermined. It only matters if you believe it is a moral imperative for everyone to have an opportunity to question the status quo, to have an opportunity for choice, to express themselves, and to create possible realities. The aim of critical pedagogy is the emancipation of the self and others to participate more fully in the experience of life. It is to develop every individual's and community's capacity through agency and empowerment. Transformative learning develops autonomous thinking and seeks meaning in both mundane and transcendent experiences. We believe these ideas are often absent in our educational institutions.

The 4Cs approach, underpinned by critical pedagogy and transformative learning, can free and transform learning by:

- *Fostering creativity in the learning and practice of teachers, students and leaders in schools to be able to imagine the possible.* Creativity is a transformative action; it is to harness what is possible. The act of creativity begins with the imagination to go beyond what we know. We have to imagine how things could be different to develop new and authentic understandings in learning. The imagination is a space of freedom where we are unfettered to create an alternative reality. Human beings with creative power to transform are then fully alive to their potential.

- *Using critical reflection as a basis for problem-based and praxis-based transformative learning and action.* Critical reflection allows the consciousness of people to emerge so they can critically intervene in their reality. Critical reflection can question ideology and recognize dominant cultural assumptions that may prevent possibility. Critical reflection is developed first from the awareness that our thinking and actions may be trapped in a box of orthodoxy or a boxed frame of reference. Through problem-posing and problem-solving, and using theory to inform practice and practice to inform theory, transformative learning in schools can be sustained.

- *Constructing collaborative learning communities and practices with teachers, students and communities in all aspects of school life.* Creativity with collaboration combines to construct a community based on dialogue and social agency through mutuality in a shared endeavour. Collaboration allows people to form communities that through their mutual zones of proximal development continue their creative capacities. Shared values through collaboration in creative and transformative practice can connect diverse and different people to challenge and share their values, to promote a 'democratic society that takes equality, justice, shared values and freedom seriously' (Giroux, 2011, p. 4).

- *Enabling the communication of all voices to collaborate, critically reflect and create as a discourse of dialogue and agency.* Communication as dialogue mediates our understanding and engagement with the world and becomes a tool of enfranchisement. It is in communication that the 'voice' of empowerment resides, for 'to speak a true word is to transform the world' (Freire, 1970/2006, p. 87). Communication is not empty slogans devoid of action and reflection. In critical pedagogy it is through the authentic and collaborative dialogue of struggle and hope that individuals and communities are transformed and humanized.

To return to Gulliver, transformation begins with the struggle to loosen the binds that hold us down.

I lay all this while, as the Reader may believe, in great Uneasiness: at length, struggling to get loose, I had the Fortune to break the Strings, and wrench out the Pegs that fastened my left Arm to the Ground; for, by lifting it up to my Face, I discovered the Methods they had taken to bind me; and, at the same time, with a violent Pull, which gave me excessive Pain, I a little loosened the Strings that tied down my Hair on the left Side, so that I was just able to turn my Head about two Inches. (Swift, 1726/2001, p. 24)

In a school we heard a student say, 'When I was researching the Renaissance I noticed something . . . we are, in a way, creating a remake of the Renaissance because we are changing the way we learn.' We knew then that transformation in the school, although a struggle, was beginning to be reborn through a reimagining of what learning constitutes.

The next chapter explores the way learning is understood and enacted in the 4Cs approach.

Understanding learning in the 4Cs approach

3

Figure 3.1 Complicite, *A Disappearing Number*

The story of Complicite's (2007) theatre production, *A Disappearing Number* (McBurney, 2008) is based on the real-life collaboration during the 1910s of two brilliant mathematicians, Srinivasa Ramanujan, a Brahmin from South India and the Cambridge don, G.H. Hardy. It is a play that connects numbers, infinity and string theory with the beauty and mystery of ideas, relationships, culture and enlightenment. It was G.H. Hardy (1940/2005) who said, 'The mathematician's patterns, like the painter's or the poet's must be beautiful; the ideas like the colours or the words, must fit together in a harmonious way. Beauty is the first test: there is no permanent place in the world for ugly mathematics' (p. 14).

It is in the beauty and harmony of the patterns and ideas of mathematics that we navigate the world through commerce, design, computer programming, physics, economics, astronomy, architecture, engineering, nanotechnology etc. Numbers and the patterns they make help us to imagine, discover and construct the world around us. They make coherence of the world because they fit ideas together in a 'harmonious way'. Similarly, *coherence makers*[1] help us to imagine and discover how to navigate and create the world through learning.

In the 4Cs approach we introduce coherence makers to illuminate and harmonize the complexity of learning and the 4C capabilities: creativity, critical reflection, communication and collaboration. This chapter explores how coherence makers work in learning, and explain how we conceive the 4Cs in relation to knowledge, wisdom and transformation. We examine the benefits of integrated curricula on learning, and introduce the Learning Disposition Wheel as a tool to develop self-regulated learners able to be empowered by the 4C capabilities. To learn and understand each capability in the 4Cs we have developed coherence makers for each (Creativity Cascade, Critical Reflection Crucible, Communication Crystal and Collaboration Circles) and these are explored in their own chapters. As coherence makers they are designed to harness and guide imaginings, questionings and discoveries about learners, learning processes, and the 4C capabilities. This chapter begins by looking at the role of coherence makers in learning.

Why do we need coherence makers in education and how do they work?

Learning is complex, and coherence makers as conceptual schemas provide order to complexity. The paradox of a coherence maker is that in its simplicity to make ideas clear, it should also open up to ideas of ever-greater complexity. A coherence maker should not render thinking reductive, limited or procedural. The simple and the complex are evident in the theorems and equations of mathematics. $E = mc^2$ (energy = mass × speed of light squared) is a seemingly simple algebraic formula that explains a profound relationship between energy and matter. While our coherence makers are not equations, nor as profound, they attempt to reveal and address the complexity of learning through simplicity.

Jerome Bruner (1960) argued that any subject of learning is more comprehensible if the fundamentals, as underlying principles or concepts are understood. From fundamentals learners can generalize, transfer, discover and intuit further learning. However, Bruner maintained that knowing fundamental ideas in a field alone is not enough. It is necessary to develop 'an attitude toward learning and inquiry, toward guessing and hunches, toward the possibility of solving problems on one's own' (Bruner, 1960, p. 20). It is therefore not just the mere presentation of coherence makers as a conceptual schema that makes sense about how learning works. There has to be a sense of discovery and excitement (and perhaps even beauty) in using the coherence maker to solve the problems of learning.

Coherence makers in learning endeavour to support and challenge teachers and students to develop a deeper mastery in the processes of learning, and allow for 'emergence' (Sawyer, 2015). By emergence we mean that the coherence makers encourage teachers and students to build new and unpredictable knowledge about learning itself. For instance, in a school community where students had difficulties with oral language and comprehension, we developed with the teachers the application of a simple teaching scaffold, 'embody, speak, write', to improve students' communication and literacy skills. The idea emerged from the coherence makers we were already using in the 4Cs approach.

Coherence makers aim to be an amalgam or synthesis of known fundamentals to make emergent discoveries about further learning. Howard Gardner (2007) argues that synthesis as a means to make connections to 'everything' must not paralyse the critical mind. It should not 'explain' everything so there is nothing to question and wonder at. Coherence makers should open up complexities through simplicity, not reduce or close down deeper understandings about phenomena. We have developed 4Cs coherence makers to open up and support the complexity of transformative learning in schools and workplaces. So what do we mean when we refer to 4C learning and the 4C approach?

The 4Cs as an organizer

The '4Cs' is shorthand for developing the capabilities of creativity, critical reflection, communication and collaboration. The 4Cs are described in brief in Table 3.1. They are capabilities that through the lens of critical pedagogy lead to empowerment. The potential and capacity to transform from 'what is' to 'what could be' are developed through skills and knowledge in the 4Cs. The '4Cs approach' aims to shape, unify and transform pedagogy, curricula, the organization of schools and the way they work. As we have already acknowledged in Chapter 1, there is nothing new about the 'Cs' as shorthand for 'twenty-first-century capabilities'. We have used the 4Cs as an organizer that synthesizes the capabilities needed to transform schools into relevant and vibrant communities that make a positive difference to those communities' social futures.

The '4Cs' representing creativity, critical reflection, communication and collaboration are an organizer to:

- Describe the capabilities that empower people to explore possibility and to change through dialogue, action and reflection.
- Focus and shape pedagogy and work practices to achieve effective, positive and inclusive outcomes.
- Develop learners in capabilities to serve their social futures.

Morality, ethics and the responsibility of being a good citizen are essential to a civil society. Education has a key role in determining and shaping responsible and active citizens that have a sense of and act for the common good. We see knowledge and wisdom being fundamentally integrated with the 4Cs capabilities. We have diagrammatically represented the relationship and the process of 4C learning with knowledge and wisdom in Figure 3.2.

The Learning Prism illustrates how knowledge, new understanding and wisdom interact with the 4Cs and become deep understanding, connected knowledge and transformative learning. The 4Cs as a 'prism' is a metaphor for representing refraction

Table 3.1 The 4Cs: creativity, critical reflection, communication and collaboration, described in brief

CREATIVITY
to craft and to inspire
Creativity is to imagine and problem-solve with possibilities by exploring the unusual and unexpected. It is not to fear failure, to learn from mistakes and to know there is a creative solution to everything. Creativity is to craft, justify, inspire and evaluate ideas and skills with others. To develop creativity learners must have a meta-awareness of its capacity and challenges as a capability. This can be explored through the creativity cascade coherence maker (pictured here).

CRITICAL REFLECTION
to question and navigate
Critical reflection is for all voices to question, elaborate and explain ideas. It is to develop thinking processes beyond asking 'what?' to asking 'why, how, what if and when?' To think critically is to first notice and then be able to reflect and re-solve problems, and meet and navigate challenges through action. Critical reflection interrogates power and how it is exercised by the student and by others. To develop critical reflection learners must have a meta-awareness of its capacity and challenges as a capability. This can be explored through the critical reflection crucible coherence maker.

COMMUNICATION
to voice and to message
Communication is to empower and respect all voices as authentic. To enable, hear and reach all voices there are multiple and integrated representations of communication to be explored and messaged. Regular and precise exhibition and feedback in learning relies on the power and purpose of communication. To develop communication learners must have a meta-awareness of its capacity and challenges. This can be explored through the communication crystal coherence maker.

COLLABORATION
to co-construct and challenge
Collaboration is engaging, negotiating and celebrating all voices to develop understandings and skills. Collaboration requires trust and openness to challenging and being challenged by others. Individual initiative and responsibility are needed for co-constructing skills, ideas and solutions with others. To develop collaboration learners must have a meta-awareness of its capacity and challenges as a capability. This can be explored through the collaboration circles coherence maker.

and changing the direction of the 'light' of knowledge and wisdom. The 4Cs are capabilities for individual and communal empowerment and they must be informed and lit up by knowledge, new understandings and wisdom. Without knowledge, new understandings and wisdom, the 4C capabilities are a prism without light, or hollow vessels without substance. Together the 4Cs and knowledge and wisdom combine into deeper and connected understandings of knowledge and possibilities for change. The refracted light ensuing from their combining continues and expands as deep understanding, connected knowledge and transformative learning.

The prism can represent experiences in learning spaces with students or it can represent the whole school. For instance, in the schools we mentor in the 4Cs approach, we use the knowledge and wisdom of effective learning. Through the prism or interaction with 4C practice and processes, teachers as learners develop a

Figure 3.2 The Learning Prism representing the interaction of knowledge, new understanding and wisdom with the 4C capabilities to develop deep understanding, connected knowledge and transformative learning

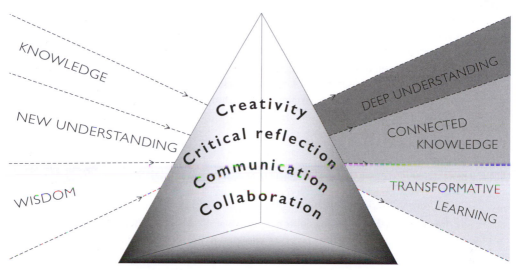

deeper understanding and connected knowledge of learning and education. They change their original assumptions of what schooling can be as they witness the struggles and transformation of students, and the transformation of themselves (Mezirow, 2009). The 4Cs capabilities are explored at length in Chapters 5 to 8, but how do we conceive knowledge, new understandings and wisdom in the 4Cs?

Knowledge as new understandings and wisdom in the 4Cs approach

Knowledge in learning is often explained as being declarative or procedural. Declarative knowledge is to know facts, concepts, principles and rules, i.e. 'knowing what', and procedural knowledge is the 'knowing how' of procedures and strategies. However, knowledge is not generative, or able to be extended and expanded and applied to new situations, unless there are 'new understandings'. From prior knowledge new understandings are made through the processes of learning.

New understanding is to know more, but as Sternberg (2003) argues, 'To be wise, one must know what one knows, know what one does not know, know what can be known, and know what cannot be known at a given time or place' (p. 153). Sternberg (2003) claims that knowing requires the wisdom of realizing what you don't know. Wisdom requires critical reflection that balances competing interests between oneself (the intrapersonal), others (the interpersonal) and other contextual aspects such as your environment, or your community (the extrapersonal). It is not wise when good outcomes can be sought for oneself but not for the good of others and their interests. Wisdom is to search, care and act for the common good of others and oneself.

Knowledge as well as ignorance can be used unwisely. Knowledge can be manipulated or mindlessly employed to have a debilitating or destructive effect on others. We view wisdom as profoundly central to 4C learning and the generating of knowledge. Wisdom improves our wellbeing and quality of life (Kekes, 1995) as it entails a mindful and deliberative approach to making judgements and taking action with the knowledge that we have (Langer, 1997). Sternberg (2003) describes the wise person as dealing with a variety of different kinds of people, seeking as much information as possible for decision-making and knowing how to weigh advice. Wisdom is about making sensible and fair judgements that take the long-term as well as short-term view of consequences.

How then do learners become wiser in their use of knowledge? Embedded in the 4Cs approach is the interwoven thread of critical reflection. This is key to the development of wisdom. Pedagogy in the 4Cs approach is characterized by questioning and critical reflection in what is being learnt and how it is being learnt, and how that informs our decisions and actions. To realize the ends to which knowledge is used, for better or worse, matters as much as knowledge itself. Students need to enquire into and understand *why* they are learning what they are learning and *how* this knowledge can be put to constructive use to improve the quality of life (Gardner, 2007). For instance, why do we learn history? Why do we need to work out and understand cause and effect and consequences of the past, to focus on the present, to understand the future? What authentic and constructive learning can students experience to realize the consequences of history on who they are and how they live, now and into the future?

Knowledge put to constructive use is often more engaging, rewarding and pleasurable anyway. Here is a history example: students created and performed a piece of promenade theatre to the community about learning at their school. They depicted education 100 years ago in different locations around the school, and compared it with their current 4C schooling. Knowledge in history, historical inquiry, literacy, drama, creativity, collaboration and communication were used to share their understanding of schooling from the past to today. From the act of sharing and taking responsibility for communicating new learning to the school community, there was a sense of pleasure and working towards a common good for the students and teachers involved in the performance as learning.

To teach for wisdom is to use critical reflection as a 4C capability to inform decisions and actions in all learning. It is to recognize explicitly that how we use knowledge infuses the way we teach. For instance how does the way we as teachers communicate, the way we collaborate, the way we critically reflect, the way we create, have an effect on others? Is that effect constructive towards a common good? How is what we learn in science, music, sport, history needed to be known to further our individual and collective wisdom? To value wisdom is to value the attainment of knowledge to achieve something good. To gain knowledge in itself is not good; knowing how to apply intelligence and creativity towards the common good is knowledge as wisdom. (Sternberg, 2003)

Another way to further the development of wisdom is to be able to construct knowledge from different points of view. Students need to consider different perspectives to make balanced, wise decisions. A more integrated approach to knowledge in the curriculum can open students to broader and deeper understandings and perspectives.

Integrating knowledge across the curriculum

In schools, students do not necessarily make links across disciplines when learning is structured and timetabled in subject 'silos'. To develop different perspectives in knowledge, learning connections can be made across disciplines when they are integrated. Disciplines can be integrated across the curriculum in any number of ways depending on the will, needs and interests of teachers and students. The implementation of curriculum integration should be unique to every learning setting, but integration can be characterized by three approaches that offer a way to design knowledge connections (Drake and Burns, 2004; Drake, 2012):

- a *multidisciplinary* approach with a central and common theme but that still focuses primarily on individual disciplines in relation to that theme,

- an *interdisciplinary* approach that organizes the curriculum around common learnings across disciplines and uses common themes, concepts and interdisciplinary skills such as literacy, numeracy, research skills etc to chunk together common learnings to emphasize interdisciplinary skills and concepts, and

- a *transdisciplinary* approach that organizes the curriculum around students questions and concerns, and students apply interdisciplinary and disciplinary skills in a real-life context (Adapted from Drake and Burns, 2004, pp. 8–14).

Integrated curricula can deepen student learning experiences by making greater sense of the many perspectives and connections that shape knowledge, and can also increase student motivation and engagement (Drake, 2012). The experience of integrating the curriculum can be described as 'dissolving the boundaries of disciplines' for as soon as one set of connections is made, another set appears (Drake and Burns, 2004). In integrating the curriculum through 4C learning (mostly through interdisciplinary and transdisciplinary approaches) we observe educators and students experiencing the deepening and widening of connections as they become more experienced in teaching and learning with integrated curricula.

We have found in schools fear and exhilaration not only in integrating the curricula, but in undertaking a 4C approach to learning as a whole. It is a transformative experience that is challenging and awakening for teachers and students. For instance, after apprehensive and confused beginnings, two teachers were very excited when they generated their third integrated programme in 4Cs learning. They were eagerly speculating about how their students would engage with and be challenged by the overall driving question they created for their integrated curricula of science, creative arts and English. The overarching question was: 'Is adaptation and change necessary for survival?' and it involved the students generating their own personal and team survivor challenge in adaptation. For instance, could they make the family meals, make all the beds at home and make their own way to school for a week? Could their parents adapt to these changes? At the same time, the students researched curiosity questions such as, why do tigers have stripes? How did humans adapt and evolve? Why do giraffes have long necks? The students were animated when introduced to the learning, and enlivened by the end of it. The inquiry tasks revealed how different perspectives across the curriculum through integration, had heightened the students' perception. It had also developed insight and wisdom in understanding the capacity of themselves, others and nature to adapt to change.

We believe that integrated curricula should not be standardized as it offers multiple and limitless pathways and experiences for teacher and student creativity (Drake, 2012). In the 4Cs approach, teachers design integrated curricula according to student needs, student interests and relevant contemporary issues. Integrated curricula are the exploration of possible and deeper connections across disciplines in learning, and as an approach to knowledge creation and learning should be both planned and emergent. Integrated knowledge can support:

- the development of making wise choices and decisions by fusing multiple and diverse perspectives across different disciplines,
- deeper connections in learning by utilizing multifaceted viewpoints from different disciplines in a real-world context, and
- emergent creative teaching and learning opportunities.

Integrated knowledge can be daunting for teachers and students; it involves taking risks, making new connections, dealing with ambiguities, encountering and solving problems and generating new ideas. It is a creative approach that encourages knowledge, new understandings and wisdom that make transformative learning possible. However, to begin and support the difficult and challenging step towards 4C transformative learning we developed a diagnostic tool for learning, the Learning Disposition Wheel (see Figure 3.3).

The capacity to develop a disposition for learning in the 4Cs

We discovered in our work with schools not only issues with learning the 4C capabilities, but problems with learning behaviours such as concentration, resilience and taking initiative. The Learning Disposition Wheel evolved as a starting point to understand and address competencies for learning, and track student progress in 4C learning.

An assumption underpinning the Learning Disposition Wheel competencies and the 4Cs capabilities is that features of human personality are malleable. This is at

Figure 3.3 The Learning Disposition Wheel is a diagnostic tool that represents the cognitive, intra and interpersonal competencies needed for self-regulated learning

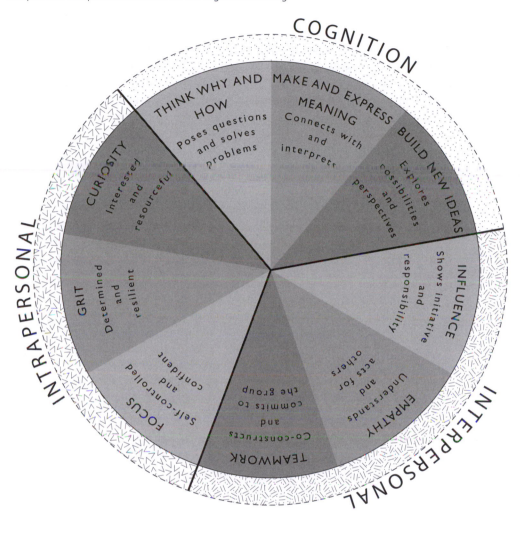

variance with the view that cognitive ability and personality traits remain fixed throughout life. There is however a recent, broad consensus based on evidence from longitudinal studies that personality traits do change (Boyce, Wood and Powdthavee, 2012). Changes in personality are as much determined by environment as by genes (Roberts, Walton and Viechtbauer, 2006). The learning environment created by schools then has the potential to shape human personality and behaviour. Almlund and colleagues (2011) argue that interventions to boost personality traits can be effective in promoting adult success and may reduce educational disadvantage. 'Although personality traits are not merely situation-driven ephemera, they are also not set in stone. We present evidence that both cognitive and personality traits evolve over the life cycle – but at different rates at different stages. Recently developed economic models of parental and environmental investment in children help to explain the evolution of these traits' (Almlund and colleagues, 2011, p. 6).

Similarly, Boyce and colleagues (2012) have shown that personality can change throughout life, and that those changes relate meaningfully to changes in subjective wellbeing. Developing the cognitive, intra and interpersonal domains of the human disposition has consequences for individual and collective wellbeing. A belief in the malleability of personality also encourages learners to be positive and open about the possibilities of being able to learn, being able to confront challenges, and being able to change (Dweck, 2000).

The malleability of human competencies resonates with Vygotsky's theories of human personality as a social, non-static concept (1983/1997a). Vygotsky argues that mastery of experiences in the world and using those experiences for future development forms personality. For example, the more people positively experience creative activities, the more creativity becomes a part of their personalities (Moran and John-Steiner, 2003; Sternberg, 2003). Here is an example of some of the behavioural and disposition changes teacher Jo noticed in her students.

> We are a team of three teachers and as we implement teaching and learning using the 4Cs we have seen individual children change in different ways. But overall, we have noticed the students have become more focused on their learning; more aware of their environment and the people with whom they interact; more capable in completing challenging tasks through collaboration; valuing their peers and understanding that diversity of perspectives is helpful in completing tasks; more confident with sharing their ideas with partners, groups and the wider grade; and more able to resolve conflict that occurs in the classroom and playground.

The contention behind the 4C approach is that a disposition for learning is malleable and strongly influenced by social constructs and interventions. In schools these constructs are built and framed around pedagogy, relationships, learning cultures, teacher and student expectations, learning spaces, technology, timetabling of learning, teacher work and professional learning practices, learning assessments, curricula choices, school leadership, community involvement, systemic requirements, government policies and legislation. All have an impact on the learner's disposition to learn. The 4Cs as capabilities and as an approach can affect all these constructs and influence how a person and a community has the capacity and opportunity to be empowered to learn, reflect, take action and transform.

The Learning Disposition Wheel as a diagnostic and assessment tool

To summarize how the Learning Disposition Wheel supports the development and progress of 4C learning, here are some typical questions and answers that demonstrate using the Learning Disposition Wheel tool to begin 4C learning at a school:

Teacher   Why are we using the Learning Disposition Wheel?

Mentor   The Wheel is a way to talk about and focus on learning, and to diagnose students' dispositions for self-regulation and self-direction.

Teacher   How do the 4Cs work with the Learning Disposition Wheel?

Mentor   We begin to develop the 4C capabilities as well, but we need to also focus on developing students' dispositions to learn. The stronger the learner is in self-direction, the stronger we can develop the 4Cs in learning and empowerment.

Teacher   How do we begin using the Wheel?

Mentor   If you look at the Wheel, what is it you think students are strong in, and what do you think they are weaker in? If you were to focus on one cognitive, intrapersonal and interpersonal competency or 'power', what would it be for your students? If it's 'focus', 'make and express meaning' and 'teamwork', that's where we begin to design learning experiences to develop the students' disposition to learn.

Teacher   Should the students use the wheel?

Mentor   The wheel is as much a tool for students as it is for teachers and parents. It gives us a way to start talking about learning, design learning experiences and assessment, and track student progress in 4C learning.

The Learning Disposition Wheel is a generic tool. It has been redesigned to cater specifically for different contexts e.g. special needs, early childhood and adult education. Here is an example from a teacher, Lucia, explaining how she, her teaching team and the students, started their development of 4C learning by using the Learning Disposition Wheel tool.

Through our initial navigation (mathematics) inquiry in line with the Learning Disposition Wheel, it became immediately apparent how the individual powers (competencies) of the Wheel were dependent on one another to deepen the learning. The actual task required students to solve an open-ended problem demonstrating a variety of measurement skills incorporating geometry, fractions and decimals and whole number understandings.

The complexities of the task immediately indicated that *grit* would be a targeted area from the Learning Disposition Wheel if the students were to successfully complete the inquiry. Through teacher observations during the beginning stages it was identified that even though students were enthusiastic and determined in their inquiry, *teamwork* was also an essential component. The learning experiences proved complex. Scaffolded learning experiences quickly drew student attention to the need to plan effectively the steps of their inquiry, which could not be done individually but as the result of working collaboratively with their team. This led to the realization that working effectively as a team meant each member had a responsibility to the team and each was held accountable to complete the mini tasks building on known understandings and skills.

During the course of their investigation students learnt that the power of teamwork relied heavily on their ability to negotiate, listen to other points of view, challenge when necessary and come to a consensus before moving forward. This was highlighted when a team member who had been absent from school, when her team explained how they had solved the problem, challenged their solution as they had not read all the information provided. She demonstrated and proved her reasoning to her team. Discussion of the roles, and responsibility of each team member to double-check solutions and challenge each other's ideas if they did not agree, rather than just accepting everything one or two teammates said, was a turning point for students allowing them to make the connection between *teamwork* and *grit*.

Another connection to the Learning Disposition Wheel that became evident to the students was *grit* and *think why* and *how*. Throughout the course of the inquiry students had to constantly check for accuracy in their measurements, and select and apply appropriate strategies to solve problems. There were numerous occasions that the students failed in their initial solutions but due to *teamwork*, which fostered *grit*, the students encouraged one another and challenged where necessary, extending each other's thinking and understanding, delving further into the learning by continually questioning, making decisions based on task requirements, proving their theories and reflecting on their learning at each stage of the inquiry.

The connection between the powers of the Learning Disposition Wheel to student learning made the learning more authentic and powerful.

The Learning Disposition Wheel emerges from the US National Research Council's report, *Education for Life and Work: Developing Transferable Knowledge and Skills in the 21st Century* (Pellegrino and Hilton, 2012). The report identifies three domains of competence that shape learning and development:

1 The cognitive – the capacity to think and reason.

2 The intrapersonal – the capacity of managing emotions and behaviours to achieve goals.

3 The interpersonal – the capacity to express, interpret and respond to messages from others.

In the Learning Disposition Wheel each cognitive, intra and interpersonal competency is equally significant and necessary to develop a disposition for deeper learning. For example, to be conscientious and show 'grit' in the intrapersonal is just as significant and valued as being able to problem-solve by 'think why and how' in the cognitive domain, as is showing 'empathy' in the interpersonal domain. The intra and interpersonal domains of human behaviour are not by-products *of* or inherent *to* cognitive learning, they are acknowledged as fundamental and interconnected *processes* in the *social practice* of learning.

It is critical to reiterate that it is the whole of the wheel that develops a disposition for learning. Without 'grit', 'new ideas' will never come to fruition; without 'influence' we cannot 'make and express meaning' effectively; without 'curiosity' we cannot 'think why and how'. Learning in the competencies on the wheel also cannot be dismembered from learning discipline specific content knowledge (as explored in Chapter 4's discussion of pedagogy).

The Learning Disposition Wheel is a tool to:

- be aware of, focus on and diagnose the integral cognitive, intra and interpersonal competencies that are needed to be a learner;
- use and develop a common meta-language between teachers, students, parents and the community, to talk about, reflect and take action about *how* to be a learner;
- understand and promote how a learning disposition is needed to develop the 4C capabilities and how the 4C capabilities can support the development of a learning disposition.

The 4Cs are also present in the Learning Disposition Wheel: creativity is 'build new ideas'; critical reflection is 'think why and how' with 'focus'; communication is 'make and express meaning'; and collaboration is 'teamwork'. The 4Cs are in the Learning Disposition Wheel as they are competencies themselves that contribute to self-regulated and deeper learning (Pellegrino and Hilton, 2012). The Learning Disposition Wheel is a tool to understand the cognitive, intra and interpersonal nature of learning, and the 4Cs as the capabilities for transformative learning and empowerment.

The relationship between all the elements in the 4Cs approach to learning is illustrated in the Transformative Spinning Wheel in Figure 3.4. We have represented the relationship between the Learning Disposition Wheel, the 4Cs, knowledge and transformative education as a wheel with interrelated and constantly spinning connections. The axle is the learning disposition that gives capacity to the 4Cs. Communication, critical reflection, collaboration and creativity as capabilities are realized and strengthened by their connection to each other. Together they spin with the creation of knowledge, new understandings and wisdom.

To encapsulate deeper learning, Fullan and Langworthy (2014) use 6Cs; the two additional Cs are character and citizenship. In our 4C organizer and approach these are inherent to the Learning Disposition Wheel and our understanding of knowledge and wisdom. Fullan and Langworthy's 6Cs illustrate how coherence and synthesis of what makes for deeper learning can be explored and communicated in different ways for different purposes.

A road map for learning in the 4Cs

Learning for teachers, students, leaders and communities in the 4Cs approach can be supported by:

● *Using 4C coherence makers and the Learning Disposition Wheel tool to focus on deeper learning and transferable knowledge to empower learners.* The coherence makers we offer synthesize fundamentals to access understanding and learning. They are also designed to open up to emergent possibilities and complexities in deeper learning and transferable knowledge. The 4C coherence makers (in Chapters 5 to 8) aim to make sense, conceptually and in practice, of

Figure 3.4 The Transformative Spinning Wheel illustrates the interconnected relationships between the Learning Disposition Wheel, the 4Cs, knowledge, new understanding and wisdom for constantly changing transformative education

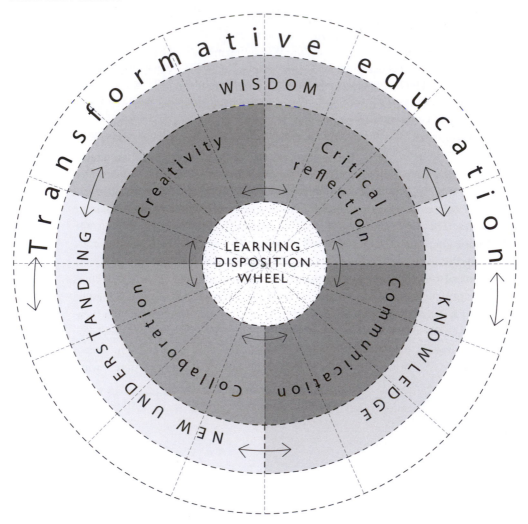

the ideas in the 4Cs approach. The coherence makers and tools can be used and understood by teachers, students and their communities.

- *Developing learners' dispositions for learning by focusing on cognitive, intra and interpersonal competencies, and the 4C capabilities, in learning and assessment.* The capacity to develop a learning disposition is a malleable entity and is dependent on developing intrapersonal and interpersonal capacities as much as cognitive abilities. The focus of much of education is solely on cognitive competencies, so teachers and learners need to develop pedagogies that nurture the learning disposition and the 4Cs within the learning of discipline-specific knowledge. Assessment and feedback are crucial tools for developing self-regulated learning through metacognition. The 4C capabilities, and the intra and interpersonal and cognitive competencies are therefore integral to assessment for learning. An example of an assessment rubric for the 4C capabilities is provided in the Appendix (assessment criteria for the Learning Wheel Disposition competencies have also been developed).

- *Developing experiences in integrated curricula to deepen student understanding and engagement.* Integrating the curriculum also develops deeper teacher engagement with knowledge and learning, as well as for students. Integrated curricula can consolidate fundamentals and transfer knowledge such as the 4Cs across the curriculum, as well as demonstrate synergies and diversities of perspectives across disciplines. Integration can deepen the connections between disciplines, and deepen the specific learning within disciplines.

- *Framing knowledge in terms of wisdom, and designing learning experiences to achieve a common good for ourselves, for others and our communities.* The 4Cs and knowledge can be empty and destructive without the morality and ethics of acting wisely. Wisdom is to acknowledge that our thinking and actions affect others and ourselves, and therefore our decisions and choices require considered and balanced judgements. Knowing why and what we learn informs how we use knowledge for a common good. Critical reflection in the 4Cs approach is crucial to developing new understandings that lead to wisdom and to transformation.

To return to the beauty of number patterns and mathematics making coherence of the world, the 'beauty' of coherence makers is to make sense of how we learn, and can transform. Learning is complex, and the Learning Disposition Wheel as a tool, and the 4Cs coherence makers, attempt to highlight how to begin to empower the learner to learn, to want to learn and to be excited by learning. The 4Cs approach aims to foster creativity to imagine the possible and to think and act with wisdom. G.H. Hardy said there is 'no place for ugly mathematics', and in schools learning should be a thing of beauty. This is what Maxine Greene (1995) has always argued for:

> We want our classrooms to be just and caring, full of various conceptions of the good. We want them to be articulate, with the dialogue involving as many

persons as possible, opening to one another, opening to the world. And we want our children to be concerned for one another, as we learn to be concerned for them. We want them to achieve friendships among one another, as each one moves to a heightened sense of craft and wide-awakeness, to a renewed consciousness of worth and possibility. (pp. 167–168)

This sense of wide-awakeness and renewed consciousness of worth and possibility is captured in the spontaneous and profound reflection of Danielle, a young primary school teacher. In response to the impact of the 4Cs approach, she said: 'The learning and the transformation starts in you and only when that's alive in you can it happen for the kids. And when it does happen in the teacher, it flows into the kids. This pedagogy works . . . it's a journey though.'

The next chapter explores the nature of the pedagogy that serves the 4Cs and empowers learners to be self-regulated, self-directed and transformed.

Note

1 We have only included a few of the coherence makers due to limited space. There are several other coherence makers including:

- The school transformation clock
- The school transformation wheel
- The 4 C pedagogy wheel
- The higher order learning wheel
- The special needs learning wheel
- The learning praxis framework

These will become available in future publications.

Pedagogy and the 4Cs approach

4

Miranda was chatting to a leader at a school, not involved in the 4Cs, about the work she was doing:

This leader is caring and dedicated in his commitment to students, and he had just returned with a group of secondary students from an intensive immersion experience in Cambodia. We were talking about inquiry-based learning and I was surprised when he said that he knew the research supported self-directed, collaborative and creative inquiry for learners, but he just didn't like it. It didn't feel right for him. I suppose he was saying the research didn't suit the kind of teacher he wanted to be. It's not to say he didn't believe in self-direction, collaboration and inquiry, because I'm sure he does. It's just the pedagogy that facilitates these skills changed the role and self-concept that he felt defined him as a teacher.

Pedagogy is at the heart of who a teacher is and the learning experiences they create for their students. In the 4Cs approach, our vision for education fundamentally impacts pedagogy. Pedagogy in the 4Cs approach is about creating the optimal conditions for students and teachers to be autonomous and self-directed in the capabilities of the 4Cs: creativity, critical reflection, communication and collaboration. In this chapter we see pedagogy as critical to empowered learners and human agency. We examine how pedagogy to develop the 4Cs requires:

- deep understanding and knowing learners and their needs,
- engaging teaching and learning as a creative process,
- deep understanding how learning is generated, and
- developing self-directed, autonomous teachers and learners.

How do we explain pedagogy in the 4Cs approach?

Pedagogy is not merely strategies and techniques for teaching, it reflects a mindset, a view of learners and learning, and what educators value as knowledge. Pedagogy must be a deliberate, strategic and mindful choice because it has profound consequences. Pedagogy reflects the type of learning, learners, schools and society we want to create. Pedagogy contributes to defining not only teachers, but to defining who learners are and can be. According to Giroux (2013), pedagogy is to link knowledge to a sense of direction for the learner: 'pedagogy goes beyond providing the conditions for the simple acts of knowing and understanding and includes the cultivation of the very power of self-definition and critical agency. . . Learning occurs in a space in which commitment and passion provide students with a sense of what it means to link knowledge to a sense of direction' (pp. 127–128).

At the heart of the 4C approach is the cultivation of self-definition and critical agency for students and teachers. Learning in the 4Cs must endow learners with a sense of direction that has purpose and hope, and a critical and creative engagement with the world. Pedagogy in the 4Cs approach must promote autonomous learners who own their learning, have choice and have a voice in their learning. To dismiss these ideas as utopian and unrealistic is to misunderstand the power of pedagogy in schools.

In the light of Paulo Freire's work, pedagogy is a social and inherently political process. It is to ask ourselves as teachers and educational leaders, do we practise what we teach? Are our schools just and democratic? Are teachers and students making and taking responsibility to promote open and critical dialogue? How are we developing a just and democratic society through our schools? Are we developing the resourcefulness to be creative and innovative in our schools? To answer these questions, teachers must continually appraise and reflect critically on their chosen and developing pedagogy through praxis, the linking of theory and practice. Through the praxis of their pedagogy, a teacher shapes the learning, the learner, and their own learning.

To create empowered 4C learners for the future, teachers have to be empowered twenty-first-century pedagogues. Teachers must be autonomous learners, learning and re-learning how to support and challenge young people authentically to prepare them for a rapidly changing and complex global environment. To do this, teachers must first know their learners by 'walking with them'.

Pedagogues 'walking with learners'

In Ancient Greece, pedagogues (*paidagogos*) were often foreign slaves who were tutors in wealthy households. They accompanied the children of the family to school, ate meals with them, and walked with them through the streets. The pedagogues carried the children's books, kept them safe and, through example, experience, conversation and discipline, taught them lessons in responsibilities, social expectations and morality. To use a metaphor derived from the Ancient Greek experience, the teacher, as pedagogue, must walk with the learner. The pedagogue gets to know the learner if they step into the learner's shoes by walking with them. Teachers understand the world of the learner by guiding them through experiences, deep questioning, discussions, actions and reflections. Pedagogy, we argue, begins with teachers building a 'collaborative' relationship with the learner.

These ideas draw from the social pedagogy tradition based on some of the following principles (adapted from Cameron and Moss, 2011, p. 9):

- There is a focus on the learner as a whole person, and support for the learner's overall development.

- The practitioner sees herself as a person, in relationship with the learner.

- Learners and teachers are seen as inhabiting the same lifespace; not as existing in separate hierarchical domains.

- As professionals, pedagogues are encouraged constantly to reflect on their practice and to apply both theoretical understandings and self-knowledge to the sometimes challenging demands with which they are confronted.

Teachers, as guides inhabiting the same lifespace, have to care for learners and gain their trust. This can only be built from collaborative relationships between teachers and learners founded on mutual respect, shared understandings and reflective practice (Greene, 1996). Without the forging of these relationships, the optimal conditions for 4C learning in a school climate cannot be fostered. To understand the differentiated individual needs and community needs of students has a relational dimension. Positive relationships are key to a school climate that is sensitive to the learner's cultural context, understands learners' histories and balances group and individual goals to ensure personal growth (Waring and Evans, 2015). The same relational dimension applies to the collaborative working conditions between teachers, between teachers and school leaders, and between teachers and their communities.

Walking with learners is a metaphor to grapple with the description of teachers as either 'sages on the stage' or 'guides on the side' (King, 1993). Teachers' as sages or guides is the dichotomy of teachers as either transmitters and fonts of knowledge or teachers as facilitators and guides of learning. The 4C approach encourages teachers to be guides on the side, but it is also an approach that supports teachers to be sages constructing the right conditions and environment for students to learn knowledge and wisdom. The 4C approach also expects learners to be sages constructing their own optimal conditions for learning, knowledge and wisdom.

To develop autonomous and sagacious learners, the relationship between teachers and learners should not be one of dependency. In the pedagogue walking with learners metaphor, autonomous learners do not walk with their pedagogue the same way every day. The pedagogue introduces learners to different paths and allows them to make choices to take paths without them. The learners know they will be met at some stage by the pedagogue, and through feedback and direction will learn from practice and the choices they make. The pedagogue too will learn from practice and mistakes, and keep exploring different and better directions for their students. For teachers and students to venture along emergent learning pathways requires relational trust, confidence and positive belief.

In this metaphor, making choices and learning from choices in learning pathways must involve critical reflection and risk taking for both pedagogues and learners. How better choices are made is learnt not from being told what is a good or a bad choice, but by thinking about the causes and consequences of choices, and why we make choices in the first place. Pedagogy is not only a result of just making choices. Teachers developing pedagogy, and students developing self-direction in their learning, have to consider what choices are made, why choices are made, and how do we learn from those choices. These types of critical reflections for the pedagogue and the learner are a feature of 4C teaching and learning.

These notions about choosing and developing pedagogy and learning designs can be synthesized for teachers and leaders in the following questions:

1 How can we know the learners better?

2 Really why are learners learning what they are learning?

3 How can what and why they are learning be put to authentic, constructive and wise use?

4 How is pedagogy and learning design shaped by the first three questions?

These questions deepen a teacher's engagement with their pedagogy.

Pedagogy as a creative process

The questions above are loosely based on the Creativity Cascade coherence maker explained in the next chapter. In the cascade, creativity is conceptualized as:

● Noticing.

● Why? Really why?

● Playing with possibilities.

● Selecting and evaluating responses.

Creativity is the ability to produce ideas that are novel, original and unexpected (Sternberg, 2003). Pedagogy has to respond to and challenge the directions that new learning forges. Pedagogy then as a creative process is novel, original and unexpected as it continually extends, enhances and challenges students to be creative in generating new knowledge.

Pedagogy in Leach and Moon's (2007) view is 'a dynamic process, informed by theories, beliefs and dialogue, but only realised in the daily interactions of learners and teachers in real settings' (p. 6). Pedagogy in the 4Cs cannot be a mechanized, formulaic and reductive practice, it must be dynamic and evolving. Pedagogy should be creative, reflective and emergent to be truly transformative in developing the needs, potential and agency of learners and teachers. Being dynamic does not infer that pedagogy is a free-wheeling, unstructured 'happening'. Learning is more effective when 'scaffolds' (Bruner, 1960; Mayer, 2004; Wood, Bruner and Ross, 1976) are deployed as loose structures to support and guide students to construct their own 'edifice of learning'. There are both structures and emergence (or improvisation) in effective pedagogy.

Structure and emergence: The pedagogy paradoxes

Sawyer (2011) describes the tension between structure and improvisation in pedagogy as the manifestation of three paradoxes. First there is the teacher paradox, the weaving together of a teacher's expert knowledge of learning plans, strategies and structures with the improvised teacher practice of responding to learning moments and emerging student learning pathways. The second is the learning paradox, a tension between guiding students with scaffolded structures but also allowing them to improvise when developing content knowledge and skills, and deeper conceptual understanding. The third is the curriculum paradox. This is the tension between the 'fixed' structure of curricula, programmes and lesson plans that direct students to desired learning outcomes. However the most effective curricula stimulate improvisational and creative learning within and beyond the curricula.

Sawyer (2011) argues these paradoxes are resolved if teachers and students balance creativity with constraint by becoming confident in adaptive, improvisational practice. For great pedagogy 'all three paradoxes are addressed through an artful dance; the direction of the class emerges from collaborative improvisation between the teacher and the students' (Sawyer, 2011, p. 3). To encourage efficacious, improvisational and autonomous learners, teachers must have efficacy in improvisational, creative practices. In 'A Call to Action: The challenges of creative teaching and learning', Sawyer (2015) argues that creative learning in schools requires the constant experience of collaborative emergence on the part of students and teachers.

In our experience, the most effective way of inculcating creative learning is, as Sawyer (2015) argues, 'not to allow learners complete freedom to improvise their own path through disciplinary knowledge; it is, rather, to guide them in a process of disciplined improvisation' (p. 27). To transform schools that foster greater creativity, skills in disciplined improvisation must be established in pedagogy and the structures of curriculum, assessment, learning goals and teacher practices. Pedagogical practices that promote disciplined improvisation and creativity include:

1 Opportunities for multiple learning pathways in a creative inquiry process.
2 Assessments that reward deeper conceptual understanding and divergent thinking.

3 Learning goals explicitly incorporating creative learning.

4 Teacher professional learning in creativity. (Sawyer, 2015)

The pedagogy underpinning the development of 4C capabilities is evident in Sawyer's (2015) vision for creative schools where students 'learn to identify good problems, how to ask good questions, how to gather relevant information, how to propose new solutions and hypotheses, and how to use domain-specific skills to express those ideas and make them a reality' (p. 29). Instead of superficial learning that results from instructionism, students participating in creative activities based on their developing knowledge learn a deeper conceptual understanding that 'prepares them to go beyond and build new knowledge' (p. 29). Through collaborative learning, students externalize their developing understandings and metacognition.

Transformation and innovation in schools requires pedagogy that provides creative, collaborative, critically reflective and communication-rich learning opportunities for students. But students also need domain-specific skills to express their ideas and to make their ideas a reality. For example, students may develop ideas about a software app that predicts the effect of building more high-density housing on temperatures and the impact on climate change. Here students must have domain-specific knowledge about temprature effects, the tools of the science of climate change and technology software. Or the students may choose to communicate their ideas about the software app through a digital video, so students need to know the domain-specific skills of digital video creation. In his vision for creativity in schools, Sawyer (2015) is also making reference to the generation of deeper transferable learning experiences as learning that 'prepares them to go beyond and build new knowledge' (p. 29). Deeper learning is central to the development of 4Cs pedagogy.

Why do we need deeper learning?

In Chapter 1 we argued that there is no longer the same demand in the workforce for routine, procedural skills. Jobs requiring low or moderate levels of competence will continue to decline, and jobs requiring more complex communication and problem-solving skills will increase (Frey and Osbourne, 2013a). To adapt to the rapid changes and complexity of new problems and situations in a connected world requires the ability to transfer knowledge.

Transferable knowledge is often described as deeper learning or twenty-first-century skills (Bellanca, 2015). These skills however have always been of value in education that empowers learners to be self-directed and adaptable. The need for deeper learning is not unique to the twenty-first century. Technology, globalization and economics and the pace of change have merely given attention to it. The quality and context of deeper learning experiences are linked to education, work, health and community outcomes (Pellegrino and Hilton, 2012). The intention of the 4Cs approach is to develop deeper learning experiences that empower people to be resourceful, resilient and creative in solving problems and transforming situations.

What is deeper learning?

Deeper learning is the process of developing durable and transferable knowledge. In deeper learning, skills and understandings are transferred to solve or do something new. Rote learning and procedural learning are good for recall and retention but poor for transferring knowledge. Deeper learning on the other hand is suited best for retention and transferring knowledge (Mayer, 2010). In cognitive psychology, deeper learning is explained by how working memory, short and long-term memories of prior learning are used, created, and accessed.

How we mentally organize knowledge affects how quickly we identify and retrieve relevant knowledge to solve a new problem. Cognitive architecture in the mind describes how the sensory, working and long-term memory acquires, stores, represents, revises and assesses information. The way knowledge is stored in the long-term memory has a profound effect on the processing and capacity of the working memory to problem-solve. The more the burden of problem-solving is moved to long-term memory, the less the burden on working memory. The deeper the learning, the more organized knowledge can be accessed from the long-term memory to problem-solve in the working memory (Moreno and Mayer, 2007).

A socio-cultural view of education explains deep learning as not just a result of an individual's cognitive functioning but also as a product of the individual's situated context and perspective. Learning takes place when individuals participate in social practices. The signs, tools, language and cultural artefacts of a community mediate an individual's learning and development. According to Vygotsky (1960/1997b) an individual's cognitive schema is an ongoing internalization of social processes, and so human and cultural development is a construct of social experiences.

Lave and Wenger (1991) view learning as a situated activity where only through social practices can learners master knowledge and skills. 'A person's intentions to learn are engaged and the meaning of learning is configured through the process of becoming a full participant in a sociocultural practice. This social process includes, indeed it subsumes, the learning of knowledgeable skills' (Lave and Wenger, 1991, p. 29). From a socio-cultural perspective, knowledge is a shared practice of knowledge creation continually being revised, elaborated and questioned. This does not just apply to the macro-view of a discipline's body of knowledge, but to the micro-view of an individual's body of knowledge. Individuals revise, elaborate and question their knowledge through social experiences.

As a social practice, deeper learning is the processing of learning, not the product of learning. It is a process both in an individual's mind and in social interactions with a community. Deeper learning is an interaction of an individual's cognitive processes and a community's social practices. The 4Cs approach requires a close examination and engagement with the cognitive and affective processes and social practices of learning. How a learner mentally organizes knowledge provides an insight into the type of learning experiences and pedagogy needed for deeper learning. Teachers have to reflect critically on *why* they teach *what* they teach, and *how* they teach *what* they teach. They then have to work out how to organize the experience of learning.

How can we organize knowledge for learning?

How to organize knowledge for learning helps teachers in developing pedagogy, programmes and learning strategies. As learners journey along the many learning pathways, how can knowledge be 'carried' along for future pathways? Mayer (2010) suggests there are five types of knowledge that work together to 'carry' knowledge. The way a learner mentally organizes these five types of knowledge influences whether the knowledge leads to transference. The five types of knowledge and how they are organized for deeper learning transference are presented in Table 4.1. To explain what these types of knowledge mean, we have used teacher learning in the 4C approach as an example of how knowledge can be organized for deeper learning.

If facts are just presented as facts they will not lead to deeper, transferable learning. But if factual knowledge is integrated with other information it is more likely to be

Table 4.1 Summary and examples of five types of integrated knowledge needed for deeper learning knowledge transference (Mayer, 2010; Pellegrino and Hilton, 2012)

Type of knowledge	How knowledge is organized for deeper learning	Example: Professional learning pedagogy working with teachers and leaders in the 4C approach in schools
Factual	Integrated, rather than isolated facts	4C learning is integrated with what teachers already know.
Conceptual	Schemas, models or general principles	4C coherence makers are schemas that synthesize and open up complexity about learning and the 4C capabilities for teachers and students.
Procedures	Automated and embedded, taking less effort and thought	Step by step experience for teachers and school leaders implementing aspects of the 4Cs approach in their teaching and learning is embedded over time.
Strategies	Specific cognitive and metacognitive strategies to be a self-directed learner	Collaborative mentoring and critical reflection in discussions, workshops and in-situ teaching promotes self-directed learning in 4C pedagogy with teachers and school leaders.
Beliefs	Positive and productive beliefs in learning	Positive belief that the development of intra and interpersonal and cognitive competencies and the 4C capabilities contribute to continued learning for teachers and school leaders.

transferred. In 4C mentoring in schools we integrate what teachers already know with what we are facilitating in 4C learning. Another type of knowledge is conceptual knowledge, and that knowledge is more likely to be transferred if it is organized around schemas and models or general principles. The 4C coherence makers we use in schools are schemas and general principles that support the deepening and transferring of the conceptual knowledge we present about the 4Cs and learning.

There is also the 'how to' of procedural knowledge. When procedures or processes are practised they are automated and embedded in long-term memory, and more readily able to be applied to new situations or problems. In our example of working with teachers, the more teachers and leaders experience and practise the ideas we develop with them, the more they understand, apply and extend the learning as procedural skills. Procedural knowledge alone does not contribute to deeper learning transfer; it works together with factual and conceptual knowledge and the other ways of organizing knowledge.

In addition to factual, conceptual and procedural knowledge there are cognitive and metacognitive strategies as a type of knowledge. These strategies are transferable when they are organized to promote and motivate self-regulation in learning. Metacognitive strategies facilitate the learner to use reflection and feedback to direct their thinking in learning. Self-regulation involves the learner being able to plan, monitor, change, reflect on and generate their own learning (Pintrich, 2003/2005; 2004). In our example of 4C learning with teachers in schools, we support teachers' cognitive and metacognitive knowledge (thinking and reflecting) through collaborative mentoring discussions, workshops and in-situ teaching of critical reflection. Teachers in collaborations with their teaching teams, and with students, also direct and progress the development of lessons and in programmes as a response to metacognition in their learning and in their students' learning.

The last type of knowledge is organizing belief in learning as something positive and productive. Learning requires being motivated to learn by valuing and believing in being able to learn (Dweck and Leggett, 1988; Dweck and Master, 2009). We have argued in Chapter 3 that a learning disposition can be nurtured and learnt through pedagogy that develops intra, interpersonal and cognitive competencies. In our example of working with teachers and leaders in schools, we hold a positive belief that the development of these intra and interpersonal and cognitive competencies and the 4C capabilities contribute to continued learning. At the core of the 4Cs approach is the empowerment of all learners to be self-directed and positive about learning.

Knowing how the types of knowledge work together and are organized helps in understanding effective pedagogy and learning strategies; it is to ask these questions about organizing knowledge:

- How are facts integrated?
- How are concepts synthesized?
- How are skills practised?
- How do strategies help self-directed learning?
- How are learners positive about learning?

How do we process learning?

Generative learning theory (Wittrock, 1974; Fiorella and Mayer, 2015) describes the way we build learning onto what we already know. Rather than examining how we *organize* knowledge, the focus with generative learning theory is how we *process* knowledge in learning. 'Organizing knowledge' can be compared to the periodic table as an organizer of elements in science knowledge. How you then *use* the periodic table for chemical experiments is the 'processing of knowledge'. Generative learning strategies are how we process material and make sense of it so that it can be applied to a new situation. This is different from rote learning, which enables remembering material, and associative learning, when responses are linked to stimuli.

Generative learning strategies are interventions that help learners to select, organize and integrate knowledge and skills. For example, a generative learning strategy is teaching. When you teach something you have to select, organize and integrate what is the best way to communicate and engage learners with a learning experience. The act of cognitively working that out, then doing it, and then reflecting on the experience, generates deeper learning. It is for the learner (as a teacher) an active rather than passive process. To return to the metaphor of pedagogues guiding and letting learners choose different pathways, generative learning strategies contribute to learners making sense of the pathways they travel, and being able to travel along new pathways.

Deeper learning for transferable knowledge and skills is what learners need to understand, question, adapt and create in new and changing situations. It focuses on the quality of the learning to achieve outcomes in transfer performance and long-term memory retention. Fiorella and Mayer (2015) present eight generative learning strategies (see Table 4.2) that contribute to learners processing learning from working memory to long-term memory. Choosing and developing appropriate and effective strategies in pedagogy is to understand why, how and when these eight cognitive strategies should be used. With most of these strategies, learners need to be trained and experienced in mastering the strategy to use them. For instance, learners need experiences in forming mental imagery to reap the benefits of learning through imagining.

These strategies alone do not foster learning; other factors such as motivation and metacognition are integral to making sense of and self-regulating the learning process. Focusing on generative learning strategies highlights the need for teachers and students to be metacognizant of strategies that inform the pedagogical and learning decisions they make. Metacognition is for teachers and students to consider, monitor and control learning strategies by first asking questions such as: What is enacting (or embodiment)? Why do we need to learn to enact in order to learn? How do we learn to enact? When do we need to enact? (Enactment as embodied cognition is discussed further in Chapter 7 as integral to communication learning.)

We focus on questioning and metacognition of learning processes to develop effective pedagogy for the 4Cs and discipline-specific knowledge. Too often pedagogy focuses solely on curriculum content and not teaching the processes and skills in how to learn. We argue that there is a policy/pedagogy gap in education in addressing the teaching of learning processes. Fiorella and Mayer (2015) also argue that greater

Table 4.2 Generative learning strategies (adapted from Fiorella and Mayer, 2015) and examples of their use in 4C pedagogy

Generative learning strategy	Description	Example of use in 4C pedagogy (where 4Cs capabilities are evident in the learning)
Summarizing	Create a summary of the learning	After a discussion or instruction, learners create three tableaus (still images) that sum up the salient features of the learning.
Mapping	Create a concept map or matrix organizer	Students collaboratively create organizers of what needs to be addressed to solve a problem and rate them red, orange and green in terms of difficulty.
Drawing	Create a drawing that depicts the learning	Numerical equations are captured as drawn visual representations and shared as online learning for critique.
Imagining	Imagine visually what depicts the learning	Personal experiences are evoked by a visualization that links to a situation and idea in literature being studied.
Self-testing	Give yourself a practice test on material learnt	Questions and answers are conceived for an interrogation of a historical character or perspective.
Self-explaining	Create an explanation of confusing parts of the learning	Learning is broken down into steps and a scaffold of questions is created to organize what is confusing or complex in a theory or procedure.
Teaching	Explain the learning to others	A group teaches by using a range of multimodal forms to solve a complex problem and questions, and is questioned by the audience.
Enacting (or embodiment)	Gesture or move objects to act out the learning	Rights and responsibilities are improvised and explored in a role play, and then evaluated and discussed.

emphasis in pedagogy should be directed to understanding and developing the processes of learning:

> We expect students to be effective learners, but we rarely help them to learn how to learn. Thus, the development of generative learning is part of what can be called the hidden curriculum – something we expect students to learn but actually do not teach. Successful students may pick up some learning strategies on their own – though perhaps not to their maximum effectiveness – whereas less successful students may not (Fiorella and Mayer, 2015, p. 201).

Generative learning is about focusing teachers and learners on being aware of and making sense of learning processes. It is about creating pedagogy and learning environments that endeavour to foster self-directed and self-regulated learners in and through the 4Cs.

How do we learn self-regulation?

Pedagogy that promotes student ownership of the learning, awareness of how to learn and positive self-belief in being able to learn, leads to self-regulation and self-direction in learning (Pellegrino and Hilton, 2012). Quite simply, learners want to learn when they are interested, have success and feel confident. The 4Cs approach aims to promote autonomous and confident learners through what is often described as a *noticing* and *questioning* pedagogy. This is because the core of the 4Cs approach enables the learner to take ownership of their learning. This is encouraged by teachers through pedagogy that heightens an awareness in close observation and critical reflection.

Students are encouraged to take notice of and responsibility for their behaviours, through the pedagogy of open questioning and increased waiting time for interactions, and peer and teacher feedback. Mindful questioning in the learning design allows learners to notice the effect their choices have on learning. Learners can make poor choices and mistakes, or good choices and achieve engagement and success, but they are encouraged and affirmed to notice and critique their choices, and the choices of others, through questioning, monitoring and evaluation.

Students lose the facility to be self-directed when teachers constantly tell them what to do and what to learn. In the 4Cs approach learners are encouraged, questioned and scaffolded to take responsibility and ownership of all learning, behaviours and aspects of school life. Commands and demands from teachers (and students) should not feature in 4C learning. The motivation to learn is affected profoundly by consistent and prominent social-psychological interventions such as promoting self-regulation through the awareness of noticing, questioning and affirmation (Yeager and Walton, 2011). Here is an example of a teacher, Dana, working and struggling with many of these ideas with secondary students who have little belief and control in their own learning abilities.

> Everyone has the capacity to achieve if you just let them. I find the challenge for me is how to make the student imagine this possibility and then believe it for themselves.
>
> Getting students to reflect on their learning by posing questions on a regular basis was difficult at first. My default was to let them know what I noticed and then provide a solution rather than allow the student to problem solve with me. Providing solutions rather than problem solving together is easier because it is

faster. In time, I found that telling them the answer to their problems didn't work. In my attempt to address their weaknesses all I did was reinforce them. I had not allowed my students to reflect on how their actions affected their learning and to communicate this with me. I had given them no opportunity to think critically about possible solutions.

With this realization, I invested time in getting students to reflect on their learning. These are students who defaulted to negative learning behaviours such as making excuses ranging from not having the right equipment, physically moving around the room, to an 'I can't' attitude. My new approach resulted in a level of positive change in the students' learning behaviours. This was by no means an overnight success. The mentoring was on a regular basis and catered to the individual at their point of need. What was simultaneously happening was I was building a relationship, and more importantly reinforcing trust with these students.

Once students made the connection with their own behaviours, or what I call the 'ah ha' moment, their success was celebrated and affirmed, allowing us to progress forward in their learning. Every possible opportunity for the student to be made aware of how they felt about their level of success was explicitly talked through. I believe strongly in building internal motivators rather than providing external motivators.

The next step for me is to find their next experience of success.

The nurturing of confidence in a collaborative learning environment is essential for a learner to believe they are able to learn (Blackwell, Trzesniewski and Dweck, 2007; Yeager and Walton, 2011). Self-efficacy and motivation for learners to learn also require learning experiences that are valued, interesting, challenging and affirming (Wentzel and Wigfield, 2009). To support self-regulation in the learner, pedagogy and learning designs have to balance challenge and affirmation. Challenge is crucial for students to achieve their full potential, but the amount and level of learning difficulty cannot overwhelm learners and destroy their confidence as learners.

Supporting, guiding and affirming learning through scaffolding aids confidence in the learner but over-scaffolding stifles improvisation and creativity in thinking and learning. Over-scaffolding also encourages learners to use surface processing strategies and to perceive deeper approaches as unnecessary (Koopman and colleagues, 2011). Effective pedagogy is evident when scaffolding is provided and withdrawn in response to students' cognitive load and expertise, and when learner self-sufficiency is developed through strategies that enable them to manage their own learning (Waring and Evans, 2015). Differentiation in the 4Cs approach is inherent to learning designs that accommodate all student interests, readiness and needs, to access and achieve learning. 4Cs learning design is inclusive, proactive and future-focused where students are active collaborators and self-regulated within the learning process.

Authentic and more 'open' learning tasks and processes linked to the student's world are also key to motivating and engaging learners to self-regulate their learning. 'Authentic learning typically focuses on real-world, complex problems and their solutions, using role-playing exercises, problem-based activities, case studies, and participation in virtual communities of practice. . . . Going beyond content, authentic learning intentionally brings into play multiple disciplines, multiple perspectives, ways of working, habits of mind, and community' (Lombardi, 2007).

We view the 4C approach and developing self-regulated learners in 4C capabilities as authentic learning for the twenty-first century. In the following example from teacher Ruth, we see evidence of developing authentic and self-directed learning experiences for her students.

As teachers we are often driven by content and compartmentalize everything, when we know that deep learning comes from integrating the curriculum to gain synergy for the students. The challenge for teachers is to let go of the teaching of content and, instead, teach children how to learn.

I had been teaching upper primary for a number of years and had always taught the Science unit on electricity in the same way, teaching the children about the different circuits and getting them to create their own models of an electrical circuit. The 4Cs approach really challenged me to explore the essence of what students really need to know and why it was important for them to know it.

As a result, we created an overall driving question across a number of curriculum areas: How do we interpret and communicate with precision? Related to that was the driving question for science: How can you clearly explain to an audience your deep understanding of energy so that it influences and changes their behaviour?

By identifying areas of the Learning Disposition Wheel that students had weaknesses in, I was able to allow the students to explore their own learning pathway, which was based on their curiosity question about energy, and not just limit their thinking to electricity.

I mindfully planned opportunities for the students to engage in the different powers of the Learning Disposition Wheel, in light of their connection to the driving question. The targeted areas of the learning wheel were 'curiosity', 'think why and how' and 'making and expressing meaning'.

Curiosity – The desire to wonder – I wanted the students to choose and explore energy phenomena that stemmed from their curiosity. This was extremely well received by students.

A student, Joseph, reflected in his Science Journal: 'During Science, instead of being assigned a topic, we got to choose our own topic and compile our own learning for the next term. We also got to answer our own questions and work with different people who were curious about the same topic we were. Instead of going home and forgetting about school and being bored, I was actually happy and excited to go and do some more research about my topic because I actually was very curious and interested in it.'

Think why and how – To design their own scientific investigation that demonstrated their chosen energy phenomena, it was necessary for the students to challenge each other and ask questions to further their learning. Scaffolds were provided in the scientific investigation process and then students were required to design, plan and carry out their own investigation, record their findings and draw conclusions based on their observations. The findings were then linked back to their curiosity question and they were able to find a solution or created more questions for their team to explore.

Making and expressing meaning – The aim for the students was to clearly articulate their thinking by communicating with precision, to effect change. This was achieved by integrating the text type language of an exposition in English with the work they were doing in Science. Students had to demonstrate how they targeted an audience to influence them in a particular way of thinking.

The feedback that the students received from the teachers and their peers directed their thinking and identified learning dispositions they demonstrated well and those that they needed to develop. The learning wheel therefore provides a common language for teachers and students to talk about the lifelong learning skills we hope that students will develop. We have never had the language or tools to support the conversations that need to take place to access deep learning

I found that students began to reflect on themselves as learners by using the language of the learning wheel, instead of whether or not they were 'good' at the content covered. Mariella, a student reflected, 'Communication and grit were my main issue due to the fact that I was shy, which meant that I was not contributing to the work of my team. We were given many opportunities to perform and that's what built my confidence. I was able to persevere with my communication goal and when I had achieved it I felt like a heavy burden was lifted off my shoulders. I learnt that it was okay to make mistakes because we learn from our mistakes.'

Self-regulation in learning requires feedback that is precise to the task and precise to the process and provides direction for improvement (Hattie and Gin, 2011). The dynamic of timely, explanatory and quality feedback and formative assessment encourages students to be responsible for their learning and improves learning progress (Black and colleagues, 2004; Black and Dylan, 2010; Gardner, 2006; Pashler and colleagues, 2005; Shute, 2008). Formative assessment uses evidence and feedback to continually improve student learning. Summative assessment diagnoses what learning needs to be improved in students, but can be used formatively if it is treated as part of the learning process. This is achieved if students are actively involved with the teacher in creating the summative testing process and success criteria (Black and colleagues, 2004).

In the 4Cs approach pedagogy is dependent on developing the cognitive (thinking and reasoning), the intrapersonal (our awareness and how we regulate our emotions and behaviours) and the interpersonal (how we relate to others) to further the effectiveness of learning in the 4C capabilities with discipline-specific knowledge.

Effective learning and pedagogy are complicated, but the 4Cs approach attempts to advocate and clarify concepts that have always been a part of deep and empowering learning experiences. Great teaching has always generated student agency, used the balance of structure and improvisational brilliance, and understood how to activate autonomous learning through cognitive, motivational and metacognitive strategies. We are only re-stating their significance. We are also acknowledging how intra and interpersonal competencies must be explicitly aligned with cognitive competencies for deeper learning and 4C capabilities to be developed.

Pedagogy for the 4Cs approach

The 4Cs approach aims to develop self-directed learners with 4C capabilities and deeper learning experiences. The Learning Disposition Wheel (see Chapter 3) as a diagnostic tool focuses on the ability to learn, and the 4Cs – creativity, critical reflection, collaboration and communication – focuses on applying learning in the wider world through the 'C' capabilities. The 4Cs approach aims to generate in learners:

- the ability to be self-directed,
- learning *in* and *through* the 4Cs capabilities, and
- skills and understandings in discipline-specific (and integrated) knowledge.

Teachers require deeper knowledge in learning, the 4Cs and discipline-specific (and integrated) content knowledge to inform the expertise of their pedagogy. This relationship is illustrated in the pedagogy diagram in Figure 4.1.

The main aims of pedagogy in the 4Cs approach are to:

- develop confidence in all student voices through embodied learning experiences to become self-directed and ethical learners in the capabilities of communication, critical reflection, collaboration and creativity, with discipline-specific (and integrated) learning;
- apply cognitive, metacognitive and affective learning strategies to the development of learning disposition competencies, the 4Cs and discipline-specific learning; and
- promote knowledge transference through curriculum and learning designs that are authentic and integrated, and use the 4Cs in problem-solving and creative tasks.

The aims of 4C pedagogy are comprehensive, and sometimes overwhelming for teachers, leaders and students. Like creativity, transformation begins as a decision. A principal Eva, who has led two schools in co-constructing 4C transformation learning, knows it is not just about ideas and aims; it is about a mindset change to pedagogy. Her key questions to teachers are: 'Who is the main holder of the pen in your room? Whose voice is mostly heard? What does it tell you about who controls the learning?'

A road map for 4C pedagogy

We believe pedagogy must be mindfully engaged with since it underpins and unifies all the choices we make as teachers. These choices affect the social, ethical, cognitive and emotional fabric of the learning environments we create. In the 'pedagogues walking with learners' metaphor, these choices affect the pathways that are chosen

Figure 4.1 The pedagogy diagram illustrates how the Learning Disposition Wheel, discipline-specific and integrated knowledge, and the 4C capabilities all inform the nature of pedagogy

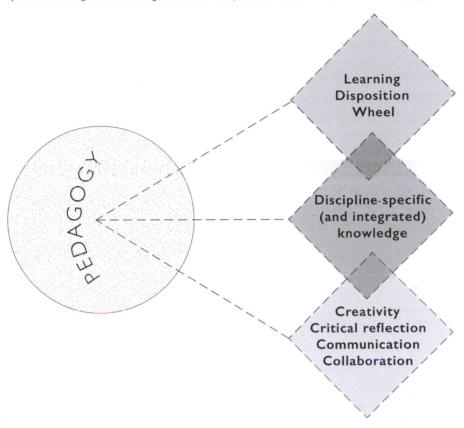

and that emerge. The way they are discovered and walked, and the way they are reflected on determine future pathways. We advocate that pedagogy fundamentally shapes what type of learners, learning, schools, communities and society we aspire to be. The 4Cs approach makes explicit the nature and development of self-regulation, learning and working with the 4C capabilities: creativity, critical reflection, collaboration and communication. Pedagogy for the 4Cs approach can be encouraged and developed by:

- *Teachers and students actively engaging with the complex mechanics of deeper learning processes to inform their decisions in pedagogy and learning.* Rigorous understanding and interrogation of how cognitive learning strategies, metacognition and motivation work together can support and encourage teachers and students to achieve better learning outcomes. Understanding how learning is processed, and why, how and when learning strategies are appropriate and effective, is critical to successful pedagogies. Pedagogy for teachers and learning for students can be monitored, controlled and created when decisions are mindfully made and critiqued. These ideas focus on the capability of critical reflection in pedagogy.

- *Teachers knowing their learners by focusing on students as whole persons, and supporting their overall development by providing them with choices and responsibilities through noticing and questioning.* Pedagogy embraced as a social process is to know learners' cognitive, intra and interpersonal needs and strengths. Supporting their overall development builds confidence and engagement by addressing their needs and furthering their strengths. Through skills in observation, critical reflection and action, teachers and learners take responsibility for their learning and make wiser choices. Communication and collaborative relationships are essential for teachers knowing and understanding learners. These ideas focus on the capabilities of communication and collaboration in pedagogy.

- *Viewing pedagogy as a creative process that collaboratively emerges between teachers and students, and fosters the learning of creativity.* A teacher responding to the new connections students make in learning is an emergent and creative approach to pedagogy. To respond to and challenge learning has both structural and improvisational elements. Disciplined improvisation in pedagogy leads to creative, collaborative emergence in learning and is a skill that develops creativity in teachers and students. These ideas focus on the capability of creativity in pedagogy.

- *Using the steps of the Creativity Cascade as a scaffold to interrogate learning programmes, lessons, evidence, curricula and school structures to further effective pedagogy in the 4Cs.* The Creativity Cascade (see Chapter 5) is a scaffold to harness understanding and skills in creativity. It is a means to critically reflect upon and then creatively problem-solve how to construct improved learning experiences and design. The Creativity Cascade helps to enquire into, and re-solve the issues teachers encounter in learning. This requires a creative approach to problem-solving pedagogy.

The big question is: How can all learners be responsible and motivated in their learning? This is an enormous issue in schools, and we believe there are effective pedagogy and learning strategies that develop autonomous and empowered learners. It begins by cultivating human agency, and the 4Cs approach aims to do this. Pedagogy is a social, cultural and political process that has wide-reaching ramifications. Giroux (2007) argues that it is the cornerstone of democracy:

> Democracy cannot work if citizens are not autonomous, self-judging, and independent – qualities that are indispensable for students if they are going to make vital judgments and choices about participating in and shaping decisions that affect everyday life, institutional reform, and governmental policy. Hence pedagogy becomes the cornerstone of democracy in that it provides the very

foundation for students to learn not merely how to be governed, but also how to be capable of governing. (p. 3)

How can education contribute to democracy? How can it empower people to be collaborators and communicators, to be creatively and critically reflective, meeting the needs of global complexity and contradictions? The next four chapters explore each of the 4Cs to make sense of how they can transform schools and learning, and how they may contribute to a just, democratic and sustainable society.

Creativity

5

The case for creativity: imagining a different future

Imagine that this generation of teachers has the opportunity to redesign and remake schooling – to make schools genuinely and intrinsically creative places. Imagine if we had schools driven by creative possibility, critical reflection, communication and collaboration instead of standardized testing and homogenized learning. How would that change how we teach and where we teach? Instead of pretending that all students and all schools can be standardized, imagine if we allowed students to create in a guided and age-appropriate way, which acknowledged that all people have the capacity for creativity in the same way that all people have the capacity to communicate.

In this chapter we want to imagine creativity as a standard expectation of schooling. To do this we will discuss the problems that persist with creative learning (including the myths that prevent its widespread adoption). We will explore how creativity effectively integrates with critical reflection, communication and collaboration and explore the evidence for creative learning being critical to schooling. In the second half of the chapter we will introduce a coherence maker for creativity learning in schools – the Creativity Cascade.

We believe a full understanding of creativity is a game changer. Dai Smith, Chair of the Arts Council, Wales agrees: 'We must, if we are to succeed economically and thrive socially, ground a quality education in both creativity as practice and culture as knowledge' (2013, p. 3). But before we begin let's examine why creativity is not currently at the centre of schooling.

The problems with teaching creativity

There are significant issues that impede the teaching of creativity in schools. In an effort to overcome these we are going to identify them in this part of the chapter and then work towards some solutions later in the chapter. The issues as we see them are:

definitional and conceptual issues; battling with the mythologies of creativity; and, perhaps most critically, the pedagogy/creativity gap. Let's begin our discussion with some of the definitional and conceptual issues in creativity learning to refute some of the persistent ambiguity around definitions that get in the way of teachers and schools making this C a priority.

Definitional and conceptual issues

Let's begin with a thought experiment. Which is the more tangible: gravity or creativity? If you said gravity you would not be alone. Many people find creativity a difficult concept to grasp, whereas we can always imagine Newton's falling apple when we are trying to imagine gravity. Perhaps the first image that comes to you is of people (perhaps astronauts), floating around without any kind of restraint, in outer space or in one of those gravity-free simulators. So we notice gravity in its absence rather than its presence. We think the same is true of creativity. We often notice the absence of creativity in our students, in our classrooms, in our schools rather than its presence. Typically, in our experience it manifests as a lack of engagement, a lack of excitement, a general lack of dynamism in places of learning and a lack of change in some school environments. We want to suggest that creativity is a definable, knowable and teachable skill that is essential to twenty-first-century learning. It is like gravity as a force that has observable constructs and can be applied to learning to make our schools and classrooms more vital and dynamic. Creativity can also provide a consistent shape for schooling in the same way that gravity shapes and organizes our physical world. To many, creativity is a kind of formless amorphous activity undertaken by genius individuals and without reference to anybody else. This kind of debilitating myth has done damage to the potential for creativity to be useful in the lives of young people. We think creativity is as real as gravity and is a solid, heavy concept. A concept that has been dogged by persistent and corrosive myths that we would now like to discuss.

Mythologies and misconceptions

One of the dominant mythologies that surrounds creativity is that it is only available to the elite genius few (Anderson, 2012). You often hear in industries such as theatre, film and advertising the term 'creatives' used. This role description is designed to divide the 'creatives' from the 'non-creatives' or the more widely used euphemism, the technicians. This dichotomy entrenches the old idea that some are born to creativity and some are born to technicality as if these two cannot interact. Of course the 'technicians' routinely practise a great deal of creativity. For instance in making film if those who are called 'creatives' have no understanding of the technical aspects of their work their creativity is likely to be unsuccessful. Creativity is a capacity that often manifests differently across learning domains (subjects) but it is present and teachable in every area of knowledge. It is not, as some argue, only present in the arts. Creativity is present wherever there is a body of knowledge that can be applied to create value for individuals and communities.

Creativity is part of our daily lives and exercised by us all. Creativity, like critical reflection, communication or collaboration, is a capacity we can learn, strengthen and develop. We all have the capacity to be creative. Craft (2002) calls this 'lifewide creativity' as it is present and demonstrated every day and seen not just in the arts. Our starting point for creativity learning is that it is a part of everyday life and should be integral to knowledge generation and learning in schools.

The Robinson report (NACCCE, 1999) nominates originality as a feature of creativity. Crucially this report defines originality as original for the individual involved in the activity. This is a fundamentally democratic approach to creativity (NACCCE, 1999) that frees educators to focus their pedagogy on all students rather than just those that might one day have the potential 'genius' required. This approach does not deny that there are different qualities of creativity; it simply argues that all students provided with the necessary resources can be creative. As Sternberg (2003) argues, 'children may generate an idea that someone else has already had, but if the idea is original to the student, the student has been creative' (p. 120).

Another myth about creativity is that it is an individual process disconnected from others – this is the myth of the heroic artist working individually in an attic (see Figure 5.1). This is sometimes called the 'creative genius' phenomenon. While we are not denying that creative geniuses exist, they are the exception rather than the rule and they almost always collaborate with others. Mozart, while obviously a creative genius, could not have been successful without the teachers, mentors and other musicians that contributed to his compositions and performances.

Research has also had a role in perpetuating the cult of the creative genius. According to Jeffrey and Craft (2001), even though a majority of research has focused on individual creativity it is consistently demonstrated in group contexts. This view of creativity as essentially collaborative is also backed by the research. Mahn and John-Steiner (2002, p. 51) argue that in collaboration, participants create mutual zones of proximal development (Vygotsky, 1978) for each other where their intellect and emotions are brought together in a unified whole. They explain for example how they think collaborative creativity actually works in the writing process: 'In producing texts partners share each other's early drafts; they strive to give shape to their communicative intent by combining precision – or word meaning – with the fluidity of the sense of the words. They live, temporarily, in each other's heads. They also draw on their mutuality as well as their differences in knowledge, working styles and temperament' (Mahn and John-Steiner, 2002, p. 51).

Another persistent myth is that creativity is discipline-free and unstructured. Creativity requires discipline and resilience to withstand the reiterations required as the project is being developed or when things do not work as planned. For instance when students are attempting to write fiction their first attempts are often uninspired and pedestrian and their work is often derivative of what they might be currently watching on television or online. The key to enhancing the writing is to encourage a culture of reiteration that

Figure 5.1 Leonid Pasternak, 'The Passion of Creation' circa 1880

develops the discipline (fiction writing). Students also need to become familiar with iteration and to accept change (or even failure) that leads to productive change. As the author of *The Book Thief*, Marcus Zusak, argues (2008), 'Failure has been my best friend as a writer. It tests you, to see if you have what it takes to see it through.'

The products of student creativity are often, initially at least, banal and plodding but the potential for creativity is enhanced when teachers are able to develop a learning environment that makes imagination, resilience, iteration and playing with possibility commonplace. Learning to be creative is an evolutionary growth that begins with the student making original discoveries (for themselves) using their imagination and then building on those discoveries by collaborating with others.

These myths (creativity is for the few, creativity is not collaborative, creativity is discipline-free) matter because they lead to people claiming that they are 'not creative'. One of the most common attitudes we face when discussing creativity is the claim by many teachers that 'I am not a creative person'. When teachers claim this deficit, it disconnects them from creativity and disempowers them from teaching it. We think one way to respond to this is to close the pedagogy/creativity gap so that teachers can see clearly how creativity can be taught.

The pedagogy/creativity gap

While there is a consensus in curriculum and policy documents that creativity is critical to our future as a harmonious and prosperous global community (Sardar, 2010), there is frequently vague 'guidance' on how teachers might implement creative learning – we call this problem the *pedagogy/creativity gap*. Perhaps even more concerning, many of the standard approaches to quality teaching do not accept that creativity is part of teaching and learning (Fleming and colleagues, 2015). It is not clear why this is the case but perhaps it relates to creativity being or appearing dangerous in some way to the order that schools and other institutions crave. As Furlong and others argue, conformity often trumps creativity: 'As many educational sociologists have observed, education is often organised in ways that facilitate control and prepare young people for a workforce in which conformity is valued over creativity' (Furlong, 2009, p. iv).

In other places several key international initiatives including Creative Partnerships in the UK and programs like it have brought the profile for creativity in primary, secondary and tertiary education to the fore (Anderson, 2015). Yet confusion persists in schools and amongst teachers about how to teach creativity. While there has been a significant shift in the discussion of creativity internationally this has not successfully filtered into the classrooms. As Ken Robinson argues, schools are part of the problem: 'if the government were to design an education system to inhibit creativity, it could hardly do better. . . . Governments throughout the world emphasise the importance of creativity, but often what they do in education suppresses it' (2001, p. 41). We, however, want to claim that schools are the primary place to make creativity a reality and a standard process in our community. We firmly believe that the compassion, imagination and ingenuity of teachers, school leaders and students are our best and most reliable resources.

Creativity and the other Cs

Critical reflection

Like so many other human capacities, creativity is neither necessarily good nor evil. There have been multiple occasions throughout history where creativity has been used to create oppression, poverty and misery. For instance the atomic bomb was an inspired piece of creativity but the pain and suffering it brought on the people of Japan has ongoing and profound ramifications internationally. Critical reflection brings an ethical dimension to creativity to help young people analyse and understand how creativity can be used to empower and disempower.

Collaboration

As we mentioned earlier, creativity in schools (and most other places) is a collaborative practice. As Fischer (2005) argues: 'Creativity does not happen inside people's heads, but in the interaction between a person's thoughts and a socio-cultural context' (p. 128). In other words creativity is almost always a collaboration between ideas, people and things. Creativity being a group process matters for education. Learning in the 4Cs is social. Creativity is most authentically understood and demonstrated with others in relational collaborative learning.

Communication

To enable deep and rich creative collaboration, students need to clearly and effectively communicate. This kind of communication is challenging because it often demands that students articulate what they had previously only imagined. For instance recently in a science and technology unit on toys, a year 5 (11-year-old) student could imagine a toy that he wanted to invent. This became difficult for him when he had to communicate what the toy would look like and what it could do. Through the use of drawings and physical representations, a group of 11-year-old students communicated with each other to understand the toy and ultimately design it. Creativity is more than just imagining something, it can also be about communicating those creative ideas with others to bring them to life.

Another aspect of communication and creativity is 'selling the idea'. The term 'cut through' has been used lately (often in politics) to describe clear and effective communication. In a world where there is no shortage of information or media, being able to communicate even the most creative ideas is a profound challenge. In the same way as students need to clearly communicate to support the development of creativity they also need to understand how to communicate in a crowded marketplace of concepts and ideas. 'Cutting through' requires students to clarify their creative process or products with a keen understanding of the audience. More significantly creativity is about inspiring others with ideas.

Having explained creativity's relationship with critical reflection, communication and collaboration we would like now to build a case for creativity being central to school learning.

Creative learning: the evidence

A few years ago a group of teacher education researchers from The University of Sydney began a research project examining the role of creativity and the arts in schooling. As we mentioned earlier creativity does not just reside in arts classrooms. Arts classrooms are however one place where creativity is 'core business' and as such this research project provided evidence to support our understanding of creativity and learning. Specifically this research considered whether active participation in the arts contributed to achievement in academic and non-academic aspects of students' lives. Our suspicion was that the inherent creative processes in the arts such as play, embodiment, improvisation, discipline and risk taking might make a significant difference to learning and that the creative capacities developed in arts classrooms may have an effect throughout schooling.

The team from The University of Sydney including Andrew Martin, Michael Anderson, Robyn Gibson and Jo Fleming wanted to know if our hunch, developed in response to several other studies, was credible. We wanted to investigate if students who do creative subjects (such as music, film, drama, visual arts and dance) are more likely to succeed in their academic and social lives. What we found was ground-breaking (Martin and colleagues, 2013). Students who study these creative subjects in school do better on a host of academic and social indicators.

They do better on:

- Adaptive motivation.
- Academic buoyancy.
- Academic intentions.
- Enjoyment of school.
- Homework completion.
- Self-esteem.
- Life satisfaction.
- Meaning and purpose.

This was no small niche study of a few classrooms. The study was undertaken with 643 primary and high school students from 15 Australian schools across social, parental income and other variables. It demonstrated that students who actively engaged in creative processes in their schooling are more likely to succeed in their academic and non-academic lives.

In the second part of the study we investigated nine of these classrooms to find out what they looked like. We found substantial and enduring features of high-quality creative learning that we think provide the basis for understanding quality learning. There were two distinctive features of quality learning in these classrooms that are relevant here: embodiment and disciplined resilience.

Embodied learning

One of the first things we noticed is that creative classrooms are embodied classrooms. The teacher worked with physical, cognitive and metacognitive strategies to make the learning engaging and authentic. That learning did not only require students to consider and review art works but critically it taught them how to embody the practices of that art form in their learning. This process of embodiment allowed them to connect with the knowledge and skills in the learning in an engaged and holistic manner. In these classrooms where students composed, choreographed, improvised, sculpted and filmed they didn't just study great composers, filmmakers, sculptors and other artists (although they did that as well), they embodied the processes of learning in these areas.

There is significant emerging evidence that embodiment is a critical untapped process for learning (Glenberg, 2008). These high-quality creative learning environments forged links for students between the funds of knowledge in their subjects and the physical manifestations of that knowledge. This has implications for creative learning beyond arts classrooms. In simple terms it is one thing to see or 'know' the facts about trench warfare in World War I. The learning becomes far more engaging and rich when, through embodying these conditions (in a simulated and safe way), students understand the personal, physical and logistical implications of this kind of warfare. There is potential for the use of embodied pedagogies in subjects such as mathematics, science and geography where this approach may unlock deeper learning for many young people.

For instance, we have been working recently with a secondary school in their science classes exploring natural disasters. This topic has been taught for years through textbook and worksheet-based approaches. In 2015 the school tried something different, trialling an approach working in partnership with a teaching artist (with a background in dance) to develop embodied understanding of the science of natural disasters. In classes, students created simulations to understand how natural forces create earthquakes, tsunamis and floods. This unit of work included the making of a news video, the use of freeze frames and soundscapes (embodied drama approaches) and an interactive forum theatre performance exploring the impacts of natural disasters on communities. Their classroom teacher Raya reflected: 'Most of the kids in this class, probably 18 out of 30, were failing science, now there's one. . . . They're doing science through theatre, through games, through play rather than books and writing and there has been a monumental improvement in results.'

Disciplined resilience

We also found that these classrooms of the arts and creativity study were often characterized by a culture of determination and grit or, as we might call it, disciplined resilience. Many of these classrooms were places where failure, retrial and reworking occurred in playful ways. Imagination, possibility and ambiguity were constant features of the learning process. This in some ways is antithetical to the common misconception of creativity being an unregulated and unrestricted form of learning. In these classrooms quite the opposite occurred. Teachers set up clear boundaries and instructions and students were encouraged to respond, respecting the disciplines of the art form and the discipline of the learning environment. While there is definitely a place for creative freedom, disciplined engagement with creative ideas is predominantly a process of iteration and discipline.

The evidence here suggests doing learning differently. To make sustainable change to prepare our students for the demands of the twenty-first century we need to work from the inside of schooling to make them creative places. To make this happen, teachers, schools and students need tangible pedagogical structures (like the Creativity Cascade) to make the learning processes explicit. In the next part of this chapter we would like to present and explain the Cascade as a coherence maker for learning and teaching creativity.

The Creativity Cascade Coherence Maker

Like all of the 4Cs, creativity is a set of capacities or processes that can be applied to the teaching of any subject matter. Coherence makers are simply ways of understanding the pedagogy of creativity (and the other Cs) so that they can be applied within and across fields of knowledge. We also need to acknowledge that the approach outlined in the cascade resembles scientific method and other well-known approaches to organizing and making knowledge. This is our intention. We want the cascade and all of the other coherence makers to be applicable as much to the arts as they are to science, geography and technology education. In that spirit the following offers an approach to creativity from a pedagogical perspective. This is the foundation of our Creativity Coherence maker.

In this coherence maker, creativity learning is imagined as a metaphorical cascade with four stages (or pools) that support high-quality learning. We are using the metaphor of the cascade because it suggests a process where one body of water (or understanding) falls (with gravitational force and disciplined but varied form) into the next and into the next. The cascade does not work unless the water flows from one part to the next. The four pools of the cascade are:

- Noticing.
- Asking why? Really why?
- Playing with possibility.
- Selecting and evaluating.

The first metaphorical pool of the cascade is 'noticing'.

Noticing

Maxine Greene described noticing as 'enabling learners to notice what is there to be noticed' (Greene, 2001, p. 6). But what does that mean? We think what noticing actually means that we take the time and energy required not only to perceive but achieve deep and connected perception. In her context she was referring to an art work but the principle of noticing is at its core 'a conversation', a concept or an idea where the student can 'nurture appreciative, reflective, cultural, participatory engagement' (Greene, 2001, p. 6). For instance. when was the last time you pondered an image for a long time (let's say more than 60 seconds)? If you are anything like us, we skip over thousands of images each day without spending any 'noticing' time. Noticing requires students to become mindfully aware (using their intellect, emotion and body) in a process of deep and critical reflection rather than just being superficially engaged.

Superficial engagement has been intensified by our screen culture, which pushes multiple messages and images into our view on a daily basis. So given this bombardment it may be possible that as a community we need to learn not only how to notice images, but how to notice relationships, ideas, connections, patterns etc. When we achieve this noticing it provides the basis for asking deep and informed questions about what we have noticed and the connectedness of the 'noticings' we have achieved. As Maxine Greene (2001, p. 6) said, teachers structure the opportunity to look deeply, and through that looking understanding begins. In essence, noticing is a skill that is required for learning (and creativity) but it is seldom taught. Noticing in these ways is communal; noticing is deepened as others (teachers or students) extend your noticing.

To explain the cascade in practice we are going to refer to some work we are doing in a Western Sydney primary school, Robinson Primary School. In some ways this example represents everyday pedagogy. It is not particularly groundbreaking but it is the kind of learning programme that schools can manage with some reorganization to orientate them towards creativity learning. Robinson Primary School has high levels of non-English speaking background children and many students who come from 'disadvantaged backgrounds'. In some ways this process could be understood as problem-based learning or others might call it a rich task. So many teachers will be familiar with the integrated approach in the learning.

The unit of work was called the data project (not a likely candidate for creative learning perhaps). This programme was designed to develop an understanding of how data and evidence are communicated, designed and understood. The year 5 students (11 and 12 years old) decided in groups on an area that they would like to understand in more depth. Some students considered the effects of climate change; some, the effects of racism in sport; and another group decided to explore the weighty topic of 'how much ice cream can you eat without vomiting?' When they decided on the task they were sent out to look for data that already existed on the topic that they had chosen. What they noticed in this process was that data is often skewed to meet the needs of those presenting that data. So already from a critical literacy perspective the students noticed that it was crucial to investigate the motives of those generating and presenting the data. What strikes us about this learning is the maturity of understanding that the students achieved. Many adults don't even consider the motivation for research. So for these students noticing has helped them understand the impetus for the production and communication of data.

Beyond this school-based example there are several other examples of noticing that illustrates its usefulness. Marina Abramović is a New York-based performance artist. Her work explores the limitations and possibilities of the body and mind. In a series of recent performances in New York, London and Sydney entitled 'The Artist is Present' (see Figure 5.2) she invites her audience as individuals to come in, sit across a table and look at her for as long or as short a time as they like.

There was a range of experiences from tears to laughter. All of this was consistent with her intention to heighten awareness in the moment. This work is based on the so-called Abramović method (Abramović, 2012) that aims to deepen noticing, sensitivity and perception in the moment. At an installation in Sydney in July 2015 the CEO of one of Australia's largest banks, Ian Narev, insisted his senior management team attend the performance. He justified the action this way: 'Take any representative collection of 20 CEOs of larger companies, and ask them what worries you most about the capability you lack, I bet creativity will come up in the top three. . . . It's really hard because the combination of what we do day to day and creative minds, often doesn't work' (Narev, 2015). Abramović's work, although seemingly a thousand miles away from schools or high finance, is actually central to the creative process. Abramović's process makes the individual slow down and open up their powers of perception or in other words their noticing.

Figure 5.2 Marina Abramović, *The Artist is Present, 2010*, Museum of Modern Art, New York, 9 March–31 May 2010

In this exercise alone many of the individuals notice their emotions, the way humans interact and the nature of time. In classrooms the same processes are available through teaching noticing in a structured and methodical manner. Perhaps these activities can be achieved initially through looking deeply into a complex painting and then listening through a piece of music and then observing closely and in some detail a leaf or an animal. Noticing is the first step in recognizing patterns, seeing relationships and behaviours and most critically for creativity provoking curiosity by formulating deep questions about what is being noticed. The second metaphorical pool of the cascade that flows directly from noticing is asking why and then going deeper to ask 'really why?'

Asking why? . . . Really why?

If we go back to the cascade metaphor, there is an actual flow from noticing to asking why. Curiosity is the basis for intrinsic learning and asking why and then really why? According to Churchill and colleagues (2016), teachers will ask up to 15 million questions in their career at a rate of 30–120 an hour (p. 276) and that takes no account of questions asked from student to student or student to teacher – clearly substantial classroom time involves questioning of one kind or another. So given that teachers spend so much time asking questions it seems critical that we endeavour to generate high-quality 'asking why' in our classrooms. In our view this means pushing our students beyond superficial questions to deep interconnections in their questioning.

For example, we could ask the question: 'Why has war been a constant throughout history?' There are simple answers such as 'because people can't get on' or perhaps 'because people are intolerant of difference'. While on one level these responses are valid they do little to uncover meaning. When we ask 'really why?' we are pushing students beyond the first superficial response. Asking 'why? Really why?' searches for deeper answers that are offered by philosophy, sociology, theology and history. In the instance of global conflict such as World War I the 'really why?' question will uncover issues of nationalism, expansionism and the rise and fall of world powers arising from the Industrial Revolution and its aftermath. In the 'really why?' phase we are looking for questions that account for, or at least acknowledge the depth and complexity, chaos and contradictions inherent in a phenomenon such as war. The 'really why?' question helps students push towards deep insights so that those insights can be employed to connect with original, novel or creative approaches to responding to the question.

Teachers should be wary of the first answer to 'why' because students often offer it superficially. Rather we should encourage our students to contemplate the deep questions to enable richer reflection. So the vision here is to provide time for students to contemplate and reflect on the questions, instead of demanding responses in milliseconds with a race to see who can answer first. Asking 'why? Really why?' provides time and space to go further and think more deeply. Teachers and students have been involved in asking why since before Socrates' time. Questioning is obviously a fundamental and longstanding process in education. Yet teachers often do not design questions that seek depth and complexity by providing enough wait time to get anything except superficial responses (Churchill and colleagues, 2016). This can severely inhibit the development of deep questions that are, in our view, the precursors for the creative process for artists and scientists. To illustrate how asking 'why? Really why?' works outside schools let's consider the work of a modern innovator.

Elon Musk is a modern day Leonardo Da Vinci. His first major innovation was to make payments on the Internet simple through a start-up company called PayPal that he sold for 1.5 billion dollars to Ebay (Vance, 2015, p. 89). The next thing he did was to buy into a company that makes electric cars feasible and affordable. That car company is called Tesla (named after the American innovator) that currently has a market capitalization of 700 billion dollars. He is now creating a factory in the Nevada desert that will produce batteries that are designed to replace the coal fired power industry and solve the problem of storing solar energy.

Elon Musk did not stop there. He is currently working on multi-planetary travel, and an innovative high-speed transport system called the 'hyperloop' where carriages that travel in a pressurized tube reach speeds of 1,200 km per hour. That would cut the trip from San Francisco to New York to 35 minutes (this trip currently takes around 48 hours by train).

Whether these projects are fantastical or probable is not really our point. Our point is that creativity requires noticing the gaps and possibilities, then asking why, and then asking really why such a thing hasn't been created. In the Elon Musk example, he asked: 'Why are Internet payments so difficult?' 'Why are electric cars not affordable and widespread?' 'Why are batteries for solar energy not being mass-produced?' He asked: 'Why is spaceflight so expensive?' He asked 'Why is ultra high-speed land travel not a reality?' While we may not necessarily be able to or even want to replicate Musk's processes in our lives or our classrooms there is evidence here of the first two pools of the Creativity Cascade. First noticing a problem and then asking 'why?' and then 'really why?' drives learning innovation deeper.

If we return to schools and the data project at Robinson Primary School, the asking 'why? Really why?' occurred when the students began generating their own data by developing surveys. In this process they had to move beyond the superficial 'why?' questions and ask the deeper 'really why?' questions to get into the complexities of these issues by exploring them in their intricacy. For instance, 'why have politicians been slow to act on climate change?', 'why does racism emerge frequently at sporting events?' and so on. These questions helped the students move beyond the superficial response, and their answers set them up to see the complexities and interconnections between ideas that are a precursor to their understanding and playing with possibility.

The first two pools of the cascade, noticing and asking 'why . . . really why?' are really just features of high-quality learning and teaching, not necessarily creative learning. It is the next pool of the cascade where the Creativity Cascade moves from high-quality learning to high-quality creative learning. The next pool in the Creativity Cascade is playing with possibility.

Playing with possibility

In 1983 three young performers, Simon McBurney, Annabel Arden and Marcello Magni (Freshwater, 2001), saw the possibility in changing the theatre. They bought an old van for £350 and played scout halls around the United Kingdom to growing but modest crowds (Trueman, 2013). The company eventually grew beyond the scout halls and out of the van to become Complicite,[1] one of the world's most successful international theatre companies. The development of their plays is a process of disciplined play with possibility. As Catherine Alexander suggests, 'The process of devising involves experimenting and discarding numerous ideas, throwing ideas together and allowing the possibility of the unexpected' (Alexander, Freedman and Gould, 2007, p. 4).

What we think is remarkable about Complicite's work is the ceaseless attempt to innovate and change what's possible in the theatre. The possibilities of the performance, text, casting, technology, bodies in space, subject matter; all of this to create theatre like nothing else the world has seen. McBurney says: 'Any play that's

Figure 5.3 Complicite, *A Disappearing Number* Rehearsal, 2007. Photographer Sarah Ainslie

making a point is less interesting than something that stays with you and suggests something further' (Trueman, 2013). We have seen several works by this ensemble and what we notice about them is their deep connection with possibility. In their play *A Disappearing Number* (which we mentioned in Chapter 3), Complicite plays with the seemingly disparate ideas of 'creativity, the passage of time, memory, cultural divides, and the way in which our past informs our present' (Abbott, 2014, p. 227).

The award-winning play explored pure mathematics in the production's content and form through a collaboration with mathematicians, dancers and actors that drew on image, mathematics, dance, physical theatre and stillness. Evident in this production was a group of artists who knew how to collaborate and play with possibility. They also demonstrated their ability to see this play as an ongoing work in progress even after it was finished. Sitting in that audience (as we did) we always had the sense that, if we came back the next night, Complicite would be reshaping and reforming the work to make it better, but always with a purpose that was precise.

Complicite might seem a long way from classrooms but their performances emerge from an imaginative playing with possibilities based on noticing and asking why about the world around them and then using these first two pools of the cascade to play with possibility. While this illustration draws from theatre we also know of many approaches in science, mathematics and geography where teachers have used these processes to make creative learning a reality for their students. We also know that when students play with possibilities in the classroom they move to a way of learning that meets the needs of the twenty-first-century citizen that is not necessarily focused on products and outcomes but on creative processes.

In our view this process begins with the nurturing of imagination. As Maxine Greene (2012) argues: 'Without imagination, you live in a small room with the windows closed. Imagination opens the windows and shows us landscapes, horizons that we would not otherwise perceive. . . . I want education to empower people to see possibility' (p. 62). Imagination is the first step in the process for playing with possibility. While imagination is predominantly an individual capacity, it feeds the collaborative creative process so necessary for learning. Imagination helps students to engage with a range of possibilities that can be shared to build collaboratively creative ideas across domains of learning. It's also critical in the development of possibility thinking. Imagination provides a palate of possibilities for students to explore and play – this is the first step in playing with possibility. As Anna Craft argued (2000):

> at the core of creative activity, I would posit the engine of 'possibility thinking' – and necessary to being creative I would specify insight. . . . What I am concerned with . . . is the kind of creativity which guides choices and route-finding in everyday life, or what I have come to term 'little c creativity'. Creativity involves being imaginative, going beyond the obvious, being aware of one's own unconventionality, being original in some way. It is not necessarily linked with a product-outcome. (p. 3)

In other words, the process is more critical than the outcome or the product in creative learning.

The foundations of the creative process are the skills of noticing and asking why. Without those two skills students can potentially be left with an uncontrolled and undisciplined process that does not build knowledge. Playing with possibility builds on these foundations but it can only be productive when the processes of noticing and asking 'why? Really why?' have been taught in a deep and interconnected manner. Playing with possibility follows the same lateral and diverse processes that Complicite employ. In their work they include improvisation, trial and error, the use of film, sound, light, puppetry and live action. When playing with possibility teachers and students frequently work in a disciplined, collaborative and generative process that is a constant iteration (Complicite's performances change from evening to evening in response to audience feedback etc). This contradicts one of the great myths about creativity – that it is discipline-free. Quite the reverse. Like gravity, creativity does rely on force and constraint. In Complicite's performances the audience's expectations and demands apply the discipline. The discipline evident in Complicite's work is the same quality we saw in our research in high-quality creative classrooms.

In the playing with possibility process at Robinson Primary School, the students used their imaginations and shared their possibilities with each other for how they would communicate their findings to their audiences. One student suggested building a museum to house all the data they had collected and present their findings. Another group shared their designs for robots that would speak to each member of the audience individually and project findings from a robotic projector head against a nearby wall. In this phase of the process the teacher supported this imaginative process by encouraging even the most outlandish ideas. This imaginative phase is key if we are to teach students to playfully engage with possibility thinking. We believe playing with possibility is critical if our classrooms and schools are to be places where productive, disciplined and generative creative processes take place. One of the ways we can deliver those teachable outcomes is enabling students to engage with responses to their creative work in a constructive and perceptive way.

Of course there comes a time when students need to make decisions about the application of their imagined possible ideas. That brings us to the last phase of the Creativity Cascade, selecting and evaluating.

Selecting and evaluating

In the first part of this stage students consider all the choices that have emerged from playing with possibility. If they have engaged creatively, all kinds of choices will have become apparent. It is at this stage that the skill of judgement to choose between all of the options. This is a kind of editing process where students apply wisdom and (prior) knowledge to make decisions between all of the creative opportunities. Simultaneous with this choice is an ongoing evaluation. The evaluation process is internal (emanating from the student) and external (listening to the evaluations of others on the choices made). Evaluation is qualitatively different however from 'listening' or 'receiving' feedback'. This phase involves an active process of discernment. A discernment of the kind and quality of the evaluations students are receiving. Evaluating requires students to consider their own judgements on the evolving creative work and the evidence being applied to make the arguments for the choices being made.

Returning to the data project at Robinson Primary School, selecting and evaluating occurred when these students had to communicate their data. The students had to move from playing with possibility (robots and museums) to consider the discipline of delivering a message to the audience (see Chapter 7). Keeping in mind the audience and the message, the students chose to communicate the data through storytelling, graphic novels, film, musical theatre and some through live experiments. The success of their presentations always depended on their ability to understand their audience, clearly explain their project, and communicate that message through the most effective medium.

This process of evaluation is essential to effective creative learning. It is not sufficient to just 'get feedback', the creative learner must make selections and seek evaluation from those with understanding of the creative project they are learning about – someone who 'gets it', engages with it and understands how to enhance the work. Then of course we are back at noticing because unlike an actual cascade we can return to the other pools to develop and extend creative learning.

In the Robinson Primary School data project teachers actively structured the learning using the Creativity Cascade to help students understand, create and communicate the data. In many ways the gift of this example is that a simple teaching sequence on a seemingly boring subject can transform into something that supports deep learning through noticing deeply, asking 'why? Really why?' to engage deep curiosity, actively playing with possibility and selecting and evaluating responses. There is nothing magical or mystical about this process. It is structured, effective pedagogy applied to the needs of students. It did provide for these students a learning experience that put creativity at the centre of learning. Here is a summary of the process:

Creativity learning starts with:

- *Noticing* – deep perception that flows into asking why, then digging deeper;
- *Asking why? Really why?* – asking penetrating complex and connected questions;
- *Playing with possibility* – imagining and engaging with the palate of possibility; and then
- *Selecting and evaluating*, which is a process of choice and discernment married with deep and perceptive evaluation (from the students themselves and from others).

If you have been convinced of the critical place creativity can have in classrooms and schools the next step is to consider how we might make creativity learning a standard expectation in learning. The concluding parts of this chapter describe the changes we think are necessary to make creativity a standard and predictable reality in schools.

A road map for creativity and learning

For many, this discussion of creativity will seem like old news. We want to acknowledge that many schools and many classrooms have been engaging with creative learning for decades. Our road map for creative schools is for teachers and school leaders who can see the potential in creativity education but feel that they are not currently meeting that potential. This road map is for those who can sense that classrooms and schools could be revitalized by making creative learning a standard practice. The evidence for change, which we discussed in Chapter 1 around our changing workforce, and the challenges that our planet faces, are, in our view, a clarion call to action for schools and schooling systems. There are three parts to our road map, a creativity audit, a creativity plan and reflective research:

- *Undertake a creativity audit.* Perhaps the best way to begin is to look at the opportunities by undertaking a creativity audit using a measure like the Situational Outlook Questionnaire (Isaksen, Lauer and Ekvall, 1999; see Chapter 9 for a discussion). Anne Harris has also developed an audit tool for schools (Harris, 2016, p. 117) For instance you might ask the following questions:

  - Are our classrooms prioritizing creativity? If not, why not?
  - Is there evidence of expertise in different kinds of creativity in the school?
  - Is there evidence of integration between curricula and non-curricula creativity offerings in the school?
  - Is student imagination encouraged and supported?
  - Are there spaces within the school that nurture and support creativity?

  Or perhaps you could use the Creativity Cascade to frame your audit. The key questions using the Creativity Cascade are:

  - What do we *notice* about the presence or otherwise of creativity in our school?
  - *Why* is this the situation? *Really why*?
  - What are the *possibilities* for creativity in our school?
  - How can we *evaluate* change in our school?

- *Develop a creativity learning action plan.* Having made these discoveries, the creativity learning action plan needs to take account of the needs of the whole school including students, parents, teachers and school leadership to make creativity central to learning and teaching. We think this will require schools to work across silos including faculties, year groupings, teaching experiences and roles in the school. Perhaps it means connecting across faculties to support creative learning. When devising this plan consider the kinds of virtual and actual resources available to schools and students. For instance we are aware of several large cultural institutions that offer free or very affordable access to creative learning resources that can be accessed at the venue or through online delivery. These kinds of resources sometimes take time to uncover but they can enrich significantly what might be possible for students.

● *Develop critically reflective research in creativity learning.* The third step is reflecting, researching and communicating what worked and what didn't. Again this requires collaboration with partners outside the school to understand how creative change has occurred, working with professional researchers from universities and other places to communicate how to make schools more creative places (see Chapter 9). A reflective research strategy will also provide evidence for the change that becoming a creative school makes to engagement and will re-shape learning strategies.

This generation of educators is entrusted to make the change. We have a clear choice, we can choose to passively accept the education system we have been 'gifted' or we can choose to change it to meet the needs of young people facing the challenges of an uncertain world. All of this discussion about creative schools is critical because getting this right has the potential to change the present and futures of the young people in our classrooms for the better. Creativity in schools has had that transformative potential ever since bell hooks was a child. hooks is one of America's leading writers, authors and social activists. In the 1960s she was a girl in a newly desegregated Hopkinsville High School in Kentucky, USA. She remembers the impact on a young mind of the opportunity to imagine a different future through the creativity of Mr Harold's art class:

> We ran to his classes. I entered the world of color, the free world of art. And in that moment I was momentarily, whatever I wanted to be. That was my initiation. I longed to be an artist, but whenever I hinted that I might be an artist, grown folks looked at me with contempt. They told me I had to be out of my mind thinking that black folks could be artists – why, you could not eat art. Nothing folks said changed my longing to enter the world of art and to be free. (1995, p. 1)

So ultimately the creative schools we imagine are not only about frameworks, systems and bureaucracies. They always, *always* come down to each individual child's human right to understand themselves and to be active and creative participants in their community. This is why creativity in schools matters, because reimagining them and remaking them will deliver untold benefits to the students who have to create tomorrow. This generation of teachers and school leaders have the opportunity and the responsibility to create schools that make that possibility a reality.

In the next chapter we are going to consider the next of our Cs, critical reflection, and how that can support young people's understanding and interpretation of the world as it is now and as it could be.

Note

1 Founded in 1983, Complicite is a London-based theatre company that tours work both nationally and internationally. Under Artistic Director Simon McBurney and Producer Judith Dimant, the Company has won more than fifty major global theatre awards.

Complicite's vision is to create work that foregrounds the crucial meeting of minds, the complicity between the performer and the audience, that is at the heart of the theatrical experience. Complicite makes work across artforms, believing that theatre, opera, film, installation, publication, radio, community art and the internet can all be sites for this collective act of imagination. Exploring the possibilities of all these media – and more – and remaining at the forefront of artistic experiment, is key to the Company's vision.

The Company began life as a collective and this spirit of collective enquiry, of collaborative curiosity as a way of working, is also central to its vision. Complicite creates work with actors, designers, writers, artists and other specialists from around the world, but has established core relationships that have spanned the last three decades. These diverse Associates – as they're known – have developed and evolved a shared creative language, which provides an anchor for the explorative work that the Company has become famous for. This commitment to developing work as an ensemble through extended periods of research and investigation is evident in every piece they bring to the stage.

'The English theatre has a fine and honourable tradition. Simon McBurney and Complicite are not part of this; they have created their own tradition and this is why they are so special, so valuable' (Peter Brook).

Critical reflection

On Friday 2 October, 2015 at around 4.30 pm a 15-year-old boy inspired by a terrorist group shot dead a police accountant in Parramatta near Sydney in Australia not far from where we live. The tragedy was exacerbated by the age of the perpetrator and his inspiration drawn from terror groups in Syria and beyond. In the ensuing media storm one of the persistent cries was that our schools needed to do more to avoid 'this kind of thing' happening again. Predictably that's where the substantive discussion relating to the role of education stopped and the relentless news cycle moved on to another story. While you may not know this story you will probably recognize the pattern. If we assumed for one moment that schools are the answer to this (in our view they are not *the* answer, they are *part* of the answer), what might we change, how might we connect young people to their world in a way that builds hope, democratic values and citizenship rather than disaffection and violence? Clearly this is an extreme example. Not all of our students are likely to be involved in 'this kind of thing'. There is however, a strong and growing body of evidence that schools are not meeting the needs of young people's social and emotional learning that may lead them to being vulnerable to poor choices that lack wisdom and create a disconnection with their community. As Durlak and colleagues (2011, p. 405) remind us: 'many students lack social-emotional competencies and become less connected to school as they progress from elementary to middle to high school, and this lack of connection negatively affects their academic performance behaviour and health'.

Social and emotional learning provides the basis for the development of wisdom, resilience (sometimes called grit) and ethical understanding. This kind of learning builds skills that support students' understanding of themselves and helps them to understand how they might contribute to a democratic and tolerant community. In our view the nurturing of social and emotional learning that leads to critical reflection and action is and always should be a mandatory feature of school curriculum. Yet many young people feel that schools are not sufficiently focused on their development as emotionally and socially competent members of society (Durlak and colleagues, 2011, p. 5).

One of the persistent features of modern society is the disconnect between people, cultures and approaches to the world. Diversity and even dissonance are necessary features of learning. Equally critical to learning is building the capacity to understand and manage this difference. When schools manage difference, respectful engagement becomes apparent in the interpersonal interactions in schools. When schools ignore the social and emotional processes related to difference it can lead to disconnection. Instead of being like the proverbial goldfish swimming around not noticing its surroundings, we need to encourage our students to understand (notice) themselves and others to help them recognize how their assumptions influence the way they see the world. We also need to support their understanding of others. We need to rethink how we can create learning that helps students to value diversity and difference and provide experiences that encourage empathy, reflection and action so that difference can be nurtured and embraced as a strength rather than a weakness.

This chapter considers the role of critical reflection in learning. We will begin by discussing the role of social and emotional learning to lay the foundation for discussion of critical reflection. Critical reflection supports students as they begin to develop understandings and generate wisdom relating to the application of subject based knowledge. Critical reflection is also central to the way students create, communicate and collaborate as it supports the growth in understanding of themselves and others as learners, and as active members of the community.

Social and emotional learning: the foundation of critical reflection

Through engaging in critical reflection students develop an understanding of how power is constructed, managed and distributed in systems and organizations (Brookfield, 2016). Formal and informal organizations have power relationships. These power relationships are sometimes obvious but they are often hidden. Critical reflection helps students to uncover these relationships and navigate power structures equipping them with tools to understand the seen and unseen social dynamics, and empowers them to act in their own contexts. For instance, year 9 students could use an understanding of critical reflection to map the ways policy is made for young people and by whom. With this mapping young people could then design and implement their own strategies drawing on their understanding of creativity, collaboration and communication to make those structures more democratic. This kind of learning depends on a growth in intrapersonal and interpersonal knowledge through social and emotional learning.

Even a casual observer would have noticed that the demands on schools have changed over the last four decades. The traditional academic priorities have rightly been joined by demands from our community to respond to the social development of students. The calls for schools to 'teach' resilience, self-confidence, empathy and other interpersonal skills have become as frequent as calls for teaching the 'basics'. Yet, as we mentioned in Chapter 1, schools in their curriculum and design reflect the realities of 50 years ago and not more contemporary demands. Part of the transformation we imagine in schools is the breaking down of the somewhat arbitrary boundaries between subjects (maths, science, human relationships, English) in learning. For many students, learning skills that prepare them for the demands of interacting with others will be far more critical than some of the content in the traditional curriculum. We are not calling for knowledge that is divided between traditional curriculum and social emotional learning. Quite the opposite. We believe that learning about literature, science, geography and history cannot and should not be de-coupled from emotional and social aspects of learning. This division seems odd and counterproductive to the development of young people and contradictory to the way students collaboratively understand and interpret their world through all their intellectual and emotional capacities.

For instance, one of the most commonly taught Shakespearean plays in the English classroom is *King Lear*. It deals with the relationship between power, emotions, loyalty and pride. These themes are also central to the learning in critical reflection. King Lear struggles to develop an authentic connection with his daughters and yet fails tragically. The play demonstrates authentically how power can destroy families, and how families can destroy power. An authentic and deep engagement with King Lear necessitates engagement with the social and emotional content of the play. Themes of love, loss, jealousy, hatred and sibling rivalry connect with the life experience of adolescents. These dynamics are not trapped in Elizabethan England, they are played out in the lives of individuals, communities and families on a daily basis. Only the context changes. In literature such as *King Lear* teachers have the opportunity to integrate the affective with the cognitive (critical reflection with literature analysis) rather than seeing them as separate and unrelated to the world around us. This connection has the potential to increase student engagement as well as offering an authentic exploration of the dynamics of power. As Durlak and colleagues (2011) argue, emotional development and relationships and the ways they fail (*King Lear* is a case study of this) are critical to the success or otherwise of each student experience at school:

> Students typically do not learn alone but rather in collaboration with their teachers, in the company of their peers, and with the encouragement of their families. Emotions can facilitate or impede children's academic engagement, work ethic, commitment, and ultimate school success. Because relationships and emotional processes affect how and what we learn, schools and families must effectively address these aspects of the educational process (p. 405).

While learning is collaborative, social and emotional, schools are not consistently organized to reflect these realities. When students lack social and emotional intelligence they can become less connected and suffer academically and non-academically throughout schooling (Blum and Libbey, 2004). When programmes that include social and emotional learning are implemented students consistently benefit. Durlak and colleagues (2011) found in a meta-analysis that these programmes: 'yielded significant positive effects on targeted socio-emotional competencies and attitudes about self, others, and school. They also enhanced students' behavioural adjustment in the form of increased prosocial behaviours' (p. 417).

We are not pretending that social-emotional learning will necessarily eradicate the kinds of incidents we discussed at the beginning of this chapter. We are however claiming that the calls from the community for schools to 'act' around these kinds of atrocities reveal a disconnection between community expectations and the current realities of schooling. In many cases communities expect that schools are equipped to meet the social and emotional development needs of students. In many schools, the curriculum and social and emotional learning (including critical reflection) are disconnected. In our view this connection becomes possible when the 4Cs are foundational to learning. One of the primary ways we feel that can take place is when students develop the capacity to engage with their world in a critically reflective and compassionate manner. For us critical reflection builds on social and emotional learning.

What is critical reflection?

Critical reflection allows students to stand 'one step back' and analyse knowledge in terms of power and agency. This ability to reflect depends on a strong foundation of social and emotional learning that fosters self-understanding. Jurgen Habermas argues that critically reflective knowledge allows a meta-understanding of learning. He claims 'critical reflective knowledge is neither behavioural nor technical, not truth establishing nor captured by a discipline. It critiques all other forms of knowledge, and in so doing, it moves beyond merely reproducing what is' (Habermas, 1978, p. 42). In Habermas's view, critical reflection helps the learner analyse knowledge. For instance when studying historical concepts, critically reflective learning seeks to understand the power relationships apparent and the implications of those relationships on others. If students are unable to understand power in their own context, they have in the study of history multiple case studies of power (its uses and abuses) for analysis. The role of nation states in the various conflicts over the last century and the influence of capital and ideology provide fertile ground for learning through critical reflection about power, its beginnings, its growth and decline. In essence what we are doing is providing students with the opportunity to analyse knowledge so that they can understand power dynamics. This process, in turn, gives students the opportunity to navigate the world (and its inherent power systems) using that understanding. Critical reflection provides a navigation tool for students. Social and emotional learning provides the foundations for critical reflection by making the learner 'awake' to their own agency and power and how the power and agency of others affect them. Social and emotional learning create sensitivity to intrapersonal and interpersonal reflectiveness that lie at the heart of critical reflection.

These self-understandings are, however, often based in personal subjectivities. We are not arguing here or anywhere in this book that subjectivity is a problem and objectivity is the answer. We argue that subjectivity needs to be accounted for and understood in learning so we can make those subjectivities apparent to students. As Fook and Gardner (2007) argue, subjectivity is critical to learning as long as it is understood and remains transparent to the individual and others, as they claim: 'being reflexive by taking into account subjectivity will involve a knowledge of who I am as a whole being (social, emotional, physical, cultural, economic, political) and understanding the effects this has on the knowledge I perceive and create' (2007, p. 29). In this view of knowledge subjectivity is not discouraged, rather it is considered a critical part of the process of assessing and understanding in learning. So, for instance, student opinions are encouraged but those opinions must be mediated by their effect on others and their effect on a community. A student who gives a presentation with sexist content in class may be exercising subjectivity but not subjectivity that is informed by critical reflection or wisdom.

Critical reflection has been consistently employed in adult learning and particularly pre-service learning for teachers and social workers. While we agree that critical reflection is an essential component of adult learning, we have not yet seen a reason why this approach could not or should not be applied to school education. The approach builds on Schön's (1983) reflective practitioner process and calls for reflection *on* and *in* action. Hatton and Smith (1995) argued that a student who critically reflects 'demonstrates an awareness that actions and events are not only located in, and explicable by, reference to multiple perspectives but are located in, and influenced by, multiple historical, and socio-political contexts' (p. 48). Critical reflection requires students to consider their experience in the context of their presumptions and their current context and then formulate action that builds on that understanding. We have included action in our conception of critical reflection to overcome one of the persistent critiques of reflection as an individualistic self-indulgence. Rather, we consider critical reflection a way of actively setting and creating a culture of proactivity.

The evidence for critical reflection

Our view is that we need a much stronger evidence base to ensure not only that critical reflection has a place in schools but that its processes and effects are accurately understood and conveyed. Reflection has been a standard expectation of teacher education for many years (Rodgers and Scott, 2008, p. 754) but has not always permeated the content of curriculum. The evidence, while not always derived from schools, does indicate that in many contexts critical reflection has strong beneficial effects on the individual and the community. In a recent summary of the research into critical reflection Jan Fook and colleagues (2015) discovered strong benefits for individuals and communities: 'These are the contributions to human flourishing: learners experience empowerment, increased competence and confidence. The capacity to deal with uncertainty, manage emotional turmoil and stress, work better in teams with colleagues, integrate theory and practice, and plan actions' (p. 99). This evidence begs the question: why have we not been making critical reflection part of what we do in classrooms and teacher education for many years? Rather than ponder what might have been, our view is that it is time to integrate critical reflection with the other key capacities: creativity, communication and collaboration to enable learners not only to create, communicate and collaborate but to understand their assumptions about knowledge to enable deep and dynamic learning.

One of the problems with terms such as 'critical' (in the same way as creativity) is that the term suffers from a lack of definitional clarity, affecting its meanings and applications. Henry Mintzberg (2005) identifies nine distinct uses of the term critical:

1 Questioning.

2 Key (as in unlocking).

3 Fault finding.

4 Judicial.

5 Providing textual variance.

6 Pertaining to crisis.

7 Crucial.

8 Grave uncertainty (like a critical injury).

9 From physics, the moment at which a substance changes form.

Given the breadth of possible meanings, we will spend some time in this chapter clarifying what we mean by critical reflection by discussing the other kind of 'critical' discourses that are prevalent and potentially useful to our understanding of the 4Cs.

What makes critical reflection 'critical'?

Critical reflection is suited to the 4Cs because it is inherently collaborative and interactive. If critical reflection is to be effective it cannot remain a cognitive process; it must lead to creative, communicative and collaborative action. Reflection that does not extend beyond the individual risks being inherently superficial, self-indulgent and disconnected from the world. Critical reflection develops, in inquiry and dialogue with others, a meta-awareness of how organizations create, communicate and collaborate to make change in the world. As Fook (and colleagues 2006, p. 9) argue, 'In this sense, critical reflection involves social and political analyses which enable transformative changes, whereas reflection may remain at the level of relatively undisruptive changes in techniques or superficial thinking.' Fundamentally, critical reflection relies on a deep and broad analysis that makes transparent each learner's presuppositions and assumptions. This is not intended to paralyse thinking but rather to contextualize learning and open the learner up to new possibilities and understandings of how power is managed and exercised across society.

Critical reflection and critical thinking

Critical thinking is, as Scriven and Paul (1987) suggest, 'the intellectually disciplined process of actively and skilfully conceptualizing, applying, analyzing, synthesizing, and/or evaluating information gathered from, or generated by, observation, experience, reflection, reasoning, or communication, as a guide to belief and action'. You may notice that many of the features of critical thinking are found in our coherence makers for creativity, communication and collaboration. The steps of noticing, asking why and then really why are essentially the processes inherent in critical thinking.

In critical reflection those 'understandings' are revisited and disrupted so that the assumptions that underpin our knowledge and learning are not left unchallenged. Rather, the process of critical reflection helps students to understand that knowledge and the application of knowledge is frequently contested and contestable. Critical reflection is a crucial part of positioning knowledge in the classroom, analysing and critiquing it to help students understand that knowledge, context and power actively and dynamically coexist and interact. For instance, recently we asked students to look through a reputable news website and count the number of articles related to business, theology, biology, dance and human relationships. On the day we undertook this exercise the articles that related to business were more frequent than all of the others put together. This simple process engaged students in critical reflection relating to what knowledge matters (at least to a national newspaper and presumably its readers). The subsequent whole class discussion examined the relative significance of different kinds of knowledge, the power and status that associated with different kinds of knowledge, and the implications for one area of knowledge being valued above others.

Critical reflection and critical pedagogy

In Chapter 2 we highlighted the centrality of critical pedagogy in developing a way of understanding schooling. By critical pedagogy we mean the process of understanding the power structures that permeate our society and how that power is exercised. Many of the schools that we have worked with as teachers, consultants, researchers and mentors have been marginalized and disenfranchised. These are the kinds of schools Paulo Freire (2000) had in mind when he said: 'Education either functions as an instrument which is used to facilitate integration of the younger generation into the logic of the present system and bring about conformity or it becomes the practice of freedom, the means by which men and women deal critically and creatively with reality and discover how to participate in the transformation of their world' (p. 34).

Freire's call for education to be a tool of creativity and change is consistent with our call for educators to think of themselves not as maintainers of the current system but rather as facilitators for students to understand and change the world and their place within it. This kind of reflection allows students to see the world as 'joined up' rather than seeing human experience as granular and disconnected. In other words they see a connection between their own assumptions and preconceptions and the role of institutions and power structures in shaping those preconceptions. For instance, when students are studying how the media is owned and operates in our community, critical reflection can provide them with an understanding of how that media ownership could influence the decision-making of governments. This has the potential to make students more reflective about the media they consume, knowing that some media owners have the potential to manipulate media messages to influence political decision-making. While there is a distinction between critical reflection and critical pedagogy, the call to analyse and question assumptions and institutions is consistent across both approaches. Essentially critical pedagogy names a movement and critical reflection names an approach to teaching.

All of this reflection and action is necessary so young people can clearly consider their choices when making decisions in their personal and social lives. For instance, when students are working with online materials a critically reflective stance prompts them to consider 'who gains' from the opinions and ideas being promoted. We see critical pedagogy as underpinning all of the 4Cs. The ability for young people to consider how power systems permeate all aspects of human experience leads to a reconsideration of knowledge and its application. As students work collaboratively, communicatively and creatively they can simultaneously (and at times metacognitively) analyse the mechanisms and the power relationships of working in these ways.

What critical reflection is not

Another (sometimes pejorative) meaning of the term critical reflection is 'fault finding'. Fook describes this sense of the term as 'scoring negative points' (Fook and collegues, 2006, p. 5). This is antithetical to our notion of critical reflection, which instead of negative criticism encourages disciplined, active and dynamic responses to knowledge. Critical reflection certainly critiques knowledge but it is not inherently negative. For instance in *King Lear* we can see the shifts in the power relationships and critique Lear's use of power while still empathizing with his plight. We are not arguing that critical reflection will not create difference or even conflict. It will. Rather we are arguing that this criticism should always seek to test and not (usually) destroy ideas. For instance, when students are challenged about the presumptions and ideas this has the potential to create conflict. In a 4Cs classroom, collaboration and communication will create a climate where this conflict becomes simply a testing and analysis of ideas rather than an attack. Critical reflection essentially strives for an analysis of knowledge and understanding that equips students to act in the world and navigate through it.

Critical reflection and the other Cs

As we have discussed throughout this book, the 4Cs are interactive and integrated throughout learning. High-quality critical reflection makes possible a learning environment where creativity, collaboration and communication can flourish. Critical reflection is able to do this because it generates a readiness to consider preconceptions and to develop learning that is analytical. Here are the ways we see this happening in schools.

Collaboration

One of the criticisms of critical reflection relates to the potential for the practice to be self-indulgent and individualistic (Fook and colleagues, 2006, p. 5). Jan Fook's (2012) work with social workers provides us with some ideas about how we might apply critical reflection in a collaborative manner. Rather than seeing critical reflection as a solitary pursuit, Fook argues that the process should be a part of the way we create a culture in our schools and in our communities (see Chapter 9 for further discussion of culture). Fook sees critical reflection as a way to understand the whole rather than all of the parts. She says, 'For me, it is about investigating someone's holistic (incorporating beliefs, emotions, and meaning) experience (through critical reflection) in a way that not only helps them learn from it anew, but also helps them learn how to learn from it' (2012, p. 232).

This process becomes necessarily collaborative when we think about the ways knowledge is created in the 4Cs – not as an isolated and self-referential process but rather as a co-construction of learning that respects diversity but also acknowledges (and often celebrates) subjectivities. For instance, a student considering refugee policy and migration may have an entrenched opinion on the issue that she cannot back with evidence. In the course of a critical reflective process the students would question each other in groups so they are prompted to analyse their subjectivities with questions such as: Who makes decisions about citizenship? Who has the right to be a citizen? Who does not have the right to be a citizen? If you needed to find a new country because of war how would you go about doing that?

This way of working opens up new spaces for dialogue and ensures that subjectivities are analysed and often challenged. This in a sense models broader democratic processes rather than isolating learners. Critical reflection is possible even within workplaces that are not necessarily critically reflective (macro cultures) to create new collaboration (micro cultures) that can help transform organizations. Fook argues that within this process 'a new microcultural space can be reshaped (within these given macrocultures) in a collaborative way. Recognizing these fundamental layers of assumptions should also enable the critically reflective gaze to be directed more effectively on oneself (as a microcosm of the broader cultural climate)' (2012, p. 223). Critical reflection is an inherently and necessarily collaborative process. While critical reflection may begin at an individual level, it must engage collaboratively with others to become effective. For transformation to take hold in classrooms, schools and communities, reflective practice needs to engage critically, creatively and collaboratively with others to transform one's own practice as well as the practice of broader social groups.

In reality, there are two phases to reflective practice. The first phase is inherently individual. This process prompts the learner to consider knowledge in the light of their conscious and unconscious assumptions and preconceptions. But the work of reflection does not stop there. If learning environments are to be effective, students must work with each other to support critical reflection by respectfully testing each other's assumptions, not as a destructive process but as a way of understanding difference and creating a kind of creative dissonance.

Creativity

In the Creativity Cascade (Chapter 4) we identified two critical components of creative learning – 'noticing' and asking 'why? Really why?'. This process does stretch beyond critical reflection but is also inclusive of critical reflection. As part of the noticing process learners should be noticing the ways they respond to different kinds of ideas. Flowing from this noticing should be a series of 'why' questions that consider their preconceptions and assumptions and the ways those assumptions form their attitudes. For instance, learners might notice that they have a strong response to discussions around creating music. If they are critically reflective they will then ask, why this response? Of course the first response might be 'I'm not musical'. When they become critically reflective (ask 'really why?') they will move beyond this to understand that this predisposition may be formed by unchallenged views or contact with music. Once these assumptions are unpacked and understood students can play with possibility to discover that music has many components in ways that they may never have considered.

Communication

Communication relies on learners being able to clearly articulate not only a message but to understand what motivates their views and assumptions. Critical reflection makes learners 'alert to messaging' so they *understand* the text, the context and subtext of the communication. This creates in students a kind of meta-awareness of communication strategies. Critical reflection enables learners to think more deeply and understand the genesis of their views and to test those views against other knowledge and opinion. As Jack Mezirow (1990) argues, in creating communication critical reflection helps us to make messages that are resistant to distortion and presupposition:

> To make meaning means to make sense of an experience; we make an interpretation of it. When we subsequently use this interpretation to guide decision making or action, then making meaning becomes learning. . . .
> Reflection enables us to correct distortions in our beliefs and errors in problem

solving. Critical reflection involves a critique of the presuppositions on which our beliefs have been built. (p. 1)

Mezirow argues here that critically reflecting helps learners to unearth their distortions and to critique what they think they know. As we make meaning in our communication and attempt to convey that meaning to others, critical reflection enables us to seek clarity and to understand how our subjectivities influence (for good and ill) communication. This approach makes the 'subtexts' (the hidden curriculum) of communication clear, leaving less room for noise and confusion. Critical reflection supports students' understanding of the motivations and the presuppositions that sometimes influence communication. Critical reflection also provides the opportunity to make subjectivities transparent to support genuine communication. Critically reflective communicators are able to analyse and clarify their own meaning making and analyse the communication strategies and approaches of others. Having considered the place of critical reflection in the 4Cs we would now like to introduce our coherence maker for critical reflection: the critical reflection crucible.

The Critical Reflection Crucible Coherence Maker

As with the other three Cs we are intent on providing a model for how critical reflection can be taught in schools. In this coherence maker we imagine critical reflection as a crucible. We have enlisted the metaphor of the crucible to emphasize the need to test and 'fire' knowledge against the heat of our reflections and the reflections of others. The metaphorical crucible ensures that what emerges is not tainted with extraneous materials but rather has integrity. The heavy and industrial nature of the analogy is deliberate. Reflection has often been marginalized as a 'soft skill' but in reality it is difficult and demanding. It is so demanding that many organizations (inside and outside education) do not manage to integrate reflection let alone critical reflection in their work cultures. By contrast, we see critical reflection (through the analogy of the crucible) as a heavy, rigorous and difficult process that requires skill and effort to create ideas that will withstand and will be supported by scrutiny.

As with the other coherence makers we have identified, the crucible is not the only way to understand critical reflection, it is however one way of visualizing a structure that can be used in the service of curriculum design in classroom learning. The crucible is in part inspired by Marilyn Taylor's model of critical reflection that identifies disorientation, exploration, reorientation and equilibrium as the key stages in the learning process sequence (Taylor, 1986, p. 60). Implicit in Taylor's model is the commitment to challenge preconceived knowledge before reconsidering that knowledge and reaching a place of equilibrium. The critical reflection crucible does not seek equilibrium in knowledge. Rather, it recognizes that knowledge is complex, influenced by our own subjectivities and that it remains dynamic. Learning is a process of layering and development. As knowledge is created, new layers and connections emerge as understanding grows. So equilibrium is not always possible or even desirable. We prefer the analogy of a crucible where critical reflection acts as the fire, refining and testing knowledge to make it resilient, strong and transparent. The phases of the critical reflection crucible are:

- ᗐ Identifying assumptions.
- ᗐ Why this? Why so?
- ᗐ Contesting, elaborating and adapting.
- ᗐ Re-solving.

The first stage in the critical reflection coherence maker is identifying assumptions.

Identifying assumptions

Learners come to learning with subjectivities that are sometimes conscious but frequently unconscious. Often these assumptions are not based on evidence or an understanding of how evidence relates to those assumptions. We have nominated 'identifying assumptions' as this makes clear to students that every individual has assumptions about knowledge (some call this 'baggage'). To move beyond those assumptions we need to understand how our views are created and how they might be recreated. We are going to return to discussions around climate change to explain how the critical reflection crucible might work in practice. Climate change is useful in understanding critical reflection as students often approach this topic with a series of opinions and attitudes they have not challenged or tested with evidence. Like any set of beliefs these views may have been influenced by their family, friends or the media and many of these views do not necessarily take account of the complexity and interconnectedness of this topic. As Wray-Lake and colleagues argue (2010, p. 83), 'We must care about young people's environmental attitudes, beliefs, and behaviours, as they are likely to be carried into adulthood, communicated to offspring, and expressed in leadership decisions as younger generations replace their elders as society's leaders.' If young people are learning about climate change in science, geography or history it is crucial that they begin by identifying assumptions. They may have assumptions about the causes of climate change, its impacts and the possible responses that are not necessarily based in evidence.

The process of critical reflection invites learners to develop understanding by contrasting their views against the evidence to understand the context of the knowledge. In science a key part of scientific process is scientific method. If students understand that findings are developed through this disciplined process it provides them with not only an appreciation of the content of the learning but also the processes of knowledge generation in the discipline. This allows them to untangle the meaning separating opinion from evidence. This matters in the climate change learning as so much of the public discourse has focused on opinions rather than evidence. The ability to untangle knowledge is a critical skill for learners facing the complexity, chaos and contradictions of the postmodern world. For this stage of the crucible we should be exploring the following questions:

- What do students believe?
- Who gains from this belief?
- How have those beliefs been formed?
- Are those beliefs and assumptions based on evidence? What is the evidence? How can students rethink their beliefs as they become aware of new knowledge and evidence?

Equally, the ability to understand our assumptions and approaches to knowledge also lays the foundation for the next feature of the crucible: Why this? Why so?

Why this? Why so?

Once learners have understood the subjectivities they bring to learning and untangled the different aspects of a given problem, the next step is to ask 'why' questions that clarify the aims of their learning. In Taylor's model this stage is called 'exploration' (1987, p. 184). We have framed this feature of the crucible as a series of questions to make a deliberate parallel between this process and creativity learning (see Chapter 5). Similar to the Creativity Cascade, this phase requires student questioning that prompts them to seek contextual and 'joined up' understanding of knowledge. If we return to the climate change question, students might ask themselves and others (potentially including climate scientists):

- Why do I hold the views on climate change that I hold? (Why so?)
- Why is climate change receiving such prominence in the media? (Why this?)
- Why do people disagree on the causes of climate change? (Why so?)
- Why are people from Geography, Science, History and the Arts examining climate change? (Why this?)

This kind of questioning develops in students an understanding that knowledge is contested, connected across disciplines and contextual. The 'why this?', 'why so?' phase of the crucible encourages learners to think deeply about the knowledge that is confronting them. For some students this may be provocative as it disrupts many of the assumptions they have made about the nature of knowledge and learning. Ultimately this leads to a stronger connection with the nature of knowledge, and not just the knowledge itself, and builds a student's capacity to contest, elaborate and adapt knowledge, having asked key questions about the nature and content of that knowledge.

In the 'why this? why so?' phase of the critical reflection crucible the following questions may arise:

- Why is this knowledge being promoted above other knowledge?
- Who is promoting this knowledge and why?
- How does this knowledge connect with other parts of learning?
- Who gets to tell the story about this knowledge? And why?

At this point students are ready to engage in the next phase of the critical reflection crucible: contesting, elaborating and adapting.

Contesting, elaborating and adapting

As we discussed at the beginning of this chapter, critical reflection is often derided as a kind of self-indulgent pondering that leads to unhelpful and endless contemplation. Our view of critical reflection encourages action and collaboration rather than contemplation alone. At the contesting, elaborating and adapting stage, ideas and knowledge are tested (or fired) to elaborate preliminary concepts and then adapt them to other problems or domains of knowledge. Returning to the climate change example, once students understand the nature of scientific evidence they are then equipped to contest scientific 'fact' using scientific method. So given the rules of the discipline they can now understand how they have been influenced by their subjectivities, how evidence is used in science to make findings and how the test–retest principle might be applied to contest that knowledge. Perhaps more usefully they now have the knowledge to make extensions and elaborations to arguments about climate change and climate science that make active connections with other knowledge domains. For instance, students could use their scientific understanding to make a film to convey a persuasive message about climate change in the same way Al Gore did with *An Inconvenient Truth* (Guggenheim, 2006). In this way knowledge is positioned as dynamic, adaptable and malleable much like the molten liquid inside a crucible. The liquid in a crucible does not remain liquid permanently. Some questions that might be useful to frame learning at this stage of the critical reflection crucible are:

- How does this knowledge conflict or agree with other available evidence?
- How can this knowledge be enhanced in the light of evidence?
- How can this knowledge be adapted to new contexts or circumstances?

The next feature of the critical reflection crucible is re-solving.

Re-solving

The term re-solving describes the active re-formulation of ideas after testing assumptions, asking critical questions, contesting the knowledge and then viewing that knowledge as a dynamic entity to be elaborated and applied before settling on a view or approach. In our view, knowledge may become firm but it is never completely solid, so the process of re-solving always accounts for the remaking and the re-application of knowledge in new circumstances and contexts. In our climate change example students may re-solve a position based on climate science evidence that sea rises will have certain effects on small pacific islands such as Tuvalu. If at a later stage the initial projections look to be shifting upwards then we can re-solve this projection through a series of recalculations. The process is conceptualized not as passive but as an active and interactive collaborative process. It seeks to collaboratively engage with expertise from the domain being studied, other learners and those with broad multidisciplinary expertise. Key questions for this phase of the critical reflection crucible include:

- How can this area of knowledge be connected to other ideas to create new knowledge?
- What is the impact of this knowledge in different contexts? Is this knowledge context dependent? (What knowledge does not transfer across contexts?)
- What factors could influence and change this knowledge in the future?
- Who has the most to gain from this knowledge?

Like all of the 4C coherence makers we have described, the process is not linear and features of the crucible overlap, occur simultaneously or become re-arranged depending on the circumstances and contexts. What does not shift however is the need for students to understand that knowledge is complex. Critical reflection provides an approach to see that knowledge is dynamic, connected and influenced by individual preconceptions. In the next section we present a road map for how we see critical reflection contributing to dealing with those demands.

A road map for critical reflection and learning

Here are our starting points for changing schools and learning into spaces for critical reflection:

- *For critical reflection to thrive in schools, teacher education must take it seriously.* As we discussed earlier, reflection is not a new concept to teachers yet it has not always permeated student learning (Rodgers and Scott, 2008, p. 754). There is, however, now an opportunity to make it not just part of teacher education but to integrate it into schools as a way of understanding how learning can take place for teachers and students. If the beginning teachers of today are to become the change makers of tomorrow they will require preparation in the key skills related to critical reflection. If schools are to reposition knowledge and prioritize and integrate social and emotional learning, critical reflection can make this happen. Social and emotional learning is foundational to critical reflection, and teacher education must make authentic links between curriculum content, social and emotional learning and critical reflection. It provides a key capacity for all teachers (and students) to unearth their own assumptions about students, schools and learning. The ultimate aim is that classrooms will be places where assumptions are transparent, ideas contested and proactivity encouraged.

- *Critical reflection moves from the periphery of education to at or near the centre of learning in the twenty-first century.* There is substantial evidence that enhancing critical reflection will have benefits across learning (Fook and colleagues, 2015). Critical reflection encourages learners to see knowledge as connected, dynamic and influenced by power and agency. Facts have become less prized in learning. What matters more for twenty-first-century learning is the application of knowledge that recognizes its complexity and interconnectedness. The rapid and near ubiquitous access to information (in the developed world) through technology makes reflection and analysis of knowledge a far more critical skill than a knowledge of the facts themselves. Critical reflection provides schools with a pedagogy to reshape their approach to knowledge and by doing so create more flexible and dynamic learning for their students.

- *Educators understand how the system is currently driven and constituted and they are the best resource for changing the education system.* One of the pathways to change in our view is to empower teachers to critically reflect to support their schools and systems to become critically reflective spaces. As John Dewey argues, teachers need to be active responders and actors in the process of change. 'It is advisable that the teacher should understand, and even be able to criticize, the general principles upon which the whole educational system is formed and administered. They are not like a private soldier in an army, expected merely to respond to and transmit external energy; they must be an intelligent medium of action' (Dewey in Goldstein, 2014, p. iii).

In the current compliance culture, which features a preoccupation with 'standards' and 'testing', this kind of teacher autonomy built on critical reflection might seem utopian. As we have argued, however, change is not coming, it is upon us, and educators risk being sidelined from the discussion that is not only crucial to our futures but the future of our schools and our students. Educators must be part of that change so that the schools of the future can be critically reflective places where knowledge is not transmitted but debated, contested and integrated across learning.

In an editorial in *Reflective Practice* in 2010, Tony Ghaye asks the question: 'In what ways can reflective practices enhance human flourishing?' He wonders whether reflective practice can help humans 'bounce back from adverse events in our lives? Would they help us be more open-minded, have more creative thoughts, enjoy better relationships with others, be more resilient?' (p. 3). While there is still no definitive answer to this question, there are increasing signs that critical reflection is beneficial and may be a necessity for the challenges we face in the twenty-first century. If we believe that human flourishing is a mission of school education, critical reflection should be at the heart of how we design and implement learning. Jan Fook claims the benefits of critical reflection are apparent: 'It can clearly be stated that there is a mounting body of well-researched claims about the benefits and outcomes of critical reflection, and that these on the whole are consistent and supportive of each other. There are contributions to "human flourishing"' (Fook and colleagues, 2015, p. 99).

If Jan Fook's claim is correct there are substantial gains to be made for learners as we integrate critical reflection in our classrooms. In the schools of the 1950s when knowledge content (facts) was a precious commodity, critical reflection may have seemed like an unnecessary process. In modern schools faced with complex and contested knowledge, critical reflection seems like a necessary capacity for twenty-first-century citizens to enable them to understand themselves and the ways they can act to benefit and strengthen their community. More critically, it provides our students with an understanding of power and the way it is exercised. In this way, critical reflection provides an understanding of how to navigate and have agency in complex systems rather than being positioned by others as a passive observer or worse still a victim. When added to the other three Cs, critical reflection offers learners ways to understand how their own backgrounds influence and enrich knowledge. They can also understand that knowledge is inherently dynamic, contested and contestable.

It is unlikely that critical reflection will stop the egregious acts of violence that we described at the beginning of this chapter. It is a hard truth that schools alone cannot influence behaviour of this kind. The calls, however, that arose after this incident and incidents like it, remind us that the community expects our schools to be places that create and nurture peaceful, tolerant and democratic values. While we would never argue that the changes we are advocating could solve this particular problem, what we have discussed in this chapter does go some of the way to connecting knowledge to social and emotional understanding. Critical reflection has a role to play in helping all of us (students, teachers, leaders and communities) to test our motivations and understandings before taking action. If we can achieve this as a standard expectation of schooling we may contribute (in Ghaye's terms) to human flourishing rather than human disintegration.

In the next chapter we explore how action can follow from critical reflection through empowered communication.

Communication

Over and over again in our work in schools we see teachers and students discovering confidence, knowledge and power through communication. We have observed how pedagogy that activates the body and enables the voice develops students' capacity to concentrate, to self-regulate their emotions and behaviours, and to learn. We have seen teachers and students explore communication across the curriculum and construct dynamic deeper learning that is interdisciplinary and multimodal. We have witnessed teachers finding courage and efficacy in their voice to lead professional learning in creativity and innovation. In the twenty-first century, communication technologies are a conduit to a connected world of knowledge and collaboration, but it is the act of communicating that profoundly impacts and empowers students and teachers to learn and transform.

Why is communicating so powerful? Miranda recalls a workshop she did years ago with the voice teacher, Rowena Balos. Rowena said to a group of teachers, 'Often you don't really know how you feel and think about something until you're stimulated to communicate. The finding of true sound opens the channel to your soul. The voice is the vehicle that expresses its content.' We think this is at the heart of communication. When we communicate authentically, our voice as our sense of self is enabled and activated to engage with the world more fully. When we communicate we express what we know, we make meaning and we shape who we think we are. For these reasons communication skills are critical learning for active and critically reflexive citizens.

We draw from Milton N. Campos's (2007; 2009) ecological meaning for communication that blends biological and cultural mechanisms. It is a critical constructivist approach informed by the learning theories of Piaget and Vygotsky, and views communication as an interaction of evolutionary, developmental and social processes. People, when communicating through any form of unmediated and mediated spoken, written, visual, symbolic and bodily language, construct and co-construct images of themselves, of one another, and of the world. Communication is therefore at the core of constructing and messaging all learning and knowledge.

In this chapter we argue that communication is:

- a capability for empowerment and twenty-first-century citizenship,
- an expression of all learning and human knowledge,
- central to all pedagogical content knowledge across the curriculum,
- multimodal and informed by pedagogy in semiotics and aesthetics,
- foundational for learning, beginning with the body and voice,
- an expression of identity and culture,
- intrinsic to the other 'C' capabilities, and
- a complex process.

Communication across the curriculum is not ad hoc or implicit; it does not just reside in some subjects, and it does not just naturally happen. Communication skills are learnt and are essential to all learning and pedagogy. Communication can only be developed if students and teachers are meta-aware and practised in the semiotics, aesthetics and complexities of communication. In the twenty-first century, teachers must engage creatively and critically with diverse communication channels. Humans are wired to learn simultaneously through their body and voice (Bruner, 1975; Dance and Larson, 1972; Vygotsky, 1934/1966; 1978) and so pedagogy for these unmediated forms of expression must be strengthened and utilized to explore communication in other technology-mediated modes.

We introduce the 'Communication Crystal' as a coherence maker to structure the development of communication as a capability. A 'crystal' with its many surfaces and angles is used to describe communication as, like a crystal, communication is multi-faceted, and refracts and reflects messaging in many ways. In our coherence maker we claim that meta-awareness and enablement of communication must be recognized as a two-way interaction and multimodal process. Being able to convey the meaning and purpose of messaging leads to the generation of action and agency. Empowerment through communication begins by considering how we conceive communication.

What do we mean by communication?

Critical constructivism in communication, as an ecology of meanings theory combines the psychology of internal cognitive and intrapersonal structures with the external natural and social environment (Campos, 2007; 2009). Through communicating we progressively and reflexively construct, co-construct and re-construct reality dependent on the influences around us. Therefore communication traverses all disciplines. According to Campos (2009):

> communication should be understood as a transversal discipline that crosses all others because it is both psychological and social and because it accounts for necessary universal and particular contingent knowledge. Communication is the

foundation of all scientific disciplines and all forms of human expression (e.g. art, common sense, codes) because it is simultaneously a condition and result of all possible human knowledge. (p. 218)

Communication as a construct of our reality encompasses all forms of human expression and knowledge. Philosophy, the arts, science, religion and day-to-day life for instance are all different forms of constructing and communicating knowledge. Communication like knowledge can, therefore, be abstract like philosophy, affective like the arts, empirical like science, mystical like religion or mundane like everyday life.

Narrowing the understanding of communication to speech, reading and writing, and communication technologies, and relegating it to a subject silo, such as 'literacy' and 'English', limits the scope and depth of communication's role in education. All learning and knowledge creation depends upon different communication symbols and codes. A climate change scientist communicates with other scientists through the symbolic representations and understandings of science, but communication on climate change with policy makers may be through the symbolic representations of rhetorical language, and communication about climate change in an art installation may be expressed as a felt or metaphorical experience.

Communication is transdisciplinary and the condition and result of all forms of knowledge. This positions communication skills as essential pedagogical content knowledge in any curriculum area. An example to demonstrate how communication is central to pedagogical content knowledge is an upper primary class learning about rights and citizenship. As part of the 4C approach the teacher began by implementing teaching strategies to develop communication skills in the body and voice. To explore citizenship she concentrated on how students could explore and communicate their rights authentically in the school and wider social context. Rather than learning *about* rights, she wanted to give them opportunities for learning *in* rights. So first students had to raise money for their excursion to the government legislature and take collective responsibility for organizing and running every aspect of a school fete. On their excursion the students visited their local parliamentary representative, and challenged him with questions that related to their local concerns. The politician was impressed with the students' communication skills and their ability to articulate and thoughtfully frame their issues. On returning to school, students explored their concerns by role-playing parliamentary debates. They believed they engaged with and debated issues more respectfully than the politicians they had witnessed in the parliament. They then had to consider what were the appropriate actions and communication channels to address the issues they had raised.

In this learning, communication skills in oracy (spoken literacy) were integral to students being confident and articulate to ask questions, listen, debate and negotiate, to act upon their rights and responsibilities. Explicit learning in communication was inherent to the learning of the content, and the pedagogy. The follow-up social action however needed skills beyond oracy; it required communication in old and new media channels, such as letter writing, media releases, blogging, video posting, online networking and crowd sourcing. In the twenty-first century, communication involves multiple semiotic modes and channels of messaging. Learning in the semiotics of multimodal communication can empower students as learners and as twenty-first-century citizens.

Semiotics and multimodal communication

Semiotics is the study of how humans make meaning for themselves and others, through multiple sign systems or codes such as words, images, videos, numbers, formulas, songs, gestures, dance etc. Semiotic theory explains that the meaning of these signs is a joint construction by multiple participants (Leeds-Hurwitz, 1993; 2009). Meaning is not intrinsic to the signs themselves; they are only given meaning and interpreted through the human connection of communication. Semiotic theory assists in analysing how this connection works, and can explain for instance the role of interdisciplinary and multimodal communication in education. In semiotic analysis, *bricolage* (Levi-Strauss, 1962/1966) and *intertextuality* (Kristeva, 1980) refer to the construction of new meaning made from the connections of multiple signs with past meanings. An example of using bricolage and intertextuality to create and communicate something new is the theatrical experimentation of Robert LePage's performance company Ex Machina based in Canada. Ex Machina's work is informed by multiple disciplines such as science, architecture, history and languages, and combines aesthetics in the recording and performing arts, using 'high tech', 'low tech' and advanced technologies to reimagine narrative codes and performance. Production manager, Michel Bernatchez describes the multiple sources of Ex Machina's inspiration:

> What is needed is a comingling of the performing arts such as dance, opera and music with the recording arts such as cinema, video and multimedia. It calls for encounters between scientists and playwrights, between scenic artists and architects, between artists from Quebec and artists from elsewhere. This intermingling would give rise to new artistic forms. That was the gamble that Ex Machina took – to become a laboratory, an incubator of a theatre capable of connecting with a 21st century audience (Caux and Gilbert, 2007, p. 10).

The semiotics of bricolage and intertextuality in Ex Machina's theatrical works and processes has created new forms of expression and new languages of staging, and a new way of exchanging ideas in the twenty-first century (LePage in Caux and Gilbert, 2007). Their work helps to explain how the semiotics of interdisciplinary curricula and integrated communication modes can also produce new and deeper learning experiences for students in twenty-first-century schools.

Using the semiotics of a multidisciplinary approach is evident in the following learning, which integrated science, English and creative arts to examine the question: 'Is change and adaptation necessary for survival?' The final exhibition and assessment of the students' learning was a group drama performance that seamlessly blended their research, experimental processes and creativity as a multidisciplinary and multimodal (linguistic, non-linguistic, mediated and non-mediated) communication experience. The students had to precisely convey, engage and persuade their audience of their evidence and findings through video blogs, live presentation, claymation animation, a rap, dramatic tableaus and documentary video footage.

As with the rights and citizenship example, communication was central to pedagogical content knowledge. The semiotics of a multimodal presentation reflected a multidisciplinary approach to content. The meaning and purpose of communication were inherent to the content knowledge. The result of the interdisciplinary curricula and integrated communication was deeper learning, as evidenced in this student's comment: 'I hadn't realized there were so many ways we could think about adaptation. And there are so many ways to get your ideas and research across.'

Skills and understandings in the semiotics of multiple modes and channels of communication are rich in creating new meaning and knowledge. Multimodal communication also has the potential to access and develop different ways of thinking to facilitate student learning (Gardner, 1999; Moreno and Mayer, 2007; Sternberg, 2003). In tertiary learning, Deanna P. Dannels (2010) advocates for programmes in multimodal communication across the curriculum (CXC) as beneficial to learning and an imperative for work engagement: 'Responding to consistent refrains from business leaders, accreditation agencies, and the popular press, CXC programs focus on helping non-communication-focused faculty and students understand the power of communication and become competent in using communication to achieve multiple goals in various settings' (pp. 56–57). We also argue that multimodal communication achieves multiple goals in the school setting. Precise and controlled learning in multimodal communication skills is integral to deeper content knowledge across the curriculum. Learning in communication not needed cannot be random and haphazard but authentically linked to meaning, purpose and audience.

We acknowledge multimodal communication and semiotics as integral to twenty-first-century education and life, but we also recognize the primacy of embodiment and oracy as foundations for learning. In low socioeconomic communities where children struggle with language, and in communities with little socioeconomic disadvantage, we begin our 4C approach to learning and transformation with a focus on communicating through the body, and the voice. This is known as embodied cognition or enactment.

Communicating using the body

As we mentioned in Chapter 5, an area of developing research is the exploration of cognition as an interplay between abstract thought and physical embodiment (Glenberg, 2008; Winkielman and colleagues, 2015). Cognition is embodied when the physical body plays a significant and causal role in cognitive processing. This runs counter to the traditional view of the mind and body being disassociated, and the body as peripheral to cognition. Psychologists and neuroscientists are increasingly exploring the role of physical embodiment on behaviour, experience and cognition (Gibbs, 2005; Meier and colleagues, 2012; Sharpiro, 2011). Embodied cognition research maintains that sensory perception and kinaesthetic action have a major role in how people perceive, learn and think. For instance, in a classroom a role-play imagining and embodying a character's possible motives in a text can support the cognitive development of inference in reading (Ewing, 2015; Saxton and Miller, 2013).

Learning through embodiment is developed as pedagogy in the 4Cs approach. It is often referred to by teachers as 'putting thinking into the body', and 'the body into their thinking'. Gibbs (2005) argues that perception, conceptual thought, memory, cognitive development, reasoning, language, emotion and consciousness are dependent on embodiment to varying extents. 'Human language and thought emerge from recurring patterns of embodied activity that constrain ongoing intelligent behaviour. We must not assume cognition to be purely internal, symbolic, computational, and disembodied, but seek out the gross and detailed ways in which language and thought are inextricably shaped by embodied action' (p. 9).

Treating cognition as only a disembodied experience has been to the detriment of using enactment as a means to learn. The 4Cs approach recognizes and explores the instrumental role of embodiment in learning. As an example of some of the ways embodiment can be used, Juliet, a teacher, describes what they have been doing with their students.

Students have enhanced their learning through embarking on a journey of the mind and body known as 'brain push ups'. This enables students to focus their mind on the task at hand. Embodiment allows preparation for learning and by integrating movement it has enabled the students to come into a state of readiness for the day. Brain push ups are created as a gateway into what the students will be working on throughout the day. For example, if students are writing imaginative texts, a brain push up could include students working in teams of four to think about and present: what does creativity look like, sound like, and feel like? As each team presents their ideas, the teacher is able to record the words or phrases heard. This is the initial introduction to students' writing.

Students incorporate movement in their initial brainstorming also. Without any background, teams or individuals are encouraged to present an idea or thought through the use of their bodies. Their audience (peers) are invited to give feedback on their interpretations or seek clarification on how a message was conveyed. They are encouraged to think about how the audience will know that they are moving from one movement to the next. We have introduced capital letters and full stops in the embodiment, as the purpose of any movement is to communicate a message with precision.

We also use embodied cognition as a checkpoint to observe and give feedback on how students are progressing and managing their learning through their research tasks. Students are encouraged to use any creative device, whether it be a mime, postcard (tableau) or rap. This allows the audience to discuss clarity in delivering a message and to suggest improvements. The teachers also give feedback on where to next in their research to guide and scaffold their learning.

We have incorporated embodied cognition across all learning disciplines to inspire, monitor and give feedback to all of our students. Those students, who in the past have been reclusive, have broadened their thinking and have been able to be empowered in the use of their bodies to convey their learning.

The power of mindful and effective experiences in embodiment is a frequently untapped resource with rich potential for learning. Learning through embodiment can involve students imagining through play, movement and breathing exercises, role-playing characters from stories and history, painting a portrait, measuring and calculating space, or undertaking a scientific experiment. The premise of putting learning in the body is that human cognition is acutely connected to kinaesthetic bodily experiences (Gibbs, 2005; Sharpiro, 2014). Cognition is linked to processes that are internal and mental, physical and bodily.

The impact of embodied learning in education is twofold. First, a concept of self, of who we are, is linked to tactile-kinaesthetic activity. Emotion and consciousness have evolved from and continue to be extensions of embodied motion (Gibbs, 2005). Second, embodied learning influences communication as a cognitive activity. Language acquisition and its use involves and is stimulated by embodied experiences (Kasckak and colleagues, 2014; Scorolli, 2014; Yu, 2014). This is evident in a programme we have introduced as part of the 4Cs approach called 'drama literacy'.

'Drama Literacy' (Jefferson, 2015) uses a range of drama processes such as dramatic play, tableaus, improvisations, role-plays, sound and movement activities, 'conscience alley', and process drama to explore, for example, learning in and through picture books, novels, poetry, history, science and the environment. We mentor teachers in how embodiment develops literacy, communication and other 'C' capabilities. Teachers comment: 'I can't believe what the students are thinking and saying in drama literacy' and 'I have never heard from this student before, they really respond to this type of learning', and 'the students' writing has really improved!' Drama is an art form of the body, gesture and spoken work, and through embodiment has the potential to develop functional, dialogical, linguistic and paralinguistic dimensions of oracy (O'Toole and Stinson, 2013). Drama pedagogy stimulates and engages other forms of literacy development such as writing and visual literacy (Anderson and Dunn, 2013; Anderson, Hughes and Manuel, 2008), strengthens verbal skills (Podlozny, 2000) and improves spontaneity, fluency, vocabulary, articulation and use of diverse language registers in language learning (Wagner, 1998). Drama pedagogical processes are an example of how learning through the body can facilitate and enhance communication skills. The positive impact of the drama literacy programme in schools illustrates an unfortunate languishing of oracy development in education. Oracy is crucial to learning, and significant in enabling people to have a 'voice' to express their ideas.

Communicating using the voice

Oral competencies are needed for the highly connected global context of the twenty-first century, but they are also pivotal in how humans learn and develop self-concept. We learn and know who we are through language acquisition and in particular through oracy (Dance and Larson, 1972). The prevalence of digital devices and time devoted to screen time has diminished children's opportunities and attendance to developing oral language skills (Ward, 2004). High stakes testing regimes that focus solely on reading and writing have also affected learning time spent on oracy (Christakis and colleagues, 2009). It is vital for students to learn and practise skills in oracy to develop language and communication processes for human interaction.

Oral language plays a fundamental role in human development. Speech allows us to communicate at a much faster rate than any other mode of human-created communication. The combining of bits of sound in a structured, grammatical way with an attached meaning allows humans to overcome the usual limits of memory (Lieberman, 1991). Sounds become symbols, and those symbols as language retain meaning over a lifetime. The meanings that individuals create for these symbols shape our thinking and are the raw material for how we perceive ourselves. The internalization of oral language mirrors our developing complex thought processes (Dance, 1982; Vygotsky, 1934/1966).

Complex thinking and self-awareness emerge from an individual's ability to talk and interact. Julie Yingling (2004) argues that human relationships affect those abilities. Through dialogue, the boundaries of the human mind interact symbolically with others, and it is through the internalizing of these experiences that a person's identity and self-perception is developed. From this perspective, thinking and identity fluctuate as communication experiences fluctuate. The nature of, and emphasis on, communication and interactions in schools have a major influence on the identity development and self-perception of students and teachers.

Oral language and enabling student and teacher 'voice' is predominant in the 4Cs approach. It fast tracks students' and teachers' confidence and belief in their abilities to think, learn and develop a sense of self. The emphasis on body, voice and multimodal communication skills is of huge consequence to developing empowerment and identity.

Communication as identity

Identity is intrinsically linked to how we communicate, and identity is influenced by how others and institutions (such as the media) communicate to us. A communication theory of identity (Hecht and colleagues, 2004; Hecht, 2009) argues that there is not one single, unified notion of self, but rather multiple identities guiding our thoughts and behaviours. Hecht (2009) argues, 'humans are inherently social beings whose lives revolve around communication, relationships, and communities and who operate from *multiple and shifting identities*' (original emphasis) (p. 139). Our multiple and shifting identities are a result of and an expression of multiple forms of communication.

These ideas about identity have ramifications for learning in and through communication at school. For example, in an integrated learning experience involving a multicultural performance, junior secondary students had the opportunity to express their sense of identity. Students elected a cultural group they identified with, and took ownership of how they communicated their culture, through dancing, storytelling, singing, visual representations etc. Different identities were explored by varying forms of cultural expression. Teachers were surprised that one boy, George, identified with a Pacific Islander group, even though he had no experience with the culture. By communicating in a new way, George explored an aspect of his 'multiple identities'. The experience of communicating through an emergent identity developed his self-concept and had a positive impact on his learning. It is critical that multiple forms of communication are explored in schools in terms of developing learner identity and self-concept.

Multiple identities are also relevant to communication technologies and connectivity. Identity, often associated with nationality, ethnicity and community is also manifest in communications technology. Old and new forms of media communication such as radio and television programmes, online communities and interactive gaming are sources for identity and locations for the expression of identity. David Holmes (2005) argues that identities in the communication technology space are an extension of the identities we develop face-to-face in relationships and communities. According to Holmes, the dominant background forms of communication that affect our lives, such as live face-to-face communication, influence the way we communicate through technology. The way we interact in the immediacy of live communication has an effect on how we receive and interact with media and communication technologies. For instance, the following electronic message from a young student, Steven, to his teachers reflects how positive face-to-face communication interactions have influenced the openness and integrity of his mediated message:

Dear Teachers,

This is probably something i've never thought i would actually be doing but i just want to confess so many things i've done wrong in regards to my education. I'm not sure myself why i suddenly had this idea of confessing nor got the courage from because of how embarrassing this is for me but, i'm sure it's a sign of something. I'm really sorry if i have disappointed all of you in regards to some school work/presentations i haven't uploaded into my google drive even making up reasons just to get away from trouble. But now, i'm done running away from the mistakes i've done and i'm prepared to make sacrifices such as focusing into more school work than social media . . .

So please, expect me to improve my grades this last term as a year 8 student, as i will be striving my best to show the things i've learnt from all of you as my teachers. No promises about the grades, but i can make sure that i will be a better person in class in relation to behaviour, grit, focus and etc. A promise i can make is that i will strive to be a top student throughout the years that's left in my schooling.

Yours sincerely,

Steven

The following microblogging exchange as homework is another example illustrating how face-to-face pedagogy has informed the respectful inquiry by one middle primary student, for more reflective thinking from another student:

Lillian   I think the book we are looking at is about how we all need to get along.

Justine   That's true Lillian, but do you think you can go a bit deeper to explain what you mean by needing to get along?

Lillian   Maybe it's saying, that different people need to get along, in different communities, and that we can enjoy the differences.

Justine   Yes, that's good thinking.

Live and mediated communications are expressions of identity, relationships and communities and they are an expression of society and culture more widely. Socio-cultural messages in communication shape and are being shaped by human behaviour. Communication as a socio-cultural phenomenon is an expression of knowledge and power, from national politics in the media, to advertising in social media, to day-to-day language in schools. Critical reflection of communication requires learners to recognize and critique the knowledge and power relations inherent in all communication and social systems. Schools are institutions that represent social forces of power or powerlessness. Through communication, schools can ingrain and normalize power and privilege, disempowerment and disenfranchisement. Power or the lack of power is embedded in the everyday talk and communication of all levels of human interaction in schools. To say, 'Year 10 at the rate you are going, you will amount to nothing,' has huge implications for power and powerlessness in schools. In critical communication pedagogy, Fassett and Warren (2007) position teachers and students to be critically reflexive of all communication practices, as well as being advocates for dialogic and democratic discursive discourse in learning.

Communication creates meaning, power, identity and relationships; it creates the culture of the classroom and the school. The 4Cs approach focuses time, energy and pedagogy to heighten awareness of, and give attention to, communication as a powerful tool *for* and *of* learning and empowerment. Communication is also connected to and informed by the other 'C' capabilities in intrinsic ways.

Communication and the other Cs

Ben Bernanke, the former US Federal Reserve (the Fed) Chairman, said in his memoir, 'monetary policy is 98% talk and 2% action' (*The Economist*, 2015, p. 37).

Bernanke's message is that communication is fundamental. His aim was to make the Fed more transparent by communicating and explaining its policies more regularly at press conferences, and in other media. Communication is key to accountability, setting an agenda and co-constructing knowledge and understanding, in the same way that communication for every individual is fundamental to co-constructing an understanding of the world: 'Each utterance makes the world; other choices would make different worlds' (Warren, 2009, p. 215). The processes and interaction of communication are staples for critical reflection, collaboration and creativity, and in turn these capabilities are embedded in communication.

Critical reflection

The ability to communicate is linked to higher order thought processes, and so without the symbols of words and other representations, humans cannot develop critical reflection. For example, in the 4Cs approach we observe how students use the language of the Learning Disposition Wheel (see Chapter 3) to formulate their critical reflection about their progress in learning. To reflect, students make meaning and develop meta-awareness by using the symbols of language for competencies on the Learning Disposition Wheel. Critical reflection in any discipline (mathematics, literature, design, physical education etc) needs the symbolic tools (numbers, words, diagrams, bodies etc) of communication, to interpret, analyse and question ideas. Without communication skills, students do not have the capacity to think with meta-awareness and reflexivity, nor the ability to co-construct thinking with others. Critical reflection requires the capability of communication, but communication cannot be developed without critical reflection. Through critical reflection, communication skills are examined, questioned and refined, to convey meaning and purpose more precisely.

Collaboration

Collaboration as a negotiated understanding between people is dependent on complex communication skills. The success of collaboration is dependent on the mutual understanding of verbal and/or non-verbal communication. Collaboration depends upon communication practices that enable all voices to co-construct joint understanding and commitment to a goal. When students and teachers encounter problems collaborating it can be due to a deficiency in communication skills.

Communication is the basis for relationships and the functioning of power between people. If communication is not a shared and compassionate collaboration between people, messaging can be purposeless or misunderstood, or an instrument of oppression or fear. Viewing communication as an ethical act of collaboration strengthens the meaning and purpose of the message, and empowers the co-communicators. In critical communication pedagogy, dialogue as method and metaphor is 'a basis for changing customary power relations and a basis for building new ways of thinking and seeing relationships' (Fassett and Warren, 2009, p. 215). The messaging of communicators and the ethical choices they make can be influenced by a humane shared vision of collaboration.

Creativity

Creative ideas, as Robert J. Sternberg (2003) argues, do not sell themselves, they have to be sold. Creative ideas disturb the status quo and so they are usually viewed with distrust, suspicion and misunderstanding. Like Ben Bernanke with monetary policy, Sternberg argues that teachers and students need to learn how to persuade people of the value of their new ideas and creative thinking.

> If children do a science project, it is a good idea for them to present it and demonstrate why it makes an important contribution. If they create a piece of artwork, they should be prepared to describe why they think it has value . . . teachers may find themselves having to justify their ideas about teaching to their principal. They should prepare their children for the same kind of experience. (Sternberg, 2003, p. 112)

Communication as rhetoric, as logic, as evidence, as possibility, persuades people of new ideas. It is, in part, the precise use of communication symbols within an area of knowledge that explains and expresses the novelty of ideas that influence individuals, domains and fields within a creative system (Csikszentmihalyi, 1996). The same applies to learning. A novel idea for a student in mathematics, for example, needs to be precisely communicated to demonstrate to others how new understandings were made.

Creative processes are inherent in the manipulation of the message and medium of different communication modes. The control and interpretation of the message and medium involves creative choices in the way messages reach and are received by others. The example of the multidisciplinary communication task integrating science, English and creative arts, highlighted students making creative choices to convey meaning and purpose to their audience. In the future, their creative choices will be strengthened through learning in controlling the messaging and aesthetics of the multimodal communication forms.

To guide awareness and understanding of the centrality and complexity of communication in learning we have developed a coherence maker, the Communication Crystal.

The Communication Crystal Coherence Maker

Crystals appear irregular in shape but in fact the crystal appearance of flat surfaces and angles is due to the regularity of layered, repeated, uniform patterns. From a universe of primordial chaos, crystals demonstrate the order of atomic arrangements. Crystal structures can explain the existence of atoms too small to see with the naked eye. Communication, like crystals and atoms, is also evidence of what can be unseen in learning. Communication is ubiquitous, but is it deeply understood and controlled in its potential for learning and transformation? Our coherence maker, the Communication Crystal, is a tangible way to explore the unseen complexity of communication. It involves the following:

- ♠ Alert to messaging.
- ♠ Enabling voice.
- ♠ Conveying meaning and purpose.
- ♠ Generating action and agency.

Crystals are multifaceted so they also suggest as a metaphor that the messages of communication can be sent and received in multiple ways. M.C. Escher's lithograph 'Order and Chaos' (1950) (Figure 7.1) illustrates the multifaceted nature of a crystal's geometry and structural order. Escher's image also demonstrates how meaning can be communicated through a visual representation rather than words.

Communication in whatever form or representation, whether through the body, voice, visual, aural, tactile, sensory, or mediated with technology, must first be *noticed* or perceived. What do we notice in Escher's picture? Why is chaos reflected in the order of the crystal? What is Escher saying when he takes such care in his drawing of both the order of the perfect crystal and the chaos of the broken and used bits and pieces? Noticing messaging is not just *what* is being represented but *how* it is being represented. The Communication Crystal coherence maker begins an understanding of communication by noticing and being *alert to messaging*.

Alert to messaging

Rather than simply being aware of sending or receiving a message, 'alert to messaging' is a heightened, reflexive state. Reflexivity is to see ourselves critically; it is to be accountable for what we say and how we say it. Alert to messaging is to consider how what we say affects others and how we receive messages affects others. This alertness is an active and energized state of awareness, and it is learnt through pedagogical strategies in metacognition, constant accountabilities (or responsibilities) and practice.

The hyper-awareness of messaging in learning spaces begins with teachers and students noticing the verbal and non-verbal dimensions of oral language. Being alert

Figure 7.1 M.C. Escher's 'Order and Chaos' © 2016 The M.C. Escher Company-The Netherlands. All rights reserved. www.mcescher.com

to the non-verbal or paralinguistic aspects of communication is to notice and interpret vocal expression, gestures and body language, proxemics (the positioning of bodies in relation to one another), energy and silences. We have observed in 4C learning students developing an alertness to how bodies facing each other improves group communication, how eyes and attentive listening to someone speaking improves the communicator's messaging, and how controlling the paralanguage of gesture and body language improves the effectiveness of their speaking.

Teachers become alert to their own vocal expression and its effect on students and notice how proxemics shapes the meaning of messaging in the learning. Standing and seated circles, for instance, create a sense of community and equality in a warm-up or discussion, and students standing and speaking to the class when giving feedback raises the students' consciousness in 'reading' a response to their feedback. In the 4Cs approach, hands-up becomes an unnecessary signal when teachers and students are alert to more subtle forms of paralinguistic messaging, such as realizing someone else wants to talk, or that others should have an opportunity to talk, or that everyone is accountable to talk.

Being alert to messaging strengthens an awareness of how communication is linked to the way we construct knowledge. Both students and teachers communicate to demonstrate their understandings of learning. Learning is deepened for instance when Pythagoras's theorem is not only demonstrated through application (fitting a tv screen measured on the diagonal, into an entertainment unit) but when students have to explain and communicate effectively how the theorem works (using the symbols of algebra, diagrams and words as precise tools of logic and reasoning). Being alert to messaging is knowing how students' explaining and teaching can be used for learning (Fiorella and Mayer, 2015).

Alert to messaging is noticing not just the significance of communication in learning, it is to notice its complexity. Salazar (2002; 2009) asserts a complex state of communication is required to generate collaborative creativity and innovation. A complex state of communication operates at the boundary of order and chaos, between the order of organized structures and the chaos of incoherence. Creativity is dependent on being on the edge of this boundary; this is where the emergence of new ideas occurs. To develop complex communication, collaborators must be alert to the frequency, procedures, roles and assumptions of the messaging in a group (Salazar, 2002).

> Whenever we see group members changing their interaction patterns, whether by changing the frequency and directional flow of communication, using new procedures to solve problems or make decisions, displaying little or no discussion typical of group member roles, or questioning or supplanting assumptions about what counts as good or bad information, the group is showing evidence of operating in a complex state. (Salazar, 2009, p. 212)

Teachers and leadership aware of and practised in complex communication processes are more likely to generate creativity and innovation in schools. In the 4Cs approach we encourage processes that generate the noticings and disrupters described by Salazar (2002). To be alert or metacognizant in the processes that engender a complex state of communication, the following questions need to be considered:

- How often has each group member spoken?
- How are new ways being used to look at ideas and issues?
- How are group members' roles shaping a typical flow and outcome in the discussion?
- What assumptions are continually being made?

Complexity in the communication processes of collaboration and critical reflection applies to students' learning too. Students alert to and practised in complex communication processes such as elaboration, evaluation and negotiation will collaborate more effectively (Webb, 2013). Complex processes in communication can only be developed if students and teachers have a reflexive awareness of noticing those processes. When communication processes are noticed, *enabling all voices* is the next step in developing communication.

Enabling voice

Enabling voice is to create the positive conditions that allow all individuals to express their thinking, and to be open to receiving others' thinking. In our definition, communication is the expression of the individual's voice through any form of messaging. We recognize the primacy of speaking and embodiment but other forms of communication – writing, reading, numeracy and representations that are visual, spatial and bodily, or mediated through instruments and technology – are also an expression of human development and human voice. It is through all these expressions that we construct a reality of who we are, who others are and what the world is (Campos, 2007). In 4Cs learning all voices must be heard, supported and challenged through expression in a range of communication modes.

Individual empowerment and the 'genius' of the group can only be realized when all voices are enabled. To enable all voices, no one voice can dominate. Through targeted pedagogy, dominant voices learn to generously let others communicate, and unconfident or unpractised communicators are given support and space to find their voices. To enable all voices in learning takes time, practice and feedback, but the fruition of these labours in pedagogy are learners with skills to be able to collaborate, reflect and create. In a primary classroom where students struggled with collaboration, the teachers used strategies such as each student in a group using a different coloured pencil to communicate their thinking, so it was visually apparent that everyone in the group had the opportunity to voice their thoughts on paper. The teachers also used embodiment exercises where groups had to communicate non-verbally by offering and yielding their ideas to create a group tableau for each person's idea, and reach a group consensus of which idea they would all agree on.

'Bus stop' strategies (also referred to in Chapter 8 as a strategy for collaborative 'offering' and 'yielding') enable all voices to reflect on learning by answering an open question, and sitting down only when they have contributed a new idea or elaborated on someone else's previous idea. The question could be: 'Why do we really need to know about earthquakes and volcanos?' The students may map and organize their ideas in small groups and then, as a class forum, stand up and construct a 'discussion' by randomly speaking one at a time and then sitting down. By close attention, no one can interrupt or repeat anything that has been previously said, they can only elaborate, extend or advance the ideas raised. Strategies like 'bus stop' highlight and enable students to voice their ideas in different ways throughout all their learning.

There are environmental, individual and group dynamic factors that can hinder the enabling of the voice in the learning situation. Based on Salazar's (2002; 2009) work on group communication, the following factors have to be addressed to enable voices in learning. The factors that Salazar (2002; 2009) argues hinder communication are:

- Time pressures.
- Organizational culture.
- Functional fixedness.
- Evaluation apprehension.
- Production blocking.
- Network structures.

Time pressures inhibit communication, as there is not enough space for group members to adequately express their thoughts. In learning, time has to be devoted to enable students to express their thinking, and for implementing strategies that develop the students' abilities to put thinking into words or representations. This includes strategies such as think, pair and share, or embody, speak and write, or brainstorm, exhibit and feedback, or the flipped classroom where students outside the classroom are exposed to new materials to develop their ideas. Pedagogical time in learning has to be spent developing the confidence and skills to communicate effectively. The aspiration for teachers and students is to acknowledge, enable and hold to account every voice in a learning session.

Another factor that affects communication is the patterns and structures of an *organizational* or classroom *culture* that prevent risk taking in thinking. Being averse to risk in learning may be indicated by students only willing to express a 'right' answer, or students reluctant to creatively problem-solve. A risk-taking learning culture values divergent and challenging thinking by students. Risk taking openly and continually acknowledges learning from mistakes. To take risks in thinking is to let go of self-censorship and the fear of making a mistake. Communicating thinking in the public sphere is taking a risk. The learning environment has to support and scaffold this leap of faith for students.

Enabling the voice can also be constrained by individual factors related to *functional fixedness*. Functional fixedness refers to a person's habitual ways of thinking in a situation. Varying communication strategies, such as drawing an abstract picture to explain your thinking, creating an embodied 'postcard' or brainstorming salient words are used to explore different ways of enabling voice, and developing flexible and divergent thinking in learning.

Evaluation apprehension is when people refrain from expressing their thoughts for fear of being judged or seen in a negative light. Voices can only be enabled and valued in a positive learning culture. Through feedback and applause from the teacher and other students, communication skills are valued and affirmed.

To enable individual voices the dynamic of group communication is navigated in terms of *production blocking*. Production blocking is the inhibition of people communicating when someone else is communicating. Put simply, we can't talk at the same time and we have to wait for our turn. This can lead to production blocking because not everyone may be able to contribute at the right time.

Network structures are the patterning of communication amongst people, for instance one person in a group may always lead discussions, another may always have the final word, or another will usually wait to be asked to contribute. These characteristics can be mindfully addressed by teachers through pedagogy, and by students when collaborating. Production blocking and network structures are addressed by varying the configurations, opportunities and types of communication. For example:

- working individually online for a group brainstorm or discussion.
- groups communicating non-verbally by constructing images or tableaus.
- small groups discussing ideas and 'jigsawing' those ideas back to a larger group.

All of these strategies enable student voices by varying the production and structures of communication.

Communication can be any form appropriate for knowledge creation and audience. Communication can be speech, discussion, inquiry, experiment, poem, report, dance, diagram, formula or code, it needs to be framed and understood as a means of communication and enablement of a person's thinking. Being alert to messaging is awareness of communication, and enabling voice provides the opportunity to communicate. Awareness and enablement allow communicators to begin to construct and co-construct meaning about themselves and the world around them. These first two aspects of the Communication Crystal scaffold are only effective if the *meaning* of the message is *conveyed* with *purpose* and control.

Conveying meaning and purpose

When a message is conveyed there has to be shared understanding between the communicator and the audience. Unless communication is considered at least a two-way process, its purpose is unclear and meaning is not exchanged or integrated. In Campos's (2007; 2009) ecology theory of communication, shared understanding is the determinant of all communication, which, 'as all biological mechanisms, is a never-ending, progressive process of disequilibrium, in which interlocutors search for equilibrium, fighting for autonomy instead of multiplicity, and shared understanding instead of conflict. Communication thus crosses science, philosophy, the arts, religion, and the daily-lived world' (Campos, 2009, p. 219). It is not enough to have an opportunity to communicate; it requires a crafting of skills to share meaning to 'search for equilibrium' with others. To convey meaning and purpose requires both the communicator and the audience to be skilled and conversant in the form of communication being used. Communication skills can be developed in learning experiences by interconnecting *making* and *understanding*. A model for collaborative communication pedagogy (based on Anderson and Jefferson, 2009) is illustrated in Figure 7.2. The model illustrates how being a communicator through 'making' is pedagogically linked or informed by a reflective and critical stance in receiving communication as understanding. The *making* and *understanding* model is based on the idea of praxis, i.e. the working together of action and reflection, practice and theory. To engage an audience requires meta-awareness and experiential practice in *crafting the message* which is interrelated to *choosing and controlling the medium*.

Figure 7.2 A model for collaborative communication pedagogy

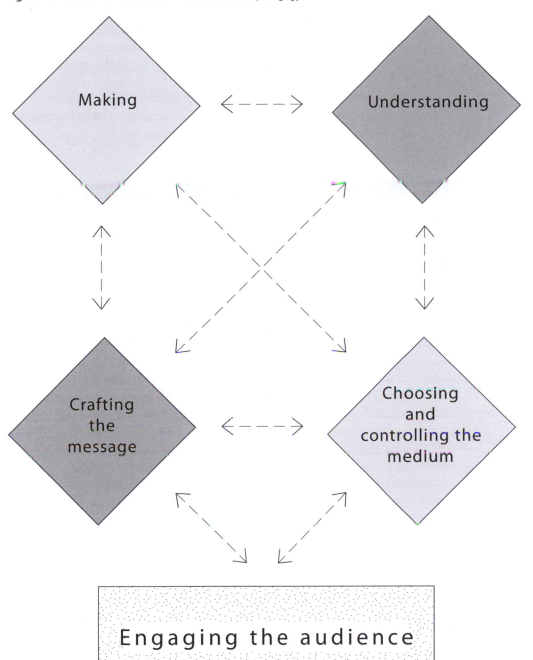

The following example illustrates how *making* and *understanding* are interconnected in developing learning in communication. In an integrated curriculum, students explored the aesthetic principles of colour, line, proportion, perspective and symbol to create the mood and essence of how they perceived themselves in a self-portrait. They studied the visual literacy of Shaun Tan's *The Red Tree* (2001) and examined how the author-artist captured the essence of the girl portrayed in the story. The students also wrote as 'art critics' and analysed how Picasso depicted identity and mood in his artworks.

Student learning in *crafting the message*, and *choosing and controlling the medium* developed through their *understanding* and reflection of the artists' works, integrated with the *making* and communicating of their own self-portrait works. Communication in the learning was not only expressed in the artworks; it was in how they communicated interpretations, reflections, analysis and feedback, to each other, orally and in writing. Learning was *in* and *through* the messaging and medium of communication in visual arts, writing and oracy. The learning was an authentic enabler of student voice by exploring perceptions of their identity and the identity of others through communication.

Technologies and new media, as Holmes (2005) argues, emerge and evolve from the complexity of social management and human behaviours. Communication mediated by technology is an aesthetic tool with which to critically reflect, create and collaborate. For instance, students using a video diary to record a science experiment on adaptation required skills to aesthetically and technically control the image and sound to capture and communicate their process. Collaboration was needed to respond to teacher and peer feedback, and critical reflection and creative thinking was needed to problem-solve the outcomes of the experiment and then to communicate it effectively to their audience. To precisely convey the meaning and purpose of the video blog was a complex interaction of learning about the science of adaptation, experimental processes, using the aesthetics of communication technology, and developing 4C capabilities.

Through making and understanding pedagogy in the aesthetics of communication, students and teachers understand and control the meaning and purpose of messaging to then *generate action and agency* as the last step in the Communication Crystal.

Generating action and agency

We view communication as a dynamic process that produces action and agency, rather than oppression and compliance. Communication in an Orwellian totalitarian state is a broadcast to maintain social and individual control through constraint and suppression. In critical communication pedagogy, communication is a social interaction that actively creates meaning, relationships, social activity and power (Fassett and Warren, 2007). Communication is more than reflecting or representing an idea, it is a multidisciplinary phenomenon that is fundamentally humanizing and enables thought, reason and identity creation (Hecht et al., 2004; Yingling, 2004).

Paulo Freire (1970/2006) argues that communication profoundly underpins an individual's empowerment and existential sense of being. Communication is a potentially transformational and humanizing force, however to be so it must be treated as a dialogue, as an act of co-constructed creation between people. If communication and dialogue are not mediated by two-way trust, humility and critical reflection, the human voice and identity are oppressed. Too often, people are ignored, dealt with abruptly, not given responsibility and told what to do. All these actions undermine trust and faith in others, and represent a lack of true communication.

In the spirit of praxis, communication generates action and agency only when infused with critical reflection and collaborative practice. Communication as action and agency should not be a form of domination and oppression, but through praxis, a thoughtful means to meet the world and challenge it (Warren, 2009). Action and agency in the world is to engage with it critically and compassionately, and to see others and ourselves as complex beings striving for meaning and purpose. Communication is a conduit for generating individual action and agency but it must be framed wisely, ethically and morally. How we communicate depends on ethical choices. According to Campos (2009), communication *is* ethics as it constructs and shapes how we love, understand, cooperate, hate, war and destroy. Communication has to be conceived as a dialogue that can construct and destroy power relations and generate new ways of thinking, being and relating to others.

How do examples in this chapter demonstrate communication generating action and agency? The students learning about citizenship communicated their rights and issues through an interaction with their local government member and a student parliament. Choosing and being responsible for the performances at the multicultural day gave George an empowered sense and expression of his identity. The electronic message from Steven illustrated his agency to communicate and change his attitude to learning. The respectful interaction of the microbloggers created mutual confidence in their ideas. The self-portrait demonstrated students had control and understanding to communicate how they perceived themselves and others, and the video blog engaged an audience with newly constructed knowledge from a science self-experiment. In all examples the power of communication generated students' self-agency, social action and knowledge.

The story of Ruth (a principal) and Juliet (a teacher) illustrates aspects of the Communication Crystal coherence maker. At a professional learning workshop in making and understanding, Ruth and Juliet were *alert to messaging* when exploring the meaning and aesthetic of Ted Hughes' poem, *Amulet* (1970). They had an opportunity to write and *voice* a poem based on their own personal amulet as a protective, re-energizing symbol. Later in the year at a 4C network professional learning workshop, Ruth and Juliet used the structure of Hughes' poem to communicate their recent experience with 4C learning and integrated it into their multimodal presentation. The poem was a creative, engaging and *purposeful* way to *convey the meaning* of their reflections to the audience. For Ruth and Juliet, the presentation was one of many steps they are taking to communicate and *generate action and agency* to transform learning at their school. This is their poem:

SYLLABUS

Inside the syllabus, the possibility of choices
Inside the possibility of choices, the confusion of questions
Inside the confusion of questions, the clarity of purpose
Inside the clarity of purpose, the essence of learning
Inside the essence of learning, the real life application
Inside the real life application, the genuine excitement
Inside the genuine excitement, the spark of curiosity
Inside the spark of curiosity, the freedom of possibilities
Inside the freedom of possibilities, the presence of scaffold
Inside the presence of scaffold, the ability to access
Inside the ability to access, the power of feedback
Inside the power of feedback, the creation of new pathways
Inside the creation of new pathways, the animated syllabus.

A road map for communication and learning

In Morreale and Pearson's (2008) study the following individual and social themes emerged as evidence of the importance of communication instruction in the twenty-first century. Communication education:

- is vital to the development of the whole person,

- helps to improve the educational enterprise,

- encourages being a responsible participant in the world, socially and culturally,

- helps individuals succeed in their careers and in business,

- enhances organizational processes and organizational life, and

- addresses concerns in the twenty-first century (health communication, crisis and communication, and crime and policing) (Morreale and Pearson, 2008, pp. 230–234).

These themes indicate how communication is an essential competency, necessary for reacting to and managing life's challenges. We argue communication must be integrated more holistically and explicitly in learning in these ways:

- *Communication's link to learning must be deeply understood as central to pedagogical content knowledge across the curriculum.* Learning and knowledge can only be expressed through the means of communication. Pedagogy that facilitates the skills of communication to explore and express knowledge strengthens capacity and engagement in learning. Teachers must be model communicators and use pedagogy that facilitates both effective communication and content knowledge in the learning experiences of their students. The heightening and enhancing of communication skills enables and develops the clarity and sophistication of metacognition and feedback for knowledge creation in learning. Practice in complex and ethical communication as a dialogue is vital to collaborative, critical reflection and creative processes in learning and transformation.

- *Communication when understood as intrinsic to identity formation has a profound impact on empowerment.* Self-perception and the construction of identity fluctuate according to communication and relationships. In schools, positive, active and enabling communication facilitated and fostered by teachers and leaders significantly influence the confidence, self-belief and empowerment of students to self-actualize their learning potential. Communication as an expression and development of self, primarily through the body and voice and then extended to other modes, has to be viewed as essential to a healthy sense of wellbeing, positive relationships and belonging to and participating in a community.

- *The multimodality and complexity of communication can serve deeper learning and teaching experiences.* Limiting communication skills to reading and writing is a reductionist approach to communication and deeper learning experiences. Skills in multimodal communication are essential competencies for the twenty-first century. The complex processes of communication as a cognitive competency can deepen learning of content, as well as develop the competencies of critical reflection, collaboration and creativity. Skills and understanding of how messages convey meaning and purpose are integral to generating action and agency in lifelong learning.

The voice teacher Rowena Balos's comment, 'Often you don't really know how you feel about something until you're stimulated to communicate' captures quite simply the fundamental role communication plays in cultivating human development and empowerment. Communication skills exist in curricula however they are not necessarily core pedagogical content knowledge across all aspects of learning. The 4Cs approach explicitly heightens communication's role as key to learning and as intrinsic to the other Cs, critical reflection, collaboration and creativity.

The Communication Crystal as a coherence maker explores how communicating can be fostered as pedagogy for student learning and as working practice for leaders and teachers in schools. Communication between humans is the striving for order and equilibrium in a world of chaos and contradictions. This is also an undercurrent theme in Escher's pictures. The more we have the opportunities and skills to communicate effectively, the better equipped we are to deal with the emergent complexities of personal, social and economic development.

The next chapter discusses the ways schools can teach and model true and deep collaboration.

Collaboration

One of the great joys for us is the creative collaboration we experience with teachers, leaders, students and school communities. A Primary teacher expressed that same joy about her teaching team. She, with two other teachers, decided to undertake the 4Cs approach in their classrooms. It wasn't a school initiative, but their school leaders supported them. The school doesn't have agile learning spaces or across class learning, but they managed to find spaces and ways to combine their three classes as joint teaching and learning ventures. Apart from the struggles and enormous gains they witnessed with their students, one of the great pleasures for the three teachers was the deep creative connection they had with each other.

The teacher, Annie, wrote about this creative connection, 'We are becoming more aware, through our engagement with the process, of the myriad ways in which real collaborative partnership can stimulate creativity and initiative, nurture and embrace difference, and enhance learning for us and the students. We feel challenged as real growth and real learning demands of us, and in turn we are challenging our students. We are learning right along with them. Not only do I feel personally more inspired, creative and purposeful but also I no longer feel like I'm in this alone.' Annie's comments resonate with the ideas of creativity scholar, Vera John-Steiner, who argues, 'Through collaboration we can transcend the constraints of biology, of time, of habit, and achieve a fuller self, beyond the limitations and the talents of the isolated self' (2000, p. 188). Through collaboration, Annie is exploring her talents beyond her isolated self.

A premise of the 4Cs approach is that through collaboration humans become their fuller selves. Through the mutuality of true collaboration we expand who we are. True collaboration is not people co-operating, sharing ideas and working together. We argue that collaboration is the beneficial mutuality of a shared vision, and the engine for creativity and emergence. Collaboration applies as much to how teachers can learn and create, to how students can learn and create. To achieve the beneficial mutuality of collaboration however requires the navigation of complex dynamics in communication and relationships. This chapter is about those dynamics. It is about how the individual self crucially develops, learns and actualizes through the oscillations of collaboration. We have synthesized collaborative processes and dynamics into a coherence maker: 'Collaboration Circles'. It is a supporting structure or scaffold to frame how collaboration can be learnt and facilitated.

Collaboration has been at the heart of human development, from the meeting of minds in the agoras of Ancient Greece to online communities of contemporary times. The lone genius propelling human development forward is a myth. It is the 'genius of the group' that generates new learning, creativity and innovation (Sawyer, 2003; 2007). Socio-cognitive and socio-cultural psychology have progressed thinking from the focus on individualism, to the social context as inextricably bound to shaping the individual in learning and creativity (Glăveanu, 2011). If 'social' processes and the 'genius of the group' are so integral to development, why isn't collaboration the orthodoxy of learning, teaching and leading in schools?

Why isn't collaboration at the centre of learning and school practice?

Collaboration is often misunderstood in terms of what it is, and how it works as a process. Without understanding collaborative practice, students working in groups can be dysfunctional and achieve little, or it can be 'busy work' with no real deep learning gains. A focus on curriculum-specific knowledge has taken teachers' attention away from domain-specific knowledge about learning itself. How we learn through collaboration is part of that domain-specific knowledge. As a result of teachers and leaders not knowing the mechanics and role of collaborative learning, group work can be discarded as ineffective, or is ineffectual when done without understanding.

The complaints of ineffective group work is that one person ends up doing all the work, or groups cannot reconcile their differences, or everyone works individually anyway. We argue that this happens because students and teachers don't know how to collaborate. Without scaffolding and modelling, and questioning and feedback in how to collaborate, the benefits from group learning are negligible (Mayer, 2010). Group projects are also questionable in their effectiveness if the pedagogy and assessment does not clarify how the collaborative processes serve individual learning (Bryan, 2004; Mayer, 2010). Teachers, students and school leaders need to understand and be confident with collaborative practice and assessment processes.

Collaboration for teachers and leaders in schools can be problematic for other reasons. The influences affecting opportunities for collaborative teacher reflection, according to Day (2004), can be:

- The paradox of productivity – In schools fewer people are doing more and so time and energy is spent dealing with solution-seeking of pressing problems rather than engaging in reflection and development.

- Isolation and contrived collegiality – The 'busyness' of the school culture and increased accountability means time is allocated to satisfy bureaucratic demands rather than collaboration.

- Feelings of bereavement – These are feelings associated with radical changes to practices that undermine a teacher's sense of professional status and esteem.

- Time – There are problems with competing demands and choosing how to use time.

- Habit – Habits and routines are difficult to break because they reach 'down into the very structure of the self' (Dewey, 1932/1985, p. 171; adapted from Day, 2004, pp. 93–95).

Even when 'collaboration' appears to be happening in school communities, the dynamics of the group 'climate' require constant examination to ensure new and positive ideas are supported to fruition. A close examination involves discerning whether there is, for example, low trust or high consensus in the working group, for both of these aspects reflect a negative climate for collaboration. For group creativity, Paulus and Nijstad (2003) argue:

> it is not very helpful when the group climate is restrictive, critical, and characterized by low levels of trust. This does not foster the sharing of unique or 'wild' ideas or the expression of divergent viewpoints. On the other hand, a very harmonious climate characterized by high levels of cohesion does not lead to high levels of group creativity because such groups may be primarily directed at maintaining group harmony, may self-censor any differences of opinion, and may fall prey to the trap of premature consensus. (p. 330)

For collaborative processes to operate effectively high levels of trust and an openness to divergent viewpoints are required. Every group member must be intrinsically motivated to realize the potential of every individual in the group. These characteristics define true collaboration and are integral to positive learning relationships and outcomes. To understand how collaboration works we would like to describe what collaboration is and what collaboration is not.

Defining collaboration

If collaboration is explained as an 'affair of the mind' (John-Steiner, 2000), then 'being a team player' or 'being cooperative' does not define collaboration. Collaboration as an 'affair of the mind' suggests an intense synergy of ideas, goals, trust and relationships between people. Moran and John-Steiner (2004) explain collaboration as the high point of a gradient that runs from social interaction, to cooperation, to working together, to collaboration. 'Social interaction involves two or more people talking or in exchange, cooperation adds the constraint of shared purpose, and working together often provides coordination of effort. But collaboration involves an intricate blending of skills, temperaments, effort and sometimes personalities to realise a shared vision of something new and useful' (p. 11).

Collaboration leads to the co-construction of something that evolves from the interdependence and mutuality of everyone's influence. Everyone in a collaborative process has a role to play, and in that role must feel equal and empowered to realize a shared and co-constructed vision. Paradoxically they should be empowered, but also feel vulnerable:

> collaboration is the necessity to be mutually vulnerable. . . . Whether you are the instigator of the project or not, there has to be a levelling of personality that goes on. There has to be an authentic acceptance of this fact, because you both decide to be equal in it. Then you have to take each other to the edge of what you individually thought you were capable of (Storey and Joubert, 2004, p. 47).

This levelling is captured in a story from a secondary school working with the 4Cs. A teacher vividly recalls the moment she sidled up to the principal who was leading the learning with 70 students, and felt the awkward courage to 'offer' another approach to the learning task to better engage the students. For her, it was an enormous step in levelling their relationship to one of collaboration. The principal 'yielded' to the better idea, and together they took the lesson forward. The principal said he felt a moment of vulnerability but then an overriding sense of beneficial mutuality in being open to another direction. The teacher later reflected:

> Applying the 4Cs breaks down hierarchical structures. If we are to collaborate, why should formal titles of roles stand in the way? Yes, we all have differing levels of experiences whether it is in years of service, qualification, backgrounds but if we are all picturing the same big picture – students experiencing levels of success – then there should be an understanding and openness of knowing that there is more than one way of achieving this. When I made the suggestion to my Principal, it was at that moment I thought of him as just another teacher in the space that I was collaborating with, rather than him being my Principal.

True collaboration is charged both cognitively and emotionally and this is why it takes you 'to the edge of what you individually thought you were capable of' (Storey and Joubert, 2004). To reach that edge or threshold requires trust, the valuing of others and joint ownership. It is being on the threshold of these very cognitive and emotional processes that make collaboration a dynamic tool for learning, identity formation, creativity and innovation. The dynamics of collaboration have to be deeply understood and practised to reap the benefits. Understanding and learning *how* to collaborate is key to positive outcomes in collaboration. *How* we collaborate can only be understood and undertaken by knowing *why* we need to collaborate.

Why do we need to collaborate?

We argue that collaboration, like the other 3Cs, is a capability for empowerment. It empowers people's potential and capacity for learning and growth. From a socio-cultural perspective, collaboration is crucial to development and learning from childhood into and throughout adulthood. Humans are predisposed to collaborate, but if the environment and social processes do not develop and enrich that predisposition, learning *in* collaboration, and learning *through* collaboration is not actualized.

In socio-cultural psychology, collaborative learning is a process seen as fundamental to socialization and human development. Vygotsky's (1978) best-known theory of a zone of proximal development (referred to in Chapters 2 and 3) explains how social processes of collaboration facilitate and consolidate individual learning. Proximal development is the dynamic threshold of what the learner is capable of learning through interaction with others, rather than the capability of what they can already achieve alone. Collaboration as the internalizing of joint activity is, according to Vygotsky, the basis for ideas and cognitive strategies for future learning and psychological development.

Collaboration is needed for learning, and learning is needed to collaborate. This interdependence is demonstrated in the essential role collaboration plays in childhood learning. From infancy, humans have a propensity to learn by imitation, the instruction of others, and through the social processes of collaboration. Skills in the interpersonal processes of collaboration are learnt from supportive interactions between adults and children. Through joint problem-solving adults 'collaborate' with children to help them develop the foundational skills they will need to develop to collaborate later on (Golbeck and El-Moslimany, 2013). Without adults collaborating through shared problem-solving, children are delayed in their development and in their socialization for learning (Bruner, 1985).

Playing to collaborate

Play is a safe and learning-rich environment where children create a zone of proximal development to try out their growing capabilities. By playing with others in the world of pretend or 'as if', children experiment and stretch themselves in a topsy-turvy world 'to become more effectively the master of the laws governing the real world' (Vygotsky, 1971, quoted in Moran and John-Steiner, 2003, p. 69). Having opportunities to play, and learning to play collaboratively, is essential for development. Through play with others, children tease out relationships, try on and practise different roles, exercise their growing capabilities and learn self-control (Vygotsky, 1984/1999; 1978). Play develops skills in the 'improvisation' of social interaction, and the language to be able to relate to others (Sawyer, 1997). Children practise skills and try out ideas within a 'make-believe' situation and are then better able to adapt to or harness real situations. Playing is critical for being able to learn, to interact with others and imagine beyond the actual to the possible. Playing with others is to be able to improvise and allow for emergence.

Developing the foundations of collaborative learning skills and collaborative problem-solving in childhood is critical to the intellectual growth and social development of children. The significance of collaboration continues throughout life in adult learning and has the potential to shape self-identity through processes that promote connection, reflection, flexibility and stability with others (Moran and John-Steiner, 2004). In adulthood the sharing of expertise and experience, and challenge and reflection through collaborations continues the expanding of the boundaries of the self through the zone of proximal development. Without collaboration we stifle the growth of the self.

In a rapidly changing world characterized by chaos, contradiction and complexity, the challenges of shifting realities are met by finding new solutions through collaboration and playing with possibilities. Collaboration and creativity are relevant and necessary for people not only in schools but in every walk of life.

> In collaborative endeavours we learn from each other by teaching what we know; we engage in mutual appropriation. Solo practices are insufficient to meet the challenges and the new complexities of classrooms, parenting, and the changing workplace. Creative collaborators provide us with important insights for ways to build joint endeavours. And their practices challenge mainstream theories whose focus is limited to the individual. (John-Steiner, 2000, p. 192)

Collaboration throughout life, like play in childhood, is an emotional and intellectual scaffold for learning and growth. Collaborative psychology goes beyond the biological constraints of independent individualism to develop and deepen understandings of human development in social terms. From a Vygotskian socio-cultural perspective, individual and social processes are profoundly intertwined. Humans can overcome their limitations through collaborative practice because it amplifies and enhances an individual's vision and purpose. Through collaboration new ways of thinking about things and new ways of doing things are conceived.

Collaboration for creative emergence

Collaboration has the power to generate the unexpected and the originality of creativity. Sawyer (2007) claims, 'When we collaborate, creativity unfolds across people; the sparks fly faster, and the whole is greater than the sum of its parts. Collaboration drives creativity because innovation always emerges from a series of sparks – never a single flash of insight' (p. 7). Collaboration ignites a series of sparks in creativity, and increases motivation and the taking of chances by 'spreading the risk' (Moran and John-Steiner, 2004). Collaboration also sparks creativity by cross-fertilizing disciplinary diversity and curiosity (Storey and Joubert, 2004). For example, in schools working with the 4C approach, the integration of teachers and disciplines across the curriculum has stimulated and excited new connections and interest in learning. Through the benefits of reciprocity, collaborations expand the potential and creativity of what individuals can achieve alone. The ultimate aim and benefit of collaboration is the emergence of thinking, ideas and actions between people as they connect and co-construct together.

Co-constructions and connections highlight how true collaboration facilitates a perpetual cycle of emergence. Emergence is the phenomenon of something emerging from the interaction of the components in a complex system. In collaborative emergence, ideas flow and emerge unpredictably from the successive individual contributions of the participants (Sawyer, 2003). It is not surprising that developing skills and understandings in collaborative emergence is fostered in a creative learning environment. According to Sawyer (2015), 'creative learning environments are those that foster *collaborative emergence,* improvisational group processes where the outcome cannot be predicted from the individual mental states and goals of the participants, and where all members of the group – teacher and students alike – participate in the unfolding flow of the encounter' (pp. 28–29; emphasis in original). Collaborative emergence is a creative process of *disciplined improvisation* (Sawyer, 2015) where original ideas and actions are generated from the co-constructing of a shared vision. Collaborative learning is also an emergent process. An individual's learning continues to be an emergent phenomenon through the collaborative co-construction of ideas. If new or emergent connections are not made, a pooling of what is already known continues to be perpetuated in working groups.

When the cognitive and emotional processes of collaboration are understood, and the skills of collaboration scaffolded and mastered, children and adults are empowered to learn, create and work with greater capacity. Collaboration requires trust and equal participation in a group, and this nurtures self-efficacy. Collaboration encourages confidence in one's own abilities and confidence in the abilities of others. To trust in the collaborative process is knowing there is a tangible process, not an informal or random experience that only works with some people. Everyone has the potential to be empowered through collaboration.

Collaboration and the other Cs

Collaboration has been at the forefront of the recent, groundbreaking detection of gravitational waves in the universe. Scientists have observed ripples in the fabric of space–time from a cataclysmic event that happened in a distant universe. It is a hugely significant event in confirming Einstein's special theory of relativity. Physicist, Rainer Weiss, said, 'The description of this observation is beautifully described in the Einstein theory of general relativity formulated 100 years ago and comprises the first test of the theory in strong gravitation. It would have been wonderful to watch Einstein's face had we been able to tell him' (LIGO Hanford Press Release, 2016). The discovery of gravitational waves reveals the role of collaboration, and the other 3Cs in a number of ways.

LIGO (Laser Interferometer Gravitational-wave Observatory) Scientific Collaboration is a group of over 1,000 scientists from 15 countries carrying out the gravitational wave research. The LIGO detectors that observed the waves are a global network constructed by an international team of technicians, engineers and scientists. The collaboration in the project is expansive and complex. And without Albert Einstein's 'collaboration' 100 years ago, the development of being able to detect and measure the tiny disturbances the waves make to space and time would not have happened. Einstein, a genius of invention, was also in his time part of a 'collaborative thought community' (John-Steiner, 2003). Einstein was a brilliant visualizer but needed the help of Marcel Grossmann to expand his mathematical understanding to support the development of his theories. Einstein's friendship with the physicist Neils Bohr was significant in challenging Einstein and his ideas. And without Einstein challenging Bohr as 'creative dissonance', knowledge in quantum mechanics and the wave-particle paradox would not have advanced. In this example of detecting gravitational waves we can observe how human collaboration over time and places, furthers discovery and knowledge. It also reveals how collaboration is intertwined with the other 3Cs.

Creativity

True collaboration profits from the diversity of different individuals coming together where co-constructed ideas emerge. Collaboration generates new ideas and knowledge as shown in the example of gravitational wave detection. It is a collaboration of scientists, engineers and technicians from around the world, and a collaboration of theoreticians and evidence practitioners over time. In the same way, new ideas can be fostered in schools, organizations and in learning through collaboration.

There are also creative processes in collaboration. Collaboration is a potentially emergent phenomenon as the participants are the parts of a complex whole. The creativity within collaboration is the possibilities that emerge from the co-construction from the individual human components. The LIGO Scientific Collaboration is an example of this.

Communication

Collaboration can only succeed through successful communication between all participants. Communication processes that may be real or virtual or captured by technology as language, signs and symbols, mediate the interaction and relationships of people in collaborations. Einstein had to capture and communicate his ideas through diagrams, mathematical formulae, words and images to collaborate with the scientific community. The network of LIGO detectors is dependent on the co-ordination of clear, open and global communication live every 24 hours.

Communication relies on messengers collaborating with each other to engage. The collaborative skills of interaction and engagement support the success of messaging through communication. Communication is a sharing of information, and collaboration focuses on *how* to share with others. Collaborative learning processes in schools focus on developing, refining and expanding communication skills.

Critical reflection

The metacognition required to navigate the complex emotional and cognitive dynamics of collaboration can only be achieved through critical reflection. Critical reflection supports awareness of the roles and actions of the individual (the self) and others in collaborative practice. In the media releases and interviews with the gravitational wave researchers, all are metacognizant of the collaborative processes that served the success of the project. In our work with schools, collaboration cannot be developed without also developing critical reflection. Through critical reflection the sophisticated roles and process of collaboration can be understood, practised and refined.

Critical reflection is strengthened through the intrapersonal and interpersonal competencies required of collaboration. For instance, the critical reflection of Einstein and Bohr as a collaboration of differing ideas allowed them to both be vulnerable and empowered by each other's approaches. In schools we have observed it is often through collaboration that a wide-awakeness to critical reflection is nurtured through the challenge and perspective of others. A very experienced teacher new to the 4Cs approach said recently, 'I have been teaching for 43 years, but I feel like a beginning teacher! It's the constant sharing of ideas and being pushed out of my comfort-zone that has made me see things so differently. It's like I'm starting again.'

The interactive processes of collaboration are integral to creativity, communication and critical reflection, and these 3C capabilities are embedded in collaboration. True creative collaboration is difficult to achieve, and can take time to establish as a way of working. We are reminded of a school where a group of school leaders and teachers had begun collaborating on the 4Cs approach, but it wasn't until they composed and sang a song together that they suddenly sensed true collaboration as an 'affair of the mind'. To assist the learning of collaboration, we have developed a coherence maker in the processes of collaborative practice. The Collaboration Circles coherence maker supports metacognition of how, what and why we collaborate.

Collaboration Circles Coherence Maker

We have constructed a coherence maker that synthesizes what we know about the processes for successful collaborations. We have used the metaphor of circles to describe collaboration. 'Circles' are groups of people with a shared interest. These groups have a strong sense of connectedness and, although they can be viewed as closed cliques, they have the capacity to create and connect with new circles. This is humorously evoked by American poet Edwin Markham's (1852–1940) epigram:

He drew a circle that shut me out –
Heretic, rebel, a thing to flout.
But love and I had the wit to win:
We drew a circle and took him In!

'Collaboration Circles' is a metaphor for connectedness and inclusion. The word 'Circle' also suggests sitting in the shape of a circle. In a circle there is no hierarchy, all faces are recognized and all voices heard. The coherence maker or scaffold for Collaboration Circles is:

○ Offering.

○ Yielding.

○ Challenging, evaluating and extending.

○ Advancing co-construction and connections.

The process of Collaboration Circles must allow for the flexibility and spontaneity of hearing all voices and ideas in the group, and the stability of structure and coherence to give order to multiple voices. Improvisers in the theatre will recognize the structure of the Collaboration Circles. Improvisers know that to create 'spontaneously' is to follow the structure of shared rules and conventions in the collaborative process. Lyn Pierse (1995), a theatre improviser, explains group improvisation in this way:

Like children, we use our imagination to spontaneously play, making everything up as we go. We find ways of listening to each other, sharing ideas and solving problems; when we don't the playing stops. To improvise productively with other people we need to agree on a set of principles which encourage play. The concept of offer and yield is integral to this process. (p. 39)

Like improvisation and play, collaboration has to allow for the spontaneous collective emergence of perceptions and propositions from the group, as well as structures and trust that ideas jointly constructed will take form and move forward. Our coherence maker helps facilitate collaboration by giving order and intention to the listening, sharing, playing, problem-solving and co-ownership of collaborative ideas.

Collaboration Circles is a coherence maker to encourage meta-awareness of what has to be achieved in the collaborative process. The steps in the scaffold are recursive, and guide learners and practitioners on a desired learning trajectory through iterative and metacognitive practice. The scaffold has social and cognitive dimensions, as both are pivotal to the success of collaborations. For instance, groups who struggle with collaboration are characterized by 'social inhibition' and 'cognitive interference'. These groups can exhibit:

● social anxiety,

● social loafing,

● an illusion of productivity,

● blocking,

- task-irrelevant behaviours, and
- cognitive load issues. (Paulus, 2000)

These characteristics are overcome by facilitating the conditions and dynamics of social and cognitive 'stimulation' in collaboration. The aim of the Collaboration Circles coherence maker is to explore processes that stimulate the social and cognitive benefits of true collaboration.

Each aspect of the Collaboration Circles scaffold will be examined in detail to reveal the complexities and advantages of collaborative practice in the way we learn, mentor, work and create. The scaffold begins the collaborative process with the verbal or non-verbal action of being able to make an 'offer'.

Offering

To offer is to be an active participant who initiates an idea or action in a group. This may be an offer of how the group will organize itself, how it will start, or the first suggestion in solving a problem to develop a new idea. Offers are the foundation of communication and provide a focus and direction for the ensuing ideas and actions of the collaboration. Offers require commitment, inclusivity and clarity of purpose, and like 'yields' are made continually throughout the collaborative process.

Offering signifies a cognitive process in communication, and emotional and behavioural processes in confidence and influence. You have to be able to communicate to offer, but without confidence and influence, the communication of the offer has no effect. Offering is a sophisticated process that necessitates:

- *Communicating*. Offering is a form of communication that has to have integrity and purpose, to affect the rest of the group as audience.
- *Risktaking*. Offering involves confidence, commitment, and overcoming the risk and fear of self-censoring, second-guessing, making a 'mistake' or dominating in the group.
- *Trusting others*. Offering demands trust in everyone's capabilities in the group to contribute to a co-constructed process and product.

The trust required for collaboration sometimes has to be built over time. For example, for a new teaching team in a school, it took substantial courage and trust for a young teacher to raise the issue of problems with collaboration when working with a senior school leader in the team. The young teacher had to overcome her fear of criticism from a senior person in a school hierarchy. For her to make the offer to address the issue of collaborative dysfunction also reflected her commitment to solving the problem openly and with integrity. It was a challenging situation for all involved, but the trust established in the group opened up possibilities and new perspectives to address the problem. In this way an offer must be recognized as both an assertive and vulnerable action, as well as involving clarity in communication.

Collaboration only succeeds with successful communication. One reason students learn effectively in collaborative learning is the active processing of information and communication while collaborating with others (Webb, 2013). To present ideas and convey information, speakers and listeners in collaboration engage cognitive processes in communication. Each step of the Collaboration Circles coherence maker develops communication skills beginning with activating dialogue in an offer. A communicator gives structure to, clarifies and extends their thinking by presenting their ideas to others in a relevant, coherent and engaging way. The communicator has to take into account the comprehension of the group as an 'audience' and this requires further explanations and justifications, further deepening the communicator's thinking (Webb, 2013).

To make an offer open to the whole group, and relevant to the group's endeavour, is the first step in a sophisticated 'dance' in communicating and developing ideas in collaboration. An offer is an attempt to be inclusive, clear and generous in launching an idea to be extended and challenged by the rest of the group. To feel open to make an offer is also dependent on relational trust in the group. The notion of everyone sharing the goals, benefits, challenges and risks of a collaborative venture is contingent on trust. Moran and John-Steiner (2004) argue, 'Trust consists of respect for another person's different perspective, an expectation of good will, and confidence in the other's ability to contribute to the common purpose. . . . Trust is the foundation for collaboration that makes possible the development of true sharing, openly negotiated conflict, and a long-term relationship despite the uncertainties and risks' (p. 21).

The 'risk' in making an offer is in trusting the goodwill of the group to consider the offer. Trust and goodwill is engendered in the equality of relational status in the group and equal participation. For children and adults the freedom to explore and challenge as equals is instrumental to collaborative learning and working. Social hierarchies are not conducive to collaboration (John-Steiner, 2000; Webb, 2013). An inclusive and confident offer cannot be made when there are issues of high and low status, dominance and submission in a group.

To offer an idea is to have confidence in the collaborative process to harness an individual's vitality and growth. The design of a collaborative task must recognize the role of the individual as adding to and enhancing the greater 'genius' of the group. The individual must be enriched through the genesis of ideas and actions that a group's collective genius can achieve. In a learning context the value-add for the individual in a collaborative task is supported by designs and pedagogy that incorporate:

- open and complex tasks that allow for multiple entry points,
- arranging group memberships to encourage productive social and cognitive dynamics for diversity and growth,
- the formulation of individual accountabilities and group goals,
- strategies for learners to know when and how to seek help from others,
- exhibition of learning gains throughout the collaborative process with regular teacher and peer feedback and questioning,

- reflections and assessment in the processes, as well as the product of the collaboration (based on Slavin, 2011; Webb, 2013).

Pedagogies and strategies in collaborative learning design need to develop students' abilities to comprehend, monitor and master the collaborative process. Collaborative learning fails when students don't know how to share explanations, coordinate communication, or seek help when needed, when they suppress other students' participation, engage in too much conflict, avoid conflict completely, and engage in negative socio-emotional behaviours (Webb, 2013). The individual has to develop skills and understandings of how to contribute, and how to allow others to contribute in the group's endeavour. This begins with being cognizant of the generosity, commitment and trust involved in making an offer, and then 'yielding' to the offer.

Yielding

A yield is the acceptance and development of an offer. A yield is not simply saying yes to another person's offer, it is taking an equal share of responsibility in supporting or shaping the focus of the offer. Yielding is to link your own thinking to someone else's previous offer. In essence, yielding is the beginning of building on from prior knowledge in the joint construction of learning and creating in collaboration. Group brainstorming as a process is a multitude of offers and yields.

The yield as a response to an offer requires:

- *Engaging.* Yielding is deep active listening and noticing of other collaborators' verbal and non-verbal contributions.
- *Joining.* Yielding means integrity in and commitment to the joint purpose of the group's collaboration.
- *Elaborating.* Yielding needs communication skills in elaboration, explaining and reasoning to instigate further discussion or actions to challenge, evaluate and extend the group's ideas.

Active listening or engaging is paramount to communication and collaboration. Attentive listening should, as John-Steiner (2000) argues, lead to hearing your own words echoed though others'. Active engagement is developed and realized by repeating others' ideas, asking questions about them, and elaborating on what has been said or done. To yield is to use these components of active engagement. An offer cannot be ignored or rejected, attentive engagement means being able to elaborate and reason with what someone has already said.

Learners who fail to attend to others' suggestions by reasserting their own thinking, or interrupting and talking over others, have to learn how to engage by connecting with others' ideas through questions, elaborations and reasoning (Webb, 2013). These communication skills teach students to notice deeply what others say, and lay the foundations for more sophisticated communication processing in the next step of the Collaboration Circles coherence maker. In yielding, learners as listeners test their understanding of the offered ideas, and identify what may be confusing or unconvincing to them. This processing helps students to link new information to what they already know and to explore new inferences and connections. Sometimes this requires sentence starter scaffolds for students such as: 'Can you elaborate to clarify what you mean? Or, did you mean . . .?'

Offering and yielding is the dialogue of a functioning group dynamic and the communication mechanism that produces collaborative learning.

> In highly coordinated groups . . . members acknowledge each other's ideas, repeat each other's suggestions, and elaborate on others' proposals. Speakers' turns are tightly connected, with group members paying close attention and responding to what other members do and say, giving space for others' contributions, and monitoring how the unfolding contributions relate to the problem-solving goal. Proposals are directly linked to the prior conversation, are acknowledged and discussed, are not ignored, and are not rejected without reasons being given. (Webb, 2013, p. 26)

These skills can be developed, for example, through the 'bus stop' learning strategy explained in Chapter 7, where learners in turn sit down from standing up when they answer an open question. Learners have to continue on and elaborate by yielding to a previous offer in the group, but cannot repeat what has already been said. In adult groups, the lack of 'bus stop' collaborative processing is apparent when the 'leader' asks what are the group's thoughts on a matter, and the responses may be connected or not, and the leader concludes, 'Thanks, I'll think about that and I'll make a decision.'

The communication mechanisms of presenting, explaining, elaborating and reasoning in the offering and yielding of collaboration is when collaborators begin to 'apply' their ideas. Learners applying their ideas through collective explanation and elaboration is positively linked to achievement (Webb, 2013). Prompts to construct explanations and reciprocal questioning support learners to enact these techniques. Learning in 'how' and 'why' to explain and question encourages learners to engage in the higher order collaborative discourse of deeper reasoning. Students also learn explanatory thinking and inquiry questioning through active teacher modelling in deeper reasoning processes in whole class interactions (Webb, 2013).

Offering and yielding form the basis of cognitive and social communication skills. Yielding is respecting, engaging and empathizing with others by acknowledging their contributions. The socially accommodating behaviours of offering and yielding must not lead however to the consensus and conformity of 'group think'. Group think is when group thinking produces its own feedback loop and suppresses 'thinking outside the group'. Schools, before they transform, are often trapped in the 'group think' space. Overcoming 'group think' depends on the third stage of the Collaboration Circles scaffold: challenging, evaluating and extending.

Challenging, evaluating and extending

'Group think' describes a 'mode of thinking that people engage in when they are deeply involved in a cohesive in-group' (Janis, 1972, p. 9). Group outcomes become constrained when group members strive for unanimity and conformity. The 'strain for consensus' in groups can lead to members fearing or second-guessing reactions from the group. Reluctance to voice dissent leads to conformity in thinking, which inhibits the group's potential for growth (Nemeth and Nemeth-Brown, 2003). Through fear of difference, adverse reactions and conflict, the 'strain for consensus' can be manifest as a silent or closed reaction of, 'we'll have to agree to disagree'. Agreeing to disagree and not co-constructing a shared vision and outcome is not collaboration. Indifference is also not a feature of collaboration. Challenging and evaluating is a feature of collaboration as it extends ideas by supporting and encouraging divergent and diverse thinking.

Challenging, evaluating and extending develop divergent thinking through skills in constructive questioning, alternatives, counter-argument, reasoning, persuasion and summarizing. Challenging, evaluating and extending ideas in collaborations requires:

- *Reflecting*. Challenging, evaluating and extending is the development of analytical, reflective, lateral and synthesized thinking.

- *Debating*. The group climate for challenging, evaluating and extending must allow for the free flow of ideas and information, fluid divisions of labour, and productive tension and debate in problem-solving.

- *Understanding*. Challenging, evaluating and extending must inhabit a 'representational space' that allows for commonalities, dissimilarities, new understandings and possibilities.

Instructional activities and prompts help to scaffold the teaching and learning of reasoning, lateral thinking and communication skills to challenge, evaluate and extend ideas with others (Webb, 2013). Students knowing why, how and when to challenge, defend and evaluate their own and others' thinking is vital to the success of the collaborative process. This involves not just cognitive scaffolding but emotional scaffolding as well (John-Steiner, 2000).

An emotional scaffold begins by acknowledging and being metacognitive of creating a behavioural climate that inculcates group social cohesion as well as individual differences in thinking and working. Free-flowing ideas and information, and fluid divisions of labour are dependent on the fostering of this climate. The climate of a collaborative group can be viewed as a microcosm of the culture of a collaborative organization. The Situational Outlook Questionnaire (Isaksen and colleagues, 1999) is a tool that uses some of the following dimensions as indicative of the climate needed for change, innovation and creativity in organizations. They include freedom; trust/openness; playfulness and humour (for a full discussion see Chapter 9). These same dimensions are needed in the emotional climate of collaboration. In collaboration there has to be an emotional 'safety zone' within which both support and constructive criticism are effectively practised (John-Steiner, 2000). As with the offer, the trust in a group is paramount for people to take the risk of honest dialogue in challenging, evaluating and extending.

Support and constructive criticism can be practised if people understand that diversity in knowledge, different temperaments and ways of working all complement and strengthen the capacity of a group's joint purpose. Individual differences have to be recognized as complementary to making up the group's 'whole'. Productive collaborations are made up of individuals with different perspectives, expertise, resources, needs and talents. Challenging, evaluating and extending in the Collaboration Circles scaffold recognizes and utilizes those differences as strengths. For some these practices are intuitively undertaken; for others challenging, evaluating and extending are a necessary scaffold to explore, practise and create a culture that utilizes the diversity of individuals. We have observed leadership teams, teaching teams and student groups gradually transforming and learning to trust the collaborative process and each other, through the openness and integrity of challenging, evaluating and extending.

Commonalities and dissimilarities in groups are vital to the enhancement of learning and working. This allows for a 'representational' space for new understandings and possibilities. Glăveanu (2011) argues that collaboration is a fusion of an individual's *personal representational space* and a group's *common representational space*. It is a fusion that gives rise to enrichment and creativity.

> It is this common representational space where the group's creative dynamics take place and it is here where different thinking styles collide and by this spark the creative process. All is achieved of course if members communicate with one another, don't withhold information and allow the free flow of ideas, and therefore both intend to share and participate in the construction of a common space. (Glăveanu, 2011, p. 13)

Moran and John-Steiner (2004) claim that the foundation and benefits of collaborative practice are in the interaction of different individuals as they challenge, evaluate and extend each other's thinking. The divergence and diversity of thinking produces a creative tension that drives the productivity of collaboration. 'Collaboration's goal is not to reach consensus, as such agreement does not lead to learning or challenge. Not only are tensions between vulnerability and security, doing and getting done, jumping in and stepping back, and collaborators' personal differences not eliminated, but preferably they are taken advantage of as a mechanism for bringing out latent opportunities of the domain' (Moran and John-Steiner, 2004, p. 12).

Through diversity, multiple perspectives and the 'fruitful cultivation of tension', individual assumptions and unexamined beliefs are examined and challenged in the group. Challenging creates the spark for latent ideas and opportunities to emerge. Evaluating as a reflective and analytical practice holds up 'mirrors' as feedback of what has been achieved by the group. Through challenge and evaluation in the collaborative process, ideas and actions are constructed and extended to their full potential. Progress is then possible to the final but ongoing step in the Collaboration Circles coherence maker: Advancing co-construction and connections.

Advancing co-construction and connections

Collaboration is more than being cooperative, it is a process to co-construct and connect knowledge that furthers what we already know or do. The act of co-

construction gives shape to the group's emergent ideas. Co-construction means taking joint ownership of the process and what has been achieved. Advancing the co-construction connects the collaboration to future learning possibilities.

Advancing co-construction and connections necessitates:

- *Sharing*. Advancing is taking joint ownership of a co-construction through a shared learning endeavour.

- *Changing*. Advancing is a dynamic that supports motivation, social cohesion and cognition and identity development as a product of the co-construction process.

- *Connecting*. Advancing is the emergence of co-constructed ideas and actions that lead to further connections.

Joint ownership of the co-construction is paramount to collaboration. Without shared meaning making in the process and product of group work, it is not collaborative. Inherent to the woven fabric of collaboration is shared meaning making. Introducing the 4Cs approach in schools for instance has to be a collaborative process of shared meaning making with teachers, leaders, students and the community. To identify with the work through ownership is a powerful motivator for learning and achievement.

In classrooms, collaborative learning beneficially affects motivation, social cohesion and cognition (Slavin, 2011). The mutual sense of purpose and social cohesion of collaboration encourages the intrinsic motivation and sense of agency to achieve (Moran and John-Steiner, 2004). Motivation and agency are evident in teacher, Annie's, story about developing collaborative teaching practices:

> I have been teaching for over 20 years and up until this year I have honestly felt that for the most part my role as 'classroom teacher' has been a very lonely and isolating path. It is also becoming substantially more challenging as the years progress. As the name of my role suggests, I have spent most of my 20 years in this role in a classroom (a big box) teaching – providing those in my care with all they need to be successful adults in an increasingly demanding world. I have felt ultimately personally responsible for the learning of 29 to 30 students every year.
>
> The pressure and daily grind of this role is completely daunting and does not only lead to despondency and incredible levels of stress for both teachers and students but is actually not an effective way of educating anyway. Each year has become more and more about mere 'survival' as the children have increasingly more challenging needs while new initiatives are thrust upon us, supposedly to make us more effective teachers.
>
> Fortunately, my colleagues and I have embarked upon another educational journey that has thankfully given us a glimpse of an alternative educational universe. This is one in which we no longer see ourselves as 'classroom teachers' but rather as collaborative educational partners, with each other and with our students. No matter where our learning space is we all have one united focus. That focus is learning and we are beginning to appreciate together that there are as many ways to achieve this focus as there are stars in the sky.

Identity and individual agency is bound up in collaboration but there is a balance between the individual losing a sense of self in the group, and the individual taking over the identity of the group. The processes of offering and yielding, challenging and evaluating suggests a balance between the autonomy and the flexibility of the individual in a group. That is not to say collaboration is without tension and struggle. If the collaborative process is clearly delineated to generate a climate of trust and confidence, the tensions, challenges and struggles, rather than be debilitating, stimulate growth and ways forward.

Our identity continues to develop throughout a lifetime (Pulkkinen and Kokko, 2000) and collaboration is a process that shapes aspects of who we are in the co-mingling with others. Helen Storey (Storey and Joubert, 2004) describes it as a 'dissembling of identity' as you bravely risk your ideas with others. The co-mingling requires opening up to others and working towards solutions rather than seeing the development of ideas as a compromise or reductionism. Co-construction should be viewed as an opening up to the possibility of something unique:

> you have to be prepared to open up and to truly take that other person into account, and not become prescriptive to them. And that is where the risk is, because they can come up with something that you don't like. The ideal scenario is that you come up with the third idea that neither of you have thought of on your own. There is something about the coming together of the two of you that produces something that is unique and when it appears it is unquestionably there. (Storey and Joubert, 2004, pp. 47–48)

Advancing co-construction and connections clarifies collaboration as not just an agreed goal and product, but a shared experience focusing on the connections between people. This is the privilege we experience in the creative collaborations we have with schools, and with colleagues with whom we write books and generate and research 4C ideas. These collaborations are the stimulation and pleasure of the 'affair of the mind' and 'thought community' that John-Steiner (2000) refers to.

A road map for collaboration and learning

For collaborative practice to be integral to the way we learn and teach we suggest:

Collaboration must be understood as a vital process for developing individual growth, knowledge and creative emergence in teaching, learning and school communities. We argue that collaboration has to be understood and practised as a process beyond co-operating and working with others. Understanding how and why collaboration is vital to human development and individual growth is necessary to facilitate its practices in teaching and learning. The emotional, cognitive and social attributes inherent to true collaboration are complex and sophisticated, and require developing skills in communication and critical reflection. Collaboration is also key to creative emergence and the synergies of diverse minds as components coming together to co-construct and create something new. The creativity of collaboration, and collaboration of creativity are integral to transforming schools.

Skills and understandings can be learnt through scaffolds and strategies that provide direction, metacognition, feedback and assessment in the processes of collaboration. Collaboration Circles is an example of a coherence maker or scaffold that can help frame the development of skills and understandings in collaboration. Metacognition of the collaborative process supports collaborators in realizing they are investing in and being responsible for the advancement of a co-constructed outcome. In learning, the design of feedback and formal assessment furthers the metacognition and skills of the collaborative processes. Feedback and assessment should reflect the individual's role in the learning and performance of the group dynamic. An example of assessing the individual's learning in collaboration is provided in the Appendix.

Technology is an enabler for collaboration and the same principles of collaborative practice apply to technologies used in the process. Twenty-first-century technologies can enhance the capacity and potential for collaboration. The pairing of humans and technology is transformational at an individual and socio-cultural level (Ihde, 1995) and this is evident in the way technologies allow faster and wider, synchronous and asynchronous opportunities for collaboration. Technologies can help to overcome the tyranny of time and space and facilitate collaboration beyond the walls of learning spaces and schools. Collaboration using technology is still a complex process involving sophisticated communication skills in trust, risk taking and developing a mindset open to diversity and possibility. The principles of the Collaboration Circles coherence maker remain the same when working through technologies.

Even with technology contracting time and space, collaboration does take time. As an addition to the work itself, time and effort must be given to the dynamics and climate of positive relationships and equal participation. The time and energy in collaboration is an investment in enriching and sustaining deeper student and teacher professional and community learning. Through collaboration, schools and their communities have an enormous capacity to generate an 'unfolding spark of ideas' to meet the challenges of the future. Or, quite simply, in Vera John-Steiner's words, 'By joining with others we accept their gift of confidence, and through interdependence, we achieve competence and connection. *Together we create our futures*' (2000: emphasis in original).

Transforming schools requires collaborative and creative leadership, and this is the focus of the next chapter.

Transformative leadership for twenty-first-century schools

9

In Chapter 1 we related the story of Peter Wentworth the school leader who had become frustrated in his leadership role. For him learning had become a series of tests and bureaucratic processes. The weight of administration had taken its toll on an otherwise inspirational teacher and leader. This resonates with many school leaders we know. Many feel assailed by various forces that diminish the opportunity for change and reform and cause them to become risk averse and disillusioned. They feel that meaningful change has become constrained by the system, by assessment-driven curriculum or by other external pressures making it all too hard (not quick, not easy). Their concerns are evidenced in the research that demonstrates change is difficult, as Pat Thomson argues: 'It is now generally recognised in professional and scholarly literatures that school change is neither quick nor easy. Reforms are begun, appear to take hold, and then fade away, leaving little or no lasting benefit. Serial reform is required in order to try to keep momentum, and to recover lost ground' (2010, p. 47).

This is more than a shame; this represents a potential crisis for schooling. When educators lose the motivation to change, they risk becoming irrelevant in a rapidly changing community. Schools do not sit outside our society, they must be critically connected with their broader communities. Our society continues to change and yet, as we have discussed earlier, schools do not always reflect effectively this change in their visions, structures and strategies. Change, however, is not an option for schools; it is essential if schools are going to be relevant to the demands of our changing community. School leaders and leadership teams need to plan, implement and sustain transformation that reflect twenty-first-century capabilities such as creativity, critical reflection, communication and collaboration. Unfortunately, we have a crisis of inertia where many educational leaders understand change is necessary but cannot find support in their schooling systems to make that change reality. This crisis is not new, as Peter Drucker prophesized in his landmark book, *Post-Capitalist Society* (1993): 'As knowledge becomes the resource of post-capitalist society, the social position of the school as "producer" and "distributive channel" of knowledge, and its monopoly, are both bound to be challenged. And some of the competitors are bound to succeed. . . . Indeed, no other institution faces challenges as radical as those that will transform the school' (p. 209). We are at a critical moment for leaders to face these radical challenges. School leadership, according to Day and colleagues (2010), is a potent factor in making change happen (the only factor more critical is the role of the classroom teacher).

There is strong and relatively consistent research about what it takes to be an effective leader in schools (Hallinger, 2011; Day and colleagues 2010). Our intention in this chapter is not to provide an exhaustive discussion on the theories or processes of school change. We intend, rather, to demonstrate how the 4Cs is a critical component of leading transformation. Hallinger's research (2011) and our experience suggests that while leadership is critical, leaders alone cannot achieve systematic and sustainable change in schools. Nonetheless leaders and leadership teams are critical to making change happen in schools. Hallinger (2011) argues:

> The principal is important, but s/he can only achieve success through the cooperation of others. The impact of the principal's leadership is mediated by the culture, work processes and people. More specifically, the 'mutual influence' model emphasizes the profound impact that the school's context has on both leadership and on learning. This perspective should be both encouraging and humbling (p. 138).

While we will be referring to the research on transformational leadership we want to contextualize this discussion around the 4Cs. The kinds of transformations we are describing here will require courageous, transformative and engaged leadership that understands the 4Cs' place in schools and can actively work towards implementing change through this approach.

Who are transformational leaders?

In our view leaders do not just have the title 'head teacher', 'principal', 'head of learning' etc. They are, rather, any member of staff that has the vision, energy and courage to engage with the transformation required in schools. In most cases this will necessarily involve the head of the school (with whatever title they take) but will also involve executive members, teachers, professional staff, parents etc. So, in short, it is anyone who understands their role as an agent of school change. The kind of school leadership we imagine follows the learning principles we have espoused here: namely school leadership is creative, critically reflective, communicative and collaborative. This chapter discusses how leadership can be understood and enacted using the 4Cs to transform learning in schools. It begins with a discussion of what transformative leadership looks like and how school communities can encourage attributes of that leadership to thrive and flourish and in doing so transform the culture of schools and schooling. We have deliberately avoided hero narratives here of principals who come in and turn around failing schools into 'hero academies'. As Michael Fullan argues:

> Charismatic leaders inadvertently often do more harm than good because, at best, they provide episodic improvement followed by frustrated or despondent dependency. Superhuman leaders also do us another disservice: they are role models who can never be emulated by large numbers. Deep and sustained reform depends on many of us, not just on the very few who were destined to be extraordinary (Fullan, 2014, p. 1).

This position is consistent with our belief about schools and how sustainable change can sustainably transform school cultures rather than just be a 'flash in the pan'. For the 4Cs to be embedded within schools deep cultural change is required. While a talented and capable leader can instigate that change, it can only be maintained over time if the culture of the school collaboratively transforms. The approach we have described here (the 4Cs) is not a one-off one-term approach. The 4Cs changes radically and deeply how schools and schooling work. Fullan argues that schools are beset with 'one-off' and frequently contradictory initiatives, policies and approaches that do not create coherent or meaningful educational change for students:

> the main problem is not the absence of innovation but the presence of too many disconnected, episodic, piecemeal, superficially adorned projects. The situation is worse for schools than for businesses. Both are facing turbulent, uncertain environments, but schools are suffering the additional burden of having a torrent of unwanted, uncoordinated policies and innovations raining down on them from hierarchical bureaucracies (Fullan, 2014, p. 109).

We believe (based on our experience of sustainable reform) that schools are changed by creative, critically reflective, communicative and collaborative teams rather than charismatic or 'hero' individuals. The individual reformer superhero may exist but we are still to meet them. As Copland argued, back in 2001:

> it is no longer reasonable or intelligent to assume that every principal can or should be able to do it all – living up to every expectation that falls out of our literature based conceptions. If schools are going to deal affirmatively with the problems of candidate supply and attract strong, competent leaders into the ranks of school administration, we must deflate the pervasive myth of principal as every thing to everyone (Copland, 2001, p. 7).

So, given the need for change that we have articulated throughout this book and the urgency attached to this change, where will it emerge? Literacy educator Peter Freebody (2015) has pointed to the growing belief among educational researchers that school systems have become beholden to party-political agenda, media panic-mongering, and managed by an educational bureaucratic class that has become policy-reactive and attentive only to minimal accountabilities (Blacker, 2013). One outcome of this is that systems find it almost impossible to effect the policy changes that have been urgent for at least a generation (Gee, 2013). A consensus among many researchers, he further argued, is that the local school site – where particular needs are experienced as priorities, and local innovative practice can be supported by staff and community – is increasingly seen as the most productive setting for innovative research and development work (Teese, 2006). If this claim is correct (and we believe it is a strong argument), individual schools are the most viable and realistic sites for change. When this change is created at school level perhaps then further change will be influential on other schools within the system. Certainly since the 4Cs approach has been developed this has been our experience.

School systems are inherently conservative and risk averse. Consequently individuals within those systems may understand or advocate for change but changing systems is akin to turning the *Titanic*. On the other hand when we have approached schools and school leadership teams many of them have immediately understood the need for transformation and responded enthusiastically to the opportunity. Many school leaders have expressed the frustrations relating to the minutiae and compliance pervasive in schools that has led to a loss of the 'mission' of schooling – which is to educate. In the next section of this chapter we are going to move from a general discussion of transformation to a more fine-grained description of how we see transformative change happening through effective leadership. Perhaps first we should discuss expectations around change, to lay the foundations for the on-going discussion of how change moves beyond an aspiration to become a reality in schools.

What does a transformed 4Cs school look like?

At the risk of being utopian, we think it's worth describing how a school transformed through the 4Cs approach might look. The school we imagine and to some extent the schools that we have observed have reformed their structures and strategies to make creativity, critical reflection, communication and collaboration the drivers for curriculum, assessment, pedagogy, student welfare and leadership. The schools have not implemented fringe and irrelevant change; they have fundamentally changed how they do education. The culture in the schools reflects a changed relationship between teachers and students that is playful, open and regularly empowers teachers and students to ask questions. Problems do not magically disappear in these schools but the way these problems are dealt with reflects the 4Cs approach to learning. In essence, our argument in this chapter and throughout this book is that transformative leadership has at its heart each of the 4Cs and works patiently and energetically to see creativity, critical reflection, communication and collaboration integrated deeply into all aspects of schooling.

Realistic school transformation

One of the legacies of the hero narrative that we discussed earlier is the tendency for some to expect transformation to happen quickly. Notwithstanding our desire for rapid change this is rarely the case. Schools who wish to transform often face issues of intransigence from staff, schooling systems, parents and others. Transformation is perceived as risky. Ironically, the risk lies, as we have discussed, in not transforming. Change, or at least sustainable change, takes time, energy and patience and as such expectations need to be managed. While there are no definitive answers across all schools and all communities what we do know is that change is difficult, time-consuming and requires persistence. Pat Thomson summarizes the research in the area:

> Whole school change is a complex and somewhat unstable notion. There are debates about what it is, why it might be done, and how it is effected. However, there is widespread agreement that:
>
> - there is no single recipe for change
> - it requires action at the local level, but also support from outside, and
> - it takes time, usually longer than is anticipated.
>
> Change has been notoriously hard to sustain, and even where there have been some gains in learning outcomes, these plateau after a relatively short period of time. This presents an ongoing challenge to schools and school systems, as well as to those who seek to support and better understand the purposes and practices of change (Thomson, 2012, p. 71).

This formulation of school change is difficult to accept in some ways. It does not offer the 'easy fixes' that some media, politicians and parents demand. It does, however, recognize that schools are complex, and that transforming schools exacerbates that complexity. Our hope is that the model of transformation that we outline in this chapter will accomplish two things. First, we hope it gives some sense of the process of transformation required to engage whole school change with the 4Cs approach to learning. Second, and perhaps more critically, we hope that this structure persuades school leadership teams that change, while difficult and complex, is achievable if that change process is led in a creative, critically reflective, collaborative and open (communicative) manner.

In an effort to explain how we conceive leadership change occurring in schools who are implementing the 4Cs approach we have developed a model and framework for change that is demonstrated in Figure 9.1.

Figure 9.1 Leading transformations in the 4Cs approach

What you will notice about this diagram is that leadership sits at the centre with the 4Cs arrayed around the term (leadership). We consider the 4Cs as component parts of effective leadership. There is no set sequence for these components to occur. Change is the process of emergence shaped by the individual context of the school, teachers, students and the community. So, in essence, effective leaders in the 4Cs approach enact creativity, critical reflection, communication and collaboration in the work of school transformation. The smaller intersecting circles in Figure 9.1 indicate the components that we consider critical to transformation. The use of the Venn diagram suggests that the 4Cs are integrated into all facets of leadership: the culture, structures, strategies partnerships, visions and research that are essential for effective change. These are obviously not the only components of change but they are from our experience, the key components that are the most problematic and therefore critical to successful transformation. The first feature of the model is the often derided term 'vision'.

Vision

The term vision is perhaps so overused that it has begun to lose its meaning but for leading change it is possibly the most critical starting point for change. As Hallinger argues in his review of 40 years of research on educational leadership and transformation: 'vision and goals are the most significant avenue through which school leaders impact learning . . . "Vision" refers to a broad picture of the direction in which the school seeks to move (e.g. educating the whole child). In contrast, "goals" refers to the specific targets that need to be achieved on the journey towards that vision' (2011, p. 129). We mean by vision a shared understanding for schooling. In some ways that should be the role of systems but given the current preference in some systems for outmoded 'one size fits all' approaches to schooling it often falls to leaders in schools to deliver necessary transformation. In the 4Cs model the vision is relatively simple: 'to make creativity, critical reflection, communication and collaboration drive the processes of learning and teaching in schools'. Simple, right? Not really, this small vision has so many deep-seated implications for how we need to change schooling. It implies deep and thorough change that will be challenging for many and painful for some. In some ways this is why vision has become so meaningless as a term because it is relatively easy to state and terrifically difficult to implement.

Vision is easy to talk and write about, but when it comes to dealing with real people in real schools, difficulties arise. The issues often result from clashes with an intransigent school culture, communities who do not understand the need for change and a system that is disinclined or unable to support innovation and change. Of course there are manifold other structural or personal factors that get in the way of any kind of change. One way to engage the whole organization is to develop a culture of collaborative vision making.

We mentioned earlier the persistent myth of the 'hero leader' with a singular vision that he (because in this mythology it is usually a 'he') makes happen. Soon after, a television mini series is made about his bravery and vision turning around a 'failing school' (this happened in Australia recently). The reality of course is that any sustainable change is achieved by a team of people who are either participants in the creation of the vision or are attracted to the vision for change or both.

Essentially collaborative leadership is a process that is inherently about:

- Providing confidence in collaborative practice.
- Developing skills across the school in collaboration, communication, critical reflection and creativity.
- Developing professional learning to enable teachers to work in collaborative and interdisciplinary teams.

- Supporting interdisciplinarity between teaching teams with resources and incentives.

- Working with systems, communities, students and parents to help them understand what collaborative transformation can achieve within and beyond the school.

As educational philosopher Maxine Greene envisioned, effective, collaborative leadership enables students, teachers and ultimately the whole school community to achieve a large discussion. Engaging in 'dialogue to involve as many persons as possible, opening to one another, opening to the world' (Goodman and Teel, 1998, p. 71). To make these visions a reality, the next step in understanding leadership for change is the development of a strong and transformative culture.

Culture

Strategy, structure and vision are critical to begin the process of change but a shift in culture is necessary for that change to be sustained. Deal and Peterson (1999, p. 10) offer this definition: 'School culture is the set of norms, values and beliefs, rituals and ceremonies, symbols and stories that make up the "persona" of the school. These unwritten expectations build up over time as teachers, administrators, parents, and students work together, solve problems, deal with challenges and, at times, cope with failures.' Isaksen and colleagues (1999) describe culture as 'the deeper foundations of the organization. According to this distinction, culture provides the foundation for patterns of behaviour that are more readily observed, described, and changed. These patterns of observed behaviour along with many other variables, e.g., management, leadership, organizational size and structure, etc., help to establish the climate within the organization' (p. 666). For experienced educators culture is the 'gut feeling' you get when you walk into the school. Often it's the intangibles such as the way teachers and students engage with each other, the condition of the physical environment or the way students present themselves. Michael Fullan (2014) argued, 'Structure does make a difference, but it is not the main point in achieving success. Transforming culture – changing the way we do things around here – is the main point, it is a particular kind of reculturing for which we strive' (p. 53).

As we have discussed in this chapter, education has been beset over the years with one-off, incoherent and inconsistent initiatives. These have become, unfortunately, part of the landscape of schools or perhaps the culture of traditional education. What we imagine by a transformed culture is a consistent and coherent series of transformations that do not underestimate the complexity of the challenge, but rather patiently and deliberately work towards shifting from old paradigm learning and teaching to placing creativity, critical reflection, collaboration and communication at the centre of learning. Culture change is, as Donato (2004) suggests, relentlessly relational and collaborative: 'Collaborative cultures simultaneously build trust, provoke anxiety and contain it, engage in raising tacit knowledge to explicit knowledge, seek connections to ideas that exist inside and outside of the group, and build coherence. . . . The result of collaboration is simultaneously the emergence of new knowledge and growth for the group' (p. 285).

There are several tangible ways to assess school culture as a way of working towards change. The Situational Outlook Questionnaire (SOQ) (Isaksen and colleagues 1999) is used to assess 'climate' through a 'Questionnaire of 50 items constructed to assess how much any particular context will support creativity and change' (p. 666). The SOQ has been used widely inside and outside of education to create a series of validated and reliable quantitative measures to support an understanding of climate and culture. The SOQ includes the following dimensions:

- Challenge and involvement;
- Freedom;
- Trust and openness;
- Idea-time;
- Playfulness and humour;
- Conflict (this is a negative indicator in the SOQ);
- Idea-support;
- Debate;
- Risk taking. (p. 668)

The potential of these kinds of tools to support change is not necessarily in the numerical scores that result from the questionnaire. Rather, the SOQ and similar tools help to define for leadership teams what creative and change-ready organizations look like and the factors that make up culture. This provides schools the opportunity to open up discussions and to make decisions about collaborative change arising from evidence. Once the context is understood and the evidence has been gathered the difficult work of shifting culture can begin.

These kinds of cultural shifts are not temporary and they are not easy to achieve. Culture change requires leadership teams to rethink their visions, structures and approaches to learning. In our experience, when these features are integrated with regard to each school's individual context, sustainable change (albeit difficult and slow) that transforms learning is achievable. Again when considering how culture can be changed by the 4Cs a series of questions may be useful:

- How can we build creativity into our school culture?
- How can we use processes of critical reflection to understand our present culture and make plans for cultural change?
- How can we communicate with the whole school community what we perceive to be our current school culture? How can we communicate a case for change?
- How can we become authentically collaborative in the way we change our culture?

One strategy that leaders can enact to make schools more open and collaborative is to develop flexible yet robust structures.

Structure

The transformations we have been discussing throughout this book only occur when we can manage the systems, resources and personalities that endure in schools. As we have discussed, schools are relatively unchanged in the structures (with a few notable exceptions) since the 1950s. The great social, economic and technological changes of the twenty-first century demand innovation in the way we do schooling, and that means innovation in our structures. Renewed focus on creativity, critical reflection, communication and collaboration is not an argument for tinkering around the edges of school structures. Rather, it imagines new school structures that recognize the realities of learning and simultaneously aspire to make schooling more engaging and relevant to the lives of students.

These changes require realignment of the structures we have taken for granted for years in school. By the way, we are not necessarily arguing that these structures are problematic in and of themselves. The problems arise when the structures are taken for granted and not assessed against the needs of students facing the demands of twenty-first-century life. Some of these structures are so assumed that they have become almost invisible to many of us. We are thinking here about the following:

- the 50-, 40- or 30-minute learning period,
- the 9am–3pm school day,
- the arbitrary divisions between knowledge areas in subjects and syllabuses,
- the physical structures of mainly disembodied classrooms,
- 25, 30 or 40 students in class,
- the difference between curriculum, co-curriculum and extra curriculum learning,
- teachers teaching one subject and one class,
- standardized assessment practices,
- age-based cohorts.

To illustrate these structural changes we would like to refer to the school we have been working with; let's call it Dumaresq High School. Instead of standard 50-minute lessons, days are themed with interdisciplinary learning, such as 'thinking like an artist', 'communicating', 'navigating', 'being me', being us' and so on. The learning occurs in a large room with the focus on different teaching strategies including pairs work, direct instruction, group work and computer-based investigations. All of this knowledge generation is supported by teams of teachers working intensively with different groups, depending on their ability, engagement and understanding of the topics. This structure provides intensive differentiation while at the same time preserving a sense of purpose around learning and the products of that learning. These kinds of structures are still a process of discovery for leadership teams, teachers and students but they do reflect attempts to change learning to reflect the kinds of capabilities required of the twenty-first-century citizen rather than the citizen of the 1950s. Beyond the need to make structures more relevant they also need to be reflective of the contextual factors in schools.

Structures will vary from school context to school context. Nonetheless we have nominated 'structure' in this discussion of leadership because it is essential to sustainable and systematic change. As Hallinger argues, an understanding of context makes transformation possible in schools: 'The capacity to read your context correctly and adapt your leadership to the needs largely determines your success. There is no one best leadership style for fostering learning in schools. We are learning more and more about the ways that leaders need to match strategies to contexts; more research on this point is needed' (Hallinger, 2011, p. 137).

In our view the right ideas are found in the right structures. These structures allow for creative collaboration of professional learning communities to explore solutions, re-define problems and create self-organizing systems that can sustain themselves when the initial burst of energy from innovation fades away. As education policy scholar Richard Elmore argued:

> structures should, at a minimum, create diversity among the energetic, already committed reformers and the skeptical and timid. . . . Certain types of structures are more likely than others to intensify and focus norms of good practice: organizations in which face-to-face relationships dominate impersonal, bureaucratic ones; organizations in which people routinely interact around common problems of practice; and organizations that focus on the results of their work for students, rather than on the working conditions of professionals. These features can be incorporated into organizations, as well as into the composition of their memberships. (Elmore, 1996, p. 20)

What we are suggesting and what Richard Elmore has long argued is that the structures in schools must reflect the qualities that pervade the learning in the context of the school. Structures that favour creativity, critical reflection, communication and collaboration, while not uncommon in current school practices, are not the norm. Leaders who wish to embrace the 4Cs must consider how to revolutionize school structures to make the learning of students consistent with the structures of schooling. The key to implementing vision, culture and structure is through strategies that are suited to the context of the school and that integrate all the components in the school transformation process.

Strategy and integration

In our view the 'heavy lifting' occurs when school leadership teams face the sometimes daunting task of putting visions and structures into practice. This is where ideas meet reality in schools and the hard work of educational change moves from being an often pleasant fantasy into a somewhat less pleasant reality. For us strategy signifies the way relationships, resources, space, time and funding drive school transformation. We are not going to claim here that we can understand each school's context. It is worth noting, however, that an understanding of the school's context is critical to making these kinds of change happen. In the process of change leaders need to build strategies that are consistent with the school context and the issues and opportunities in the culture of the school. Strategies provide the ways and means for implementing the structures and visions for changing that school. The 4Cs provide a set of organizers that school leaders could consider when devising strategies for school change. For instance:

- How can we use creative processes to reimagine the spaces and the places in our school?

- How can we critically reflect on the strategies we are using to change our school?

- How can we alter strategies when our critical reflection reveals issues, problems, opportunities?

- How can we improve communication so that the members of our school community understand what's going on during and after the change process has begun?

- How can we collaborate deeply to make decisions about school welfare policies?

The 4Cs are a good starting point but they must be implemented with a deep understanding of context. Context is critical and an understanding of different contexts will enable change. For instance, a strategy that works in one phase of transformation will not work in another. A school that has extensive refugee and English as an additional language student populations requires a focus on language and literacy to support the development of communication skills. While the school would not neglect creativity, critical reflection and collaboration, communication learning strategies may be emphasized to meet the specific needs of these learners. In another school context where students have English as a first language it is possible to create strategies that focus on the needs of that school. Recently we have worked with schools in a middle-class area that reflects this profile. One of the concerns of the leadership in the school was that students lacked an understanding of authentic and meaningful diversity. In this school context it was possible to implement strategies that explore diversity and engaged with the 4Cs.

Change has rhythms and momentum that differ throughout the process. Day and colleagues (2010) argue in their meta-analysis, 'Ten strong claims about successful leadership', that the layering of strategies within a context is critical to lasting change: 'Effective heads [leadership teams] make judgments, according to their context, about the timing, selection, relevance, application and continuation of strategies that create the right conditions for effective teaching, learning and pupil achievement within and across broad development phases' (p. 15).

To illustrate the role of strategy we might consider the context of a newly established school and a school that is 30 years old. These schools will differ in terms of staffing profile, physical learning spaces, resourcing, and student, parent and community expectations. These differences may seem obvious but many systems create policy that ignores context and then wonder why the policy fails. While the vision and perhaps the structures may be similar in both of these contexts the strategies will need to be designed and implemented to meet the needs of each school specifically. Older schools often require patient and sometimes painstaking consultation to engage with the cultural expectations that have been established over many years. In the context of the new school, change may be possible faster but that change and creating that culture will require different kinds of strategies. Key to the understanding of strategy and its implementation is integration. Integration is the skill of knowing how and when and what scale to implement which strategies and with whom.

Any transformation requires a layering and balancing across complex areas of school life. Change is never as simple as deciding on a series of strategies and then implementing them one after the other. This coordination is a strategic challenge that is similar to 'playing chess in three dimensions' yet integration is critical to changing school culture in a sustainable and lasting way.

Each school has its own set of contexts that dictate and drive decisions about how strategies are implemented and coordinated. For instance changing approaches to teacher professional learning will necessarily impact on teaching and learning strategies. Changing approaches to classroom learning strategies has an impact on learning spaces, timetabling and the way the school day is arranged. Integration is the coordination and layering of strategies to create a coherent and logical process of change that inspires confidence in the change process.

As Richard Elmore (1996) argues, issues of integration (which he refers to here as scale) must recognize that there are human beings in the process. He says: 'A basic prerequisite for tackling the problem of scale, then, is to insist that reforms that purport to change practice embody an explicit theory about how human beings learn to do things differently. . . . Furthermore, these theories have to make sense at the individual and at the organizational level' (pp. 24–25). Elmore's observation highlights the complexity of integration. Understanding which strategies to enact and when is a major challenge for leadership teams. For instance, a school we have been working in is considering engaging with the 4Cs. This school has a history of very high academic achievement that parents (and some staff) at the school are very protective of. This leadership team has a series of choices about how to implement changes and at what stage to communicate these changes to parents, teachers and students. This school must, however, integrate those decisions in a way that reassures parents, teachers and students and at the same time make a coherent argument for the change being made.

This is the challenge of integration: getting the layers and the rhythms of change coordinated and enacted in ways that inspire confidence at a school level. Michael

Fullan and Maria Langworthy (2014) provide some advice about the qualities inherent in successfully integrated transformational leadership:

> These new change leaders will have to operate under conditions of dynamic change. We see the process as consisting of: directional vision, letting go, and reining in across iterative cycles. Such leaders will need to open up the possibilities with directional ideas but not necessarily concrete plans at the early stage. As this 'invitational stage' unfolds, leaders – again at all levels – will need to be open to new explorations while supporting people under conditions of ambiguity. In this sense, leaders 'let go' as new ideas and practices are explored, which happens in rapid order. As the process unfolds, leaders will need to help others identify, refine and spread what is working. This is a change process of the likes we have never seen, and a major theme of it is the rapid inclusion of more and more partners in the process. (p. 48)

In other words, and consistent with the approach throughout this book, transformational leaders will need to exhibit and employ high level creativity, critical reflection, communication and collaboration as they manage this difficult process.

In a school we have been working with recently the leadership team is integrating change with the 4Cs. In this school the teachers are open to ideas because they keep asking more and more questions. They are motivated to 'figure out' the most effective way to integrate deep learning and to try new and sometimes unfamiliar pedagogical approaches. They are being critically reflective, communicating, collaborative and starting to feel free to be creative. Partnerships are a feature of open and engaged schools.

Partnerships

Often, introducing partnerships will open up the school to new ways of thinking and new ways of working. Partnerships allow schools to expand what learning can mean by engaging with the rich storehouse of resources and ideas beyond their front gate. For partnerships to be effective, schools (and partners) need to have a deep understanding and commitment to creativity, critical reflection, communication and collaboration. In a sense, partnerships are the 'embodiment' of the 4Cs approach. Partnerships often help students to understand that learning has implications in the real world. Partnerships allow students to connect their learning with real-life applications of that learning.

One way for schools to engage with this opportunity is to recalibrate so that partnerships are embedded in the learning from the beginning rather than 'bolted on' at the end. This approach necessitates an 'outward facing' school that is open and equipped to engage in all sorts of partnerships from many places including parents (professional skills, drawing on life stories), cultural institutions (The Lincoln Centre, The Sydney Opera House) to international organizations (The United

Nations, NASA, The Metropolitan Opera). The emergence of accessible and pervasive technologies allows unprecedented access to partners (and their resources) all over the world. This is an opportunity that can change learning fundamentally. Partnerships can take many forms from working with the local community to engaging with international agencies.

To illustrate how the 4Cs can work in partnership let's use the simple example of a school project to build a local community garden. A school interested in partnerships and the 4Cs might engage with their local community to design (creativity) a community garden in partnership with a local landscape architect. In the construction phase they might work with builders, local gardeners, biologists from a university (collaboration) to construct the garden. When the garden is finished they might work with a local advertising agency to design (creativity) a campaign to bring people to the garden (collaboration and communication). To understand the effectiveness of all of these phases in the project, students could critically reflect with environmental scientists from the local council about the effectiveness of the garden for the community.

This simple example of the community garden design and construction positions learning as a partnership with the community. In this instance learning is not restrained by the resources of the school, rather it harnesses the resources of the broader community to make learning deep, complex and engaging.

Partnerships are and always have been a critical part of education but they are not without difficulties. Anyone who has been involved in schools knows that they are busy places and anyone who has been involved in a partnership of any kind knows that they are time-consuming. Often schools become so busy that partnerships seem too time-consuming and too difficult. For us, this seems like a substantial missed opportunity.

Perhaps rather than asking what partnerships might cost schools in time and effort, schools could consider what *not* engaging with these partnerships will cost in terms of lost student learning and engagement. Rather than exhaustively discuss how each partnership might work we thought we might reflect on some of the issues that can strengthen or challenge partnerships in schools.

Trust and respect

Many issues in partnerships stem from a basic lack of trust or respect. Often the lack of trust or respect is not malicious or personal in nature – it is not that the partners and schools necessarily distrust or disrespect each other – but more likely that they do not know enough about the kinds of work each other does, and therefore do not place the same value on the same things. Additionally, many schools have had little experience with partnerships and therefore are not necessarily equipped to deal with the demands that partnerships present. For example, when undertaking partnerships with universities, it is worth understanding that academic work and teaching in universities is qualitatively different to teaching in schools (there are different motivations and different remits). For instance many academics do not have a background in classrooms and most are not trained teachers and may not have a realistic understanding of knowledge and practice of teachers and the realities of schools. This has the potential to create the perception of a lack of respect that could lead to a lack of trust between schools and the partnership organization. As always, the key is clear and sustained communication to maintain trust and respect.

Communication

Unsurprisingly, lapses in communication can often cause friction in partnerships. Equally disruptive can be mis-communication, particularly if it causes mistakes. Although communication seems as though it should be so easy these days – with email, online networks, Twitter, teleconferencing and so on, it is critical to recognize that people working in different organizations and roles have different types of access to, and routines for, communication. The best way to avoid mis-communication or frustrating lapses in communication is to establish a plan for contact and communication early in the partnership. A 'contact person' who has easy access to the necessary communication tools in each site is often a good solution.

Apathy and disorganization

This is a difficult issue to overcome and the solutions are often dependent on the reason for the apathy or disorganization. Overwork is a common reason for disorganization. The rhythms of schools are often quite different from the rhythms that partnership organizations are used to. This can cause misunderstanding and requires skill to close the gap between each organization's expectations.

Apathy is altogether a more difficult issue as it often stems from a disinclination to change or actively engage with new ideas. Apathy sometimes comes about when the partnership is imposed rather than the whole school community 'opting in' to the partnership. Sometimes teachers are involved in an initiative because they have been subtly told they have to be (rather than because they want to be). This is not only an ethical issue, but can also lead to other areas of conflict such as competing agendas or lack of trust. This is mostly overcome in our experience by working with the willing rather than the resistant in partnerships through building consensus and demonstrating the benefits of partnerships.

Competing agendas

There are frequently mismatches between the needs of the partner and the needs of the school. Rarely do partners (or schools for that matter) come to partnerships with exactly the same motivations, approaches and agendas. While trust and explicit discussion can overcome potential problems here, these competing agendas do have the potential to create conflict. It is critical that all parties to partnerships are explicit about why they are participating and that these discussions are had early in the planning phase – different agendas in partnerships are commonplace; competing agendas can cause problems. As we have discussed, the 4Cs are integral to the success of partnerships in schools. The following questions may assist schools in the development of sustainable partnerships:

- Which partners can provide support for students to extend and integrate creativity in science, visual arts, mathematics, geography or music?
- How can we create partnerships that are genuinely collaborative?
- How can we model effective communication strategies for students?
- How can we use processes of critical reflection to understand the potential opportunities and problems for partnerships?
- Who can help us transform schools through the 4Cs?

Research and evaluation

Even a cursory glance at the 4Cs approach will reveal the emphasis we place on authentic research and evaluation. When we are considering leadership, evaluation and research become critical to making evidence-based decisions about change and renewal in schools. There is not sufficient space here to explain the processes and approaches that can deliver systematic, sustainable and realistic research and evaluation (for a comprehensive discussion see: Anderson and Freebody, 2014; Cohen, Manion and Morrison, 2000; Denzin and Lincoln, 2005; Freebody, 2003; O'Toole, 2006) but we think it is worth providing a rationale for evaluation and research within a leadership context. This section is designed for the understanding of the complexities of research as it relates leadership. Many transformations that are driven by so-called 'evidence' have failed in the long run because those implementing the change at a school level have not understood the limitations of the research. Leaders can avoid this by understanding the uses of research and the complexities of applying large-scale research to specific contexts.

Understanding context through evaluation

One of the persistent challenges of leadership is connecting context with a viable change strategy. School change has suffered from a series of imposed reforms that often do not take sufficient account of the context of the school. The 4Cs as a model only has the capacity to effectively change practice if the context is comprehensively understood. In our conversations with school and systems leaders we commonly hear 'We really didn't take enough time to understand the context, before we implemented change on that school.' We believe 4Cs are a logical and relevant framework for school transformation. They are, however, pointless unless they are fitted to the context of each individual school.

Contextual evaluation has many parts. An evaluation of a school should take into account factors such as:

- the history of the organization,
- the capacities of the teaching staff,
- engagement level of parents,
- the role of partnerships.

Evaluation can help to create a picture made up of these factors. There are many evaluation instruments that school leaders can enlist in to support this process. One example that we have used with schools to assess student motivation engagement is the MES scale developed by Andrew Martin (2009). This instrument develops a profile of student motivation and engagement and provides cohort measures to support leaders to understand what is happening in each year group of any given school. This kind of instrument and the data it produces has its limitations. The data explains the 'what' but not the 'why' of the context. Qualitative approaches such as focus groups and interviews can provide insights into the 'why'.

Again, when looking at student capabilities and the 4Cs there are some qualitative analytical tools available. In some schools we have used a series of surveys to analyse student understandings of the 4Cs. There are at least two ways to use tools such as this. Schools considering implementing the 4Cs can use these kinds of instruments to analyse student readiness for the 4Cs. The second approach is to use the instrument to track growth and development in student understanding and capabilities over time. Using the instrument in this way, schools could evaluate students before any change occurs (as a baseline) and several times as the changes are being implemented. Leaders can use evaluation tools such as these to understand the context and track the shape of the change going on in the schools. These strategies are most effective when they are married with qualitative evaluation strategies.

Qualitative evaluation strategies

In a school we have been working with recently the issue of staff capability arose. The leadership team wanted to understand the likely attitude of the staff to the 4Cs. Qualitative evaluation strategies can provide insights into the attitudes and beliefs of the teaching staff beyond the summary statistics that quantitative strategies offer. This information can assist leadership teams to formulate effective structures and strategies in the school context as they take into account the complexities related to transformation strategies.

The evaluation strategies here have limitations, which we will discuss further. These tools can, however, provide leadership teams with an understanding of the 'what' and the 'why' of the context. The next part of this chapter deals with issues relating to research. We have included a section on research in the leadership chapter because 'data-driven decisions, 'effect sizes' and 'evidence-based practice' have become pervasive in schools (often driven by system imperatives). There are however some very real risks and opportunities here that leaders must be aware of when they are engaging with evaluation and research in schools.

Building theory through research

One of the major challenges for researchers in education is to build theoretical models that allow research to reach beyond the confines of classrooms or schools. Theory can be defined as a coherent description and explanation of observed phenomena that can also produce predictions about the behaviour of individuals or groups. Theory is a way that teachers in different contexts can speak about the way learning occurs. Theory allows researchers to cross borders, boundaries and subjects. Given the usefulness of theory as a way to have rich and deep conversations you might think it would be a standard fixture in education. The reality, according to Kettley (2010), however, is that we are in a state of crisis when it comes to innovative research: 'the crisis of theory building in education studies arises from the failure to encourage original interpretations of data among new researchers. Cleaving to existing concepts and isolated paradigms is not imaginative thinking' (p. 9). Perhaps one of the unfortunate implications of school change is that school leaders tend to look inwards at their own contexts. Kettley's call for 'original interpretations' and 'imaginative thinking' is to move beyond themselves in their own schools to explore new ways of contributing to research discussions theory building that can nourish educational change more broadly. For us, that involves finding research methodologies that match the needs of schools and that do not dogmatically adhere to one approach.

The methodological 'tug o war'

In the current climate there is a televised 'tug o war' between the public good, which requires simple questions, answers and solutions that are reportable, fundable and easily understood. These are sometimes expressed in metrics such as 'effect sizes'. On the other side is the complex, messy, busy reality of educational practice that through its myriad different contexts and circumstances makes research certainty questionable. Those involved in educational research and evaluation are required to navigate between public expectations while maintaining integrity in their research. Research decisions, particularly about methodology, are influenced by this 'tug o war'.

We are not claiming that one approach should be favoured above the other; rather, that the methodologies respond to the variety of questions that educators need answers for. We should not be deluded into thinking that the complex questions that arise in education can be responded to with methodologies that do not take account of that complexity. At its core, evaluation and research is a process of untangling the many variables to understand how educators can make a difference in the lives of students. This untangling is a particular challenge for those working in quantitative research. Their role is to untangle the complexities and distil those complexities into mainly numerical measures. On the other hand, qualitative research methods can provide researchers with the tools to understand and reflect on the complexities of school learning.

The capacity to analyse and reflect complexity, however, can also lead to confusing and muddled outcomes. What we are saying here, without getting into an unedifying and ultimately pointless discussion around the relative benefits of different approaches, is that the research methods chosen depend entirely on the what is being explored, the research question and the research contexts. Complexity is a feature of schooling that cannot be wished away (nor should it). It is part of the educational research landscape that makes it unique and an exciting place to work.

The politics of evidence-based practice

At first glance it seems reasonable, perhaps even axiomatic, that we should require evidence to make changes in practice or policy in education. A critical issue, however, is what counts as evidence and what evidence counts? Evidence-based research is a contested term in this field. Lyn Yates prefers the term 'scientifically-based' (2004, p. 24) research to avoid the issues that surround the use of the term 'evidence' and so cuts to the heart of what is really meant by the term: that it is research based on empiricism. Denzin and Giardina (2008, p. 11) argue that there is a concerning new trend in research that privileges certain types of evidence over others:

> Like an elephant in the living room, the evidence-based practice model is an intruder whose presence can no longer be ignored. Within the global audit culture, proposals concerning the use of . . . experimental methodologies, randomized control trials, quantitative metrics, citation analyses, shared databases, journal impact factors, rigid notions of accountability, data transparency, warrantability, rigorous peer-review evaluation scales and fixed formats for scientific articles now compete, fighting to gain ascendency in the evidence-quality-standards discourse. (pp. 11–12)

When school leaders are considering the kinds of change that we've been discussing in this chapter, research and evaluation have clear benefits. These benefits, however, can only be realized if the research and evaluation is understood in its complexity. Research and research methodologies have their advantages and disadvantages and those that claim objective truth should be regarded with scepticism. Schooling and especially school transformation is context-driven, messy, unpredictable, complex and difficult. Research and evaluation can support a leader in this process if it is understood and implemented in a systematic and critically reflective way. The 4Cs also have a role in the ways schools can frame their research and evaluation strategies. The following questions are designed to assist schools as they build their research and evaluation:

- How can we understand student and staff readiness for creative learning through arts-based research approaches?
- Can we develop collaborative approaches for research through partnerships with universities?
- How can we effectively communicate that new understandings develop through research? What other possibilities are there of theory creation from school-based research?

- How can critical reflection be central to research and evaluation processes at our school?

A road map for transformative leadership

- *Establish a vision for change that integrates the 4Cs into the school culture.* As we have claimed throughout this book, the 4Cs offer a different view of learning and working in organizations. The demands of the twenty-first century mean collaboration, creativity, critical reflection and communication become critical skills in an evolving society and economy. Part of the role of decision-making is crafting arguments that make that reality clear to those around us. It is no longer simply acceptable to assert that the 4Cs matter. Part of the vision must be driven by convincing arguments about the role of schools in a changing and evolving society. We can build a vision if we have effective arguments based on research evidence that convinces parents, students, teachers and systems of the need and the urgency of this change.

- *Embed the 4Cs in the process of leadership and change.* We have detailed throughout this chapter the ways we think the 4Cs can be embedded into leadership for transformation. As we hope we have made clear it is not just a process of teaching the 4Cs, they need to be inherent in the culture, structures, vision, partnerships and strategies in each school.

- *Develop a culture of creativity, critical reflection, communication and collaboration.* As we have discussed, cultural change is difficult and it is likely to take years rather than months to achieve. One of the implicit arguments throughout this chapter has been that the 4Cs are actually critical to effective transformative leadership. When schools transform to make the culture experimental, playful, creative and open, change is not only possible it is probable. If our aspiration is that our students learn through and with the 4Cs, school leaders will need to reflect and model them in their school structures and cultures.

Transforming schools has never been a simple task. Schools are complex and multilayered organizations and they differ from context to context. While the aim of 4Cs learning is to change schools across all systems, the reality is that school change is more likely to occur in individual schools when teachers, students and parents recognize the old models of learning based on the old realities are no longer relevant. As schools transform into places where twenty-first-century learning is explicitly and deeply integrated (exhibited through the 4Cs) other schools will take notice. Systems seem, for the large part, no longer able to make the changes that are required. If schooling is to remain relevant this change is critical. As we have discussed in this chapter, leadership is not the only factor in transforming schools but creative, critically reflective, communicative and collaborative leadership does have a substantial role to play in transforming schools. Even if it is one school at a time. This is no small matter. If schools are to transform they will need leaders who understand and can enact the kinds of change we have identified here.

The next chapter will make some concluding reflections about the implications for transforming schools and freeing learning.

Freeing learning

Implications for transforming schools through the 4Cs

You will notice that our blueprint for school transformation is both hopeful and aspirational. Aspirations are critical in education so that we can imagine a future that moves us beyond the transmission pedagogy and high stakes testing that currently persist in many schools. But at the same time we understand the classroom realities of transformation. As we have been writing this book we have had an internal 'teacher voice' guiding us; asking us questions, provoking us and reminding us of the classroom realities. One of the persistent questions that the 'teacher' asks is 'how does this work in the real world – in real classrooms?' This chapter discusses some of the implications for making the 4Cs transformation work in classrooms, schools and communities. We want to open the possibilities for change, and support schools to transform through coherent and comprehensive frameworks (coherence makers, Learning Disposition Wheel etc.). Our motivation for writing this book was the need to reconcile classroom realities with urgent need for transformation. The education writer Stephen Heppell (2011) offers this provocation for schools and schooling:

> If education is looking perilously like a structurally declining industry, society has embraced learning as über cool. The media are full of people learning to cook, learning to dance, learning to learn. Whole genres of new media – such as reality TV – are built on the ambiguity of presenting dull and D-list stars with unexpected circumstances and watching them cope. Process has replaced product as the focus of our curiosity. It is the beginning of a new renaissance in learning; but sadly, education doesn't look likely to be around long enough to learn from it. (p. 41)

Added to the rise of learning that Heppell describes here are the postnormal conditions in our communities, nations and beyond that we referred to in Chapter 1. Chaos, complexity and contradiction (Sardar, 2010) has created pressure for change in our society, and our schools are not immune to that pressure. In the face of this rapid change, one thing is clear to us. We need to articulate a way of learning, built on the substantial resources that already exist in schools, that responds effectively to the needs of the twenty-first century. We also realize that we need to propose approaches to learning that teachers see as realistic and possible in their own classrooms. We are aware that some of the ideas we have here may appear utopian. We do not imagine a perfected future but one of the attractions of utopias is that they are implicitly hopeful as they give us a possible future to 'sail towards'. As Oscar Wilde (2007) said: 'A map of the world that does not include Utopia is not worth even glancing at, for it leaves out the one country at which Humanity is always landing. And when Humanity lands there, it looks out, and, seeing a better country, sets sail. Progress is the realisation of Utopias' (p. 247). While the modernist concept of 'progress' may need further examination, the general point is well made: that in response to overwhelming change, education must navigate towards a better metaphorical 'country'. That is not to say that the country that exists currently is not worthwhile. We think schools are one of the most critical institutions for creating equity and change in our communities. They are not, however, excluded from the external pressures that are forcing change across our communities.

In this final chapter we are going to examine the impacts and implications of the 4Cs for schools and learning. You will notice that we remain critically hopeful about the future of learning. As Freire argued: 'Hope is a natural, possible, and necessary impetus in the context of our unfinishedness' (1998, p. 69). We are undeniably hopeful in our approach. We also recognize that transformation is a relational human process that happens with real people in real schools and presents real problems. Transformation is a collaborative process that only works when teams comprising leaders, teachers and the community members all recognize the potential that the 4Cs has for making school better for all. In short, we recognize that transformation has to be relational as well as hopeful. In the next few pages we want briefly to address some of the issues that have arisen as we have spoken to teachers and school leaders about school transformation and the 4Cs.

The 'how' of transformation

One of the issues with utopias is that there is never really an understanding of how society transitions from its current situation to a utopian state. As you have seen in our 'road maps' at the end of many of the chapters, our motivation is to make explicit how schools might implement creativity, critical reflection, collaboration and communication. A primary motivation for writing this book was to close the gap between aspiration to teach the 4Cs and the lack of guidance for schools and teachers on how to teach the 4Cs in classrooms (that's one reason we have included teacher and student voices throughout this book). The coherence makers we present in this book are our contribution to closing the gap between aspiration and action in teaching twenty-first-century capabilities. The following is a list (in no particular order) of the features of schooling that we think will be impacted by transformation. This list is not exhaustive but it will provide a 'rough guide' to prepare the traveller for this transformative journey.

Transformed schools will teach as well as *live* the 4Cs

The changes we have foreshadowed in this book are not just about changes to pedagogy. Schools that deeply understand the 4Cs will need to change the shape of much of what they do. Capacities such as creativity, critical reflection, communication and collaboration are not only relevant to effective pedagogy, they are inherent to the practices and processes of effective schools. So for instance effective schools that foster creativity will include structures, strategies, pedagogy and leadership that explicitly models creative processes and practices in its approaches to assessment, student welfare policies, communication with parents and staff professional learning. Often in our work with schools we hear that claim: 'the 4Cs are fine in theory but we don't have the time'. We recognize that schools are busy places and that transformation involves looking at all of the functions of schools and then prioritizing them. Many of the schools we have worked with spend inordinate and inefficient amounts of time and resources on tasks that do not really contribute to the learning or the welfare of students. The time taken to implement the 4Cs is likely to bring deep benefits for some of the functions schools see currently as critical. For instance taking time for critical reflection will assist school leaders, teachers and students to consider what actually contributes to the quality of the school environment. In short, schools need to not only teach the 4Cs they need to be the 4Cs.

Transforming schools will change the partnerships between parents and the community

As McNeal (2014) argues, there has been a substantial discussion about the role of parents and the communities in 'fixing' schools. This approach often considers parents as possible saviours for a failing system rather than in a partnership with educators to create high-quality learning for students. He argues that 'much of this attention can be attributed to there being something inherently appealing in the notion that increased parent involvement will help remedy the continued problem of poor academic performance ... in many ways, it is the attempt to help "fix" a faltering education system without fundamentally restructuring schools, redistributing students, raising standards for teachers, or investing more resources' (2014, p. 564).

The 4C approach imagines parental involvement in a different way. Instead of parents being 'fixers' of schools we see them working in partnership with school leaders, teachers and students by doing what they do best: encouraging their children to engage with twenty-first-century capabilities. This will require some persuasive communication on behalf of the school. A clear rationale for the 4Cs should be established and argued coherently so parents can understand why it matters and how it will make a difference for their children. Some parents consider their school experience as the best model for the schooling of their children. Yet even in the last two decades (since they attended school) what schools are and what they are expected to do has changed dramatically. One school we have been working with ensures that parents understand the approach the school takes by explaining the Learning Disposition Wheel (see Chapter 3) to parents during the intake interview. When parents understand the alignment between the 4Cs and twenty-first-century learning, they are far more likely to engage and support that learning. We are not suggesting that this is easy or that every parent become a 'convert' but partnerships with parents are critical in the transformation process of schools.

In Chapter 9 we discussed the benefits for schools of creating partnerships with the community. In our view this is putting collaboration into practice in schools. Beyond the piecemeal and insubstantial partnerships that some schools are engaged with, these deep community partnerships become integral to a transformed school's learning environment. To make these partnerships a sustainable part of school life, resources, policies and practices need to be reconsidered and reallocated. As we have mentioned, partnerships are difficult, however connections with the community create an environment where schools are connected to partners all over the world. Community partnerships are not new to schools. Practices such as 'work experience' have been a regular part of schooling for decades. We are suggesting that the processes inherent in community partnerships that already exist in schools (finding partners, matching them with supervisors etc.) could be adapted, applied and multiplied in new partnerships with communities in science, geography, design, mathematics etc. This will contribute to partnerships becoming the rule rather than the exception in schools.

Learning will transform approaches to assessment

The current preference schooling systems have for high stakes testing has meant that learning, testing and assessment have become increasingly disconnected. As Val Klenowski and Claire Wyatt-Smith (2012) claim, this approach has now become a tool of public accountability and international competition rather than an integral part of learning: 'The move to foreground the accountability purpose of testing that occurred in England almost 20 years ago is here in Australia today, with schools and teachers being judged on published results and schools being placed in league tables. This focus has been driven largely by the media and political decision-making at both state and federal levels' (p. 65). High stakes testing only measures a small slice of learning that is easily testable. These nationwide testing regimes distort learning in schools; driving it towards the test and the consequent rankings rather than the needs of twenty-first-century learners.

We are not arguing for the abolition or even the diminution of assessment. Assessment is critical to analysing the effectiveness of learning and supporting each individual student's development. The problems arise when high stakes testing is considered a panacea for system improvement and applied by those (often outside education) for purposes other than learning (such as ranking, making unfair comparisons between schools, funding and defunding). Klenowski and Wyatt-Smith (2012) argue that educators need to challenge the current connection between testing and redesign assessment: 'It is time to critique the flawed thinking associated with an assumed connection between testing and learning improvement. . . . As many have argued, the challenge for the educational community is to ward off this pressure, focusing instead on providing support for the long-term professional development change necessary to effect actual pedagogical change and improved outcomes and a more equitable society' (p. 79).

We think that the 4Cs offer abundant possibility to make these changes. The assessment rubrics that we have provided in the Appendix detail the expectations of learners during each stage of learning in the 4Cs from 'awakening' to 'adept'. These rubrics provide a viable framework for recalibrating and reconsidering assessment. Assessment must be aligned with the learning needs of students for it to be effective and useful. It needs to be redesigned to make it interdisciplinary, multidisciplinary and transdisciplinary so it engages authentically and relevantly with real-world problems (that are in nature interdisciplinary). The problems of climate change, poverty, refugee displacement and international conflict relate to history, mathematics, science, geography and English. If we ultimately seek authenticity in our learning and assessment practices, schools will need to create more joined-up approaches to both.

When schools are implementing the 4Cs they need to explore ways of reworking assessment to create connected tasks that assess creativity, critical reflection, collaboration and communication as well as knowledge, wisdom and new understanding. We acknowledge that there is some work to do in the development of assessment tools for creativity and collaboration and critical reflection. There are viable models in schools that can be adapted to assess the 4Cs. For example we already have reliable and valid approaches to collaboration in physical education, music and drama. There are equally strong assessment strategies for creativity, critical reflection and communication available.

You have probably heard the saying 'what matters gets tested'. At the moment what gets tested is a very narrow band of understanding in schools, potentially disenfranchising and discouraging students who cannot achieve in that narrow band. Assessments for creativity, critical reflection, communication and collaboration should not supplant these areas of domain-specific knowledge (such as science, geography, dance). Rather, we should develop assessment practices that integrate this knowledge with the broader skills students require for their twenty-first-century lives.

School spaces and resources will change

For the last several decades (with notable exceptions) learning spaces in schools have been designed and built in much the same way. The classrooms of today look very similar to the classrooms of the 1950s. For the most part, students sit in rows that face the front. A teacher sits at a slightly larger desk facing the students or writes on the board (or the modern equivalent: interactive whiteboard). We can think of almost no other place (except for universities) where this kind of practice persists. The resilience of this design tells us something about the way schools work. The transmission model of teaching (teachers speak and students listen) is still deeply embedded within the fabric of our schools. This is even more remarkable when you consider the technologies that now pervade every other part of our lives that have not disrupted substantially our learning and teaching spaces. As learning space innovator, Stephen Heppell argues: 'this isn't the time to use technology to refine the model we had before; this is the time to harness technology to let children go as far as they want' (Victorian Department of Education and Early Childhood Development, 2014, p. 9).

Rather than discussing this further in deficit terms we argue that 4Cs learning can be the impetus for making school spaces and resources work more efficiently, effectively and authentically. Spaces that complement and support 4C learning enable collaboration, playfulness, embodiment and creative practice. These spaces look more like science labs, drama studios or visual arts spaces rather than the standard chairs and tables set up in neat rows. When chairs and tables are required for learning they should be flexible, allowing students to work with each other and to work as a whole group. The key to 4C learning is allowing different models of classroom organization that can be flexibly and rapidly redeployed and reconfigured to meet the needs of the learning and learners.

A school that we have been working with has created large open spaces where groups of 70–80 students can work independently, in pairs or in groups with teams of teachers supporting their learning. This allows a variety of learning strategies to occur in the same room. In this flexible classroom some students are involved in large group work, some students with high literacy needs are working with support teachers individually or in small groups. The key to this space is flexibility so that learning configurations can be changed quickly and effectively to meet the individual and group needs of students. These spaces need to cater for students having more autonomy as self-regulated learners so they can use the space to meet their own learning needs. This is preferable to the traditional chair and table set-up as it allows teachers to use learning strategies that favour creativity, critical reflection, communication and collaboration. The key in these configurations is accepting learning is more than transmission. In a conventional classroom the design and physical resources act as an obstruction to flexible and differentiated learning. And rather than being 'bolted on', technology is layered within this learning space so it is available to students as they need it. In these classrooms technology is not an end in itself. Technology always serves the needs of the students and the teachers and ultimately the learning. These spaces are not just a possibility, we have seen them working effectively in several schools to promote learning through the 4Cs. This approach to learning spaces will change what is possible for learners and teachers and will ultimately deliver a more effective, engaging and relevant learning experience for students.

School organization will change

Schools are complex systems. Therefore when one part of schooling changes, such as learning, it has a real implication for the other components of schooling. When schools implement the 4Cs they realize it is not simply a matter of changing pedagogy. This approach changes the way schools are run and organized.

For instance one school changed from compartmentalizing subjects into 50-minute blocks to having whole-day interdisciplinary learning sessions that integrated several knowledge domains including numeracy, geography, drama, commerce and science under the learning theme: navigating. This has implications for the way schools timetable and arrange students, organize teaching staff and manage different learner abilities. Paradoxically teaching in a large team allows learning to become differentiated as some teachers in that team focus on those who need support while others can focus on those who need extension.

Integrating partnerships in a meaningful and effective way is also a challenge to the school organization. It is reasonably simple to create ad hoc connections with the community but designing partnerships authentically into the lives of schools (in the way we are suggesting) requires strategy, energy and a willingness to rethink school structures. Arranging the resources and support to bring in and manage partnerships (whether they are delivered through technology or in person) will have organizational and staffing implications for schools. Many educational organizations have teaching staff devoted to creating and fostering these partnerships so that they are meaningful and connected in a deep and enduring way to the learning and culture of that school.

Leadership in schools will change

We have already devoted Chapter 9 to the issues related to leading transformation. We do, however, want to recognize and discuss the implications for school leaders. Leadership in the 4Cs is intrinsically collaborative. It does not necessarily rely on hierarchies but rather on a system that values mutual respect. We are not arguing here that systems of responsibility or even seniority should be abolished, quite the opposite. It is critical that schools maintain lines of responsibility that are understood and clearly defined so that supportive relationships and structures can be sustained.

As we mentioned earlier, leadership does not rely solely on one individual. Schools need to build leaders of learning at every level of the organization. In our experience leaders do not just hold titles. Leaders understand the need for change and will work with others from across subject areas, year groups and teaching approaches to develop authentically collaborative approaches to learning. Leadership in the 4Cs approach seeks to create structures that make collaborative relationships integral to schools. This kind of leadership also values emergent structures and processes that respond and reflect internal and external challenges. Leadership in the 4Cs is inherently respectful, emergent, collaborative and responsive.

Teaching will change

As we have mentioned earlier the role of the teacher changes from individual transmitter of knowledge to become a collaborative designer, learner, facilitator, responder and deliverer of deep and connected learning. Rather than individual teachers locked away in their classrooms, this approach to learning is more likely to see teachers working in multidisciplinary and transdisciplinary teams. This has implications for the way teachers work together in terms of timetabling, subject disciplines taught, planning and working spaces (staff rooms) and for staff supervision. Working in traditional ways as the transmitter of knowledge, at least superficially, always seems more straightforward than teamwork. Unfortunately this way of working has serious limitations that have limited schools exploring flexible and more effective approaches to learning. Team approaches to learning and teaching take more time in the design and critical reflection phases and are more complex to deliver. They do, however, create a learning culture that reflects more closely creativity, critical reflection, communication and collaboration.

Schools will also need to develop professional learning that supports teachers as they transition from their traditional teaching roles to the 4Cs. The professional learning required is in some ways reasonably straightforward and logical. If teachers are teaching the 4Cs they will need to build capacities in creativity, critical reflection, collaboration and communication. While many teachers may feel they already have these skills we have found (as we begin working with schools in the 4Cs) that in some cases teachers need more support than students in developing these capacities. This stands to reason. If you have been teaching in your own classroom for several decades this 'change in gear' will not necessarily come naturally or easily. In fact all teachers have experienced 'old ways' of teaching all their lives (because everyone goes to school). Transforming practice is always challenging. It is critical, however, that teachers and school leaders demonstrate as well as articulate transformation by reflecting the 4Cs in their teaching and non-teaching roles.

These approaches will also mean that the old demarcations between teaching and welfare must change. 4C learning is likely to uncover students who are vulnerable and at risk. In these circumstances all teachers have the responsibility for welfare, not just 'head teacher welfare', 'dean of students' or the 'year coordinator' (who have traditionally been responsible for welfare in schools). Currently students deemed to be 'at risk' are referred elsewhere in many schools. The reality is, however, that all teachers have always a responsibility for the wellbeing of their students. This approach simply formalizes that responsibility so that when teachers notice issues with students they can take those issues to the whole team and create an appropriate series of supports for those students.

This has implications for teacher preparation. Teaching the 4Cs will mean that initial teacher education will need to focus in a more concentrated way on developing skills of collaborative and multidisciplinary teaching. While the 4Cs have featured in some teacher education courses over the years they have not been integrated effectively into initial teacher education or in postgraduate professional learning (Masters courses). Teacher education must respond to the challenge of twenty-first-century learning and incorporate the 4Cs into its practices if it is to remain relevant to schools and ultimately to our community.

Learning *must* change

As Stephen Heppell (2011, p. 41) argued at the opening of this chapter, schools have become disconnected with the learning needs of the twenty-first century. While learning in the popular media remains as strong as it ever has been, learning in schools looks distinctly 'last century'. The blueprint for learning contained in the 4Cs provides schools with a set of explicit and coherent frameworks that can be employed to make learning more authentic, relevant and engaging for students. This is not an easy transition for schools, school leaders and teachers to make. The simple truth is, however, that we have no choice. Our communities are changing rapidly in response to the realities of the twenty-first century and schools need to change to meet those challenges.

Beyond the macro level of politics, schools and schooling systems, there are millions of micro stories (students) who are the most compelling reasons for change: to give them the opportunity to participate in learning that is relevant and engages with the future that will be their reality. We have seen evidence of transformative change in schools who engage with the 4Cs. These schools demonstrate growth in empowerment for staff, students and school leaders. For students and teachers, the 4Cs authentically open up human potential through confidence in their diverse capabilities (not just narrow capabilities judged thorough a high stakes test).

To meet this challenge schools need to move beyond a tendency towards conformity and engage an approach that frees learning. Liberation theologian Richard Shaull, in his foreword to Paulo Freire's classic book, *Pedagogy of the Oppressed*, also explored this tension between freedom and conformity:

> There is no such thing as a neutral educational process. Education either functions as an instrument which is used to facilitate the integration of the younger generation into the logic of the present system and bring about conformity to it, or it becomes 'the practice of freedom', the means by which men and women deal critically and creatively with reality and discover how to participate in the transformation of their world. (p. 14)

What was true for Richard Shaull and Paulo Freire in 1970 is perhaps more persuasive now, almost 50 years later. If schools are going to deliver access and equity to the most vulnerable and marginalized in our community they need to transform and reorient themselves to deliver quality, relevant education for all. The 'practice of freedom' can only be achieved by our schools when we leave behind the sometimes comfortable traditions that suited another age and reset our institutions to meet the needs of today's young people. For those that care about equity this is non-negotiable. It will not be those who have access to social capital and power that are defeated by the changes to come in the mid to late twenty-first century. It will be those who are left with an out-dated and outmoded education system.

Our argument throughout this book has been that communities and societies matter and they don't just happen by accident. Schools are a critical model and site of social learning so young people can understand and engage with the skills and understandings required to build community. Jonothan Neelands calls this process pro-social learning. He argues: "young people are beginning to model the conditions for a future society based in the necessity of learning how to live with the grave importance of our interdependence as humans" (Neelands, 2009a, p. 176). The 4Cs approach puts the pro-social at the centre of the schooling experience so that our interdependence can be successful, not only in schools but in our communities and society generally.

While it may seem like an overreach to suggest that the future of schools is tied to the future of global wellbeing, there are challenges we face now that we may have faced before but not at the rate of intensity we are currently experiencing. So the changes and the blueprints that we have outlined here matter on the macro level for our community and our 'global village' but they also matter because each child in each school has a right to an education that has been designed to meet their needs now and into the future. We, as educators, can choose to meet those needs with energy, enthusiasm, determination and creativity. The alternative, which is the breakdown of schools, will be our inheritance if we do not act now. We need to transform learning to make schools creative, critically reflective, communicative and collaborative places.

Appendix: Assessment continuums for the 4C capabilities

CREATIVITY continuum				
Awakening	**Applying**	**Accelerating**	**Advanced**	**Adept**
Attempts to engage with familiar ideas but has difficulties perceiving, reflecting and imagining the possibility of new ideas. Is unsure of the capacity and challenges of creative practice.	Attempts to reflect on and imagine possibilities, but has difficulty exploring iteratively and laterally a number of ideas, and then selecting and refining the best new idea. Shows an awareness of the capacity and challenges of creative practice.	Shows discipline and flexibility in iteratively and laterally reflecting on, playing with and developing new ideas, and attempts to select and refine the best idea for a particular purpose. Is developing reflective and active processes in creative practice.	Is playful, resilient and persistent when exploring, developing and refining possibilities, and uses critically reflective, collaborative and communication processes to discern and evaluate the best ideas and their purpose. Is critically reflective and active in realizing the capacity, challenges and ethical understandings of creative practice.	Embraces ambiguity and uncertainty to explore the unexpected and unknown, and generates interest and excitement by making new connections and challenging ideas using critically reflective, collaborative and communication processes. Is insightful using critical reflection, ethical reasoning and action to realize the capacity and challenges of creative practice.

CRITICAL REFLECTION continuum

Awakening	Applying	Accelerating	Advanced	Adept
Attempts to identify problems but has difficulty framing and responding to questions that develop thinking processes to find solutions and take action.

Is unsure of the capacity and challenges of critical reflective practice. | Attempts to frame and respond to questions that address identified problems, but has difficulty recognizing assumptions or acting to manage and re-solve problems.

Shows an awareness of the capacity and challenges of critical reflective practice. | Recognizes assumptions to frame questions and attempts to manage and re-solve problems by contesting and elaborating ideas to make reasoned judgements and decisions to take action.

Is developing reflective and active processes in critical reflective practice. | Reassesses judgements, decisions and actions by contesting and adapting ideas to manage and re-solve problems, and attempts to interrogate the influence of assumptions and power in thinking and acting.

Is critically reflective and active in realizing the capacity, challenges and ethical understandings of critical reflective practice. | Frames critical questions to explore own and others' judgements, decisions and actions and continues to manage and re-solve problems through reasoning, reassessment and imagining how assumptions and power can be transformed.

Is insightful using critical reflection, ethical reasoning and action to realize the capacity and challenges of critical reflective practice. |

COMMUNICATION continuum

Awakening	Applying	Accelerating	Advanced	Adept
Attempts to engage with or craft a message but has difficulty being aware of controlling mediums used for making and expressing meaning.

Is unsure of the capacity and challenges of communication practice. | Engages with or crafts messages with intent of purpose for an audience but has difficulties making and conveying precise meaning through the control of mediums.

Shows an awareness of the capacity and challenges of communication practice. | Enables and crafts messages to convey purpose and attempts to choose and control mediums that engage and connect with an audience with greater precision of meaning.

Is developing reflective and active processes in collaborative practice. | Interacts with and enables more sophisticated crafting of messages by choosing and manipulating mediums to create active and connected meaning for an audience.

Is critically reflective and active in realizing the capacity, challenges and ethical understandings of communication practice. | Interacts with and generates crafted and complex messages through the manipulation of mediums to create dynamic meaning, action and agency for participants.

Is insightful using critical reflection, ethical reasoning and action to realize the capacity and challenges of communication practice. |

Messages can be communicated through mediums that are oral, aural, written, read, visual, verbal, non-verbal, spatial, sensory, affective, symbolic, multimodal, technology.

COLLABORATION continuum				
Awakening	Applying	Accelerating	Advanced	Adept
Attempts to communicate with others, but has difficulty negotiating and taking responsibility for a shared understanding of a group's joint purpose. Is unsure of the capacity and challenges of collaborative practice.	Engages with others and attempts to negotiate a shared understanding of the group's goals, but has difficulties taking responsibility and influencing the outcome of the joint venture. Shows an awareness of the capacity and challenges of collaborative practice.	Is committed to reflecting on and influencing the outcome of the group's joint purpose, but needs to support the group's direction by challenging and evaluating to deepen the outcomes. Is developing reflective and active processes in collaborative practice.	Contributes to challenging and evaluating the group's free-flowing ideas leading to productive outcomes, but possibilities could be explored further by extending ideas and connections in the group's shared endeavour. Is critically reflective and active in realizing the capacity, challenges and ethical understandings of collaborative practice.	Is highly motivated in fostering and opening up possibilities, and allows ideas to emerge and take form into action that is co-constructed and leads to further connections and agency through the group's shared endeavour. Is insightful using critical reflection, ethical reasoning and action to realize the capacity and challenges of collaborative practice.

References

Abbott, S. (2014). 'Simon McBurney's ambitious pursuit of the pure maths play'. *Interdisciplinary Science Reviews, 39*(3), 224–237.

Abramović, M. (2012). *The Abramović method.* Italy: 24 Ore Cultura.

Alexander, C., Freedman, N. & Gould, V. (2007). A *Disappearing Number* resource pack. http://www.complicite.org

Almlund, M., Duckworth, A. L., Heckman, J. J. & Kautz, T. (2011). 'Personality psychology and economics'. In E. A. Hanushek, S. Machin & L. Wößmann (Eds), *Handbook of the economics of education.* Amsterdam: Elsevier (pp. 1–181).

Anderson, M. (2012). *MasterClass in drama education: Transforming teaching and learning.* London: Continuum.

Anderson, M. (2015). 'Drama, creativity and learning'. In S. Schonmann (Ed.), *International yearbook for research in arts education 2015: The wisdom of the many – key issues in arts education.* Munster: Waxmann (pp. 235–240).

Anderson, M. & Dunn, J. (Eds) (2013). *How drama activates learning. Contemporary research and practice.* London: Bloomsbury.

Anderson, M. & Freebody, K. (2014). *Partnerships in education research: Creating knowledge that matters.* New York: Bloomsbury Academic.

Anderson, M. & Jefferson, M. (2009). *Teaching the screen: Film education for Generation Next.* Sydney: Allen and Unwin.

Anderson, M., Hughes, J. & Manuel, J. (2008). *Drama and English teaching: Imagination, action and engagement.* Melbourne: Oxford University Press.

Anyon, J. (2011). *Marx and education.* New York and London: Routledge.

Barnett, W. S. (2000). 'Economics of early childhood intervention'. *Handbook of Early Childhood Intervention, 2,* 589–610.

Bellanca, J. A. (2015). 'Advancing a new agenda'. In J. Bellanca (Ed.), *Deeper learning: Beyond 21st century skills.* Bloomington, IN: Solution Tree Press (pp. 1–18).

Black, P. & Dylan, W. (2010). ' *"Kappan Classic":* Inside the Black Box – Raising standards through classroom assessment'. *Phi Delta Kappan, 92*(1), 81–90.

Black, P., Harrison, C., Lee, C., B. & Wiliam, D. (2004). 'Working inside the black box: Assessment for learning in the classroom'. *Phi Delta Kappan, 86*(1), 9–21.

Blacker, D. J. (2013). *The falling rate of learning and the neoliberal endgame.* Hants, UK: Zero Books.

Blackwell, L., Trzesniewski, K. & Dweck, C. (2007). 'Implicit theories of intelligence predict achievement across an adolescent transition: A longitudinal study and an intervention'. *Child Development, 78*(1), 246–263.

Blum, R. W. & Libbey, H. P. (2004). 'Executive summary' in *Journal of School Health, 74*(7), 231.

Boal, A. (1979/2000). *Theatre of the oppressed.* London: Pluto Press.

Bottrell, D. (2015). 'Schools and communities fit for purpose'. In H. Proctor, P. Brownlee & P. Freebody (Eds), *Controversies in education: Orthodoxy and heresy in policy and practice.* New York: Springer (pp. 27–38).

Bottrell, D. & Goodwin, S. (2011). 'Schools, communities and the achievement turn: The neoliberalisation of equity'. In D. Bottrell & S. Goodwin (Eds), *Schools, communities and social inclusion.* Melbourne: Palgrave Macmillan (pp. 22–37).

Boyce, C. J., Wood, A. M. & Powdthavee, N. (2012). 'Is personality fixed? Personality changes as much as "variable" economic factors and more strongly predicts changes to life satisfaction'. *Social Indicators Research*, *111*, 287–305.

Brookfield, S. (2016). 'So what exactly is critical about critical reflection?' In J. Fook, V. Collington, F. Ross, G. Ruch & L. West, *Researching critical reflection: Multidisciplinary perspectives*. London and New York: Routledge (pp. 11–22).

Bruner, J. S. (1960). *The process of education*. Cambridge, MA: Harvard University Press.

Bruner, J. (1975). 'From communication to language: A psychological perspective'. *Cognition*, *3*, 255–287.

Bruner, J. S. (1985). 'Vygotsky: A historical and conceptual perspective'. In J. Wertsch (Ed.), *Culture, communication, and cognition: Vygotskian perspectives*. Cambridge: Cambridge University Press (pp. 21–34).

Bryan, C. (2004). 'Assessing the creative work of groups'. In D. Miell & K. Littleton (Eds), *Collaborative creativity: Contemporary perspectives*. London: Free Association Books (pp. 52–64).

Cameron, C. & Moss, P. (Eds) (2011). *Social pedagogy and working with children and young people: Where care and education meet*. London: Jessica Kingsley.

Campos, M. N. (2007). 'Ecology of meanings: A critical constructivist communication model'. *Communication Theory*, *17*, 386–410.

Campos, M. (2009). 'Critical constructivism'. In S. Littlejohn & K. Foss, *Encyclopedia of communication theory*. London: Sage.

Caux, P. & Gilbert, B. (2007). *Ex Machina: From page to stage*. Trans by N. Kroetsch (2009). Vancouver: Talon Books.

Centre for Economic Development Australia (CEDA). (2015). *Australia's future workforce?* Melbourne: CEDA.

Christakis, D., Gilkerson, J., Richards, J., Zimmerman, F., Garrison, M., Xu, D., Gray, S. & Yapanel, U. (2009). 'Audible television and decreased adult words, infant vocalizations, and conversational turns: A population-based study'. *Archives of Pediatrics and Adolescent Medicine*, *163*(6), 554–568.

Churchill, R., Ferguson, P., Godhino, S., Johnson, N., Keddie, A., Letts, W., Lowe, K., Mackay. J., McGill, M., Moss, J., Nagel, M. & Shaw, K. (2016). *Teaching: Making a difference* (3rd ed). Australia: Wiley.

Cohen, L., Manion, L. & Morrison, K. (2000). *Research methods in education*. London: Routledge Falmer Press.

Copland, M. A. (2001). 'The myth of the superprincipal'. *Phi Delta Kappan*, *82*(7), 528.

Craft, A. (2000). *Creativity across the primary curriculum*, London: Routledge.

Craft, A. (2002). *Creativity and early years education*. London: Continuum.

Csikszentmihalyi, M. (1996). *Creativity: Flow and the psychology of discovery and invention*. New York: Harper Collins.

Dance, F. (Ed.) (1982). *Human communication theory: Comparative essays*. New York: Harper & Row (pp. 120–146).

Dance, F. & Larson, C. (1972). *Speech communication concepts and behaviours*. New York: Holt, Rinehart and Winston.

Dannels, D. (2010). 'Communication across the curriculum problematics and possibilities: Standing at the forefront of educational reform'. In D. L. Fassett (Ed.), *The SAGE handbook of communication and instruction*. London: Sage (pp. 55–79).

Darling-Hammond, L. (2004). 'Standards, accountability, and school reform'. *Teachers College Record*, *106*(6), 1047–1085.

Day, C. (2004). *A passion for teaching*. London and New York: Routledge.

Day, C., Sammons, P., Leithwood, K., Hopkins, D., Harris, A., Gu, Q. & Brown, E. (2010). *Ten strong claims about successful school leadership*. Nottingham, UK: The National College for School Leadership.

Deal, T. E. & Peterson, K. D. (1999). *Shaping school culture: The heart of leadership*. San Francisco, CA: Jossey-Bass.

Denzin, N. K. & Giardina, M. D. (2008). *Qualitative inquiry and the politics of evidence*. Walnut Creek, CA: Left Coast Press.

Denzin, N. K. & Lincoln, Y. S. (2005). *The SAGE handbook of qualitative research*. Thousand Oaks: Sage Publications.

Dewey, J. (1932/1985). Ethics. In J. A. Boydston (Ed.), *John Dewey: The later works, vol 7*. Carbondale, IL: Southern Illinois University Press.

Dickinson, E. (1924). *The complete poems of Emily Dickinson*. Boston, MA: Little Brown.

Donato, R. (2004). 'Aspects of collaboration in pedagogical discourse'. *Annual Review of Applied Linguistics*, *24*, 283–302.

Drake, S. M. (2012). *Creating standards-based integrated curriculum: The common core state standards edition* (3rd ed). Thousand Oaks, CA: Corwin.

Drake, S. M. & Burns, R. C. (2004). *Meeting standards through integrated curriculum*. Alexandria, VA: Association for Supervision and Curriculum Development.

Drucker, P. F. (1993). *Post-Capitalist society*. New York: Harper Business.

Durlak, J. A., Dymnicki, A. B., Taylor, R. D., Weissberg, R. P. & Schellinger, K. B. (2011). 'The impact of enhancing students' social and emotional learning: A meta-analysis of school-based universal interventions'. *Child Development*, *82*(1), 405–432.

Dweck, C. (2000). *Self-theories: Their role in motivation, personality, and development*. Philadelphia, PA: Psychology Press.

Dweck, C. S. & Leggett, E. L. (1988). 'A social cognitive approach to motivation and personality'. *Psychological Review*, *95*(2), 256–273.

Dweck, C. S. & Master, A. (2009). 'Self-theories and beliefs about intelligence'. In K. R. Wentzel & A. Wigfield (Eds), *Handbook of motivation at school*. New York: Routledge (pp. 123–140).

The Economist. (2015). 'More talk, more action'. Ben Bernanke, page 37 of *The Economist*: 17 October 2015.

Eisenhower Study Group. (2011). *The costs of war since 2001: Iraq, Afghanistan, and Pakistan*. Providence, RI: Watson Institute, Brown University.

Elmore, R. (1996). 'Getting to scale with good educational practice'. *Harvard Educational Review*, *66*(1), 1–27.

Ewing, R. (2015). 'Dramatic play and process drama: Towards a collective zone of proximal development to enhance language and literacy'. In S. Davis, H. G. Clemson, B. Ferholt, S-M. Jansson & A. Marjanovic-Shane (Eds), *Dramatic interactions in education: Vygotskian and sociocultural approaches to drama, education and research*. New York: Bloomsbury Academic (pp. 135–152).

Fassett, D. & Warren, J. (2007). *Critical communication pedagogy*. London: Sage.

Fiorella, L. & Mayer, R. E. (2015). *Learning as a generative activity: Eight learning strategies that promote understanding*. New York: Cambridge University Press.

Fischer, G. (2005, April). 'Distances and diversity: sources for social creativity'. In *Proceedings of the 5th conference on Creativity & Cognition* (pp. 128–136). ACM.

Fleming, J., Gibson, R., Anderson, M., Martin, A. & Sudmalis, D. (2015). 'Cultivating imaginative thinking: Teacher strategies used in high-performing arts education classrooms'. *Cambridge Journal of Education*. Online first.

Fook, J. (2012). *Social work: A critical approach to practice*. London: Sage.

Fook, J. & Gardner, F. (2007). *Practising critical reflection: A resource handbook*. London: McGraw-Hill.

Fook, J., Psoinos, M. & Sartori, D. (2015). 'Evaluation studies of critical reflection'. In J. Fook, V. Collington, F. Ross G. Ruch & L. West (Eds), *Researching critical reflection: Multidisciplinary perspectives*. London and New York: Routledge (pp. 90–104).

Fook, J., White, S. & Gardner, F. (2006). 'Critical reflection: A review of contemporary literature and understandings'. In *Critical reflection in health and social care*. Maidenhead: Open University Press (pp. 3–20).

Freebody, P. (2003). *Qualitative research in education: Interaction and practice*. London: Sage.

Freebody, P. (2015). *Critique, schooling and education: A literacy researcher's perspective*. Plenary address, Critical Studies in Applied Theatre Unit, Annual International Conference, Auckland, New Zealand, October 2015.

Freire, P. (1970/2006). *Pedagogy of the oppressed (30th anniversary ed)*. New York: Bloomsbury Academic.

Freire, P. (1979). *Pedagogy of the oppressed*. New York: Continuum.

Freire, P. (1994). *Pedagogy of hope: Reliving pedagogy of the oppressed*. New York: Continuum.

Freire, P. (1998). *Pedagogy of freedom: Ethics, democracy, and civic courage*. New York: Rowman & Littlefield.

Freire, P. (2000). *Pedagogy of the oppressed*. London: Bloomsbury.

Freshwater, H. (2001). 'The ethics of indeterminacy: Theatre de Complicite's "Mnemonic"'. *New Theatre Quarterly, 17*, 212–218.

Frey, C. & Osborne, M. (2013a). 'The future of employment: How susceptible are jobs to computerisation?' Retrieved from http://www.oxfordmartin.ox.ac.uk/downloads/academic/The_Future_of_Employment.pdf (Date accessed 20 September 2015).

Frey, C. & Osborne, M. (2013b). 'Improving technology now means that nearly 50 percent of occupations in the US are under threat of computerisation'. *LSE American Politics and Policy (USAPP) blog*. Retrieved from http://blogs.lse.ac.uk/usappblog/2013/09/30/computerisation-50-percent-occupations-threatened (Date accessed 20 September 2015).

Fullan, M. (2014). *Leading in a culture of change: Personal action guide and workbook*. San Francisco, CA: Jossey-Bass.

Fullan, M. & Langworthy, M. (2014). *A rich seam: How new pedagogies find deep learning*. London: Pearson.

Furlong, A. (2009). Foreword in Wyn, J., *Touching the future: Building skills for life and work*. Victoria: ACER Press.

Gardner, H. (1983). *Frames of mind: The theory of multiple intelligences*. New York: Basic Books.

Gardner, H. (1999). *Intelligence reframed: Multiple intelligences for the 21st century*. New York: Basic Books.

Gardner, H. (2007). *Five minds for the future*. Boston, MA: Harvard Business School Press.

Gardner, J. (Ed.) (2006). *Assessment and learning*. London: Sage.

Gee, J. P. (2013). *The anti-education era: Creating smarter students through digital learning*. New York: Palgrave.

Ghaye, T. (2010). 'In what ways can reflective practices enhance human flourishing?' *Reflective Practice, 11*(1), 1–7.

Gibbs, R. (2005). *Embodiment and cognitive science*. Cambridge: Cambridge University Press.

Giroux, H. (2003). 'Critical theory and educational practice'. In A. Darder, M. Baltodano & R. Torres (Eds), *The critical pedagogy reader*. London and New York: Routledge (pp. 27–56).

Giroux, H. (2007). 'Introduction: Democracy, education and the politics of critical pedagogy'. In P. McLaren & J. Kincheloe (Eds), *Critical pedagogy: Where are we now?* New York: Peter Lang (pp. 1–5).

Giroux, H. (2011). *On critical pedagogy*. New York: Continuum.

Giroux, H. (2013). *America's education deficit and the war on youth*. New York: Monthly Review Press.

Glăveanu, V. P. (2011). 'How are we creative together? Comparing sociocognitive and sociocultural answers'. *Theory & Psychology, 21*(4), 473–492.

Glenberg, A. M. (2008). 'Embodiment for education'. In P. Calvo & T. Gomila (Eds), *Handbook of cognitive science: An embodied approach*. San Diego, CA: Elsevier (pp. 355–372).

Goggin, G. (2006). *Cell phone culture: Mobile technology in everyday life*. London: Routledge.

Golbeck, S. L. & El-Moslimany, H. (2013). 'Developmental approaches to collaborative learning'. In C. E. Hmelo-Silver, A. Chinn, C. K. K. Chan & A. M. O'Donnel (Eds), *The international handbook of collaborative learning*. New York and London: Routledge (pp. 41–56).

Goldstein, D. (2014). *The teacher wars: A history of America's most embattled profession*. New York: Anchor.

Goodman, J. & Teel, J. (1998). 'The passion of the possible: Maxine Greene, democratic community, and education'. In W. F. Pinar (Ed.), *The passionate mind of Maxine Greene: "I am. . . not yet"*. London and New York: Taylor & Francis (pp. 60–75).

Gordon, M. (2015). 'Patrick Dodson's heartfelt plea to Tony Abbott: Change course on indigenous policy before it's too late'. *Sydney Morning Herald*. Retrieved 4 May 2016 from http://www.smh.com.au/federal-politics/political-news

Greene, M. (1993). 'The passions of pluralism, multiculturalism and the expanding community'. *Educational Researcher, 22*(1), 13–18.

Greene, M. (1995). *Releasing the imagination: Essays on education, the arts and social change*. San Francisco, CA: Jossey-Bass.

Greene, M. (2001). *Variations on a blue guitar: The Lincoln Center Institute lectures on aesthetic education*. Williston: Teachers College Press.

Greene, M. (2012). 'Imagination, inquiry, and innovation'. Conference at College of New Rochelle.

Guggenheim, D. (2006). *An inconvenient truth: A global warning* [DVD]. Hollywood: Paramount.

Habermas, J. (1978). *Knowledge and human interests* (2nd ed). London: Heinemann.

Hallinger, P. (2011). 'Leadership for learning: Lessons from 40 years of empirical research'. *Journal of Educational Administration, 49*(2), 125–142.

Hardy, G. H. (1940/2005). *A mathematician's apology*. University of Alberta Mathematical Sciences Society: Hargreaves.

Hargreaves, A. (2003). *Teaching in the knowledge society: Education in the age of insecurity*. Williston: Teachers College Press.

Harris, A. (2017). *Creativity and Education*. London: Palgrave.

Hattie, J. & Gin, M. (2011). 'Instruction based on feedback'. In R.E. Mayer & P.A. Alexander (Eds), *Handbook of research on learning and instruction*. New York: Routledge (pp. 249–271).

Hatton, N. & Smith, D. (1995). *Reflection in teacher education: Towards definition and implementation*. The University of Sydney: School of Teaching and Curriculum Studies.

Hayes, D. (2017). 'Teachers' work in high-poverty contexts: Curating repertoires of pedagogical practice'. In J. Lampert & B. Burnett (Eds), *Teacher education for high poverty schools*. New York: Springer (pp. 211–222).

Hecht, M. (2009). 'Communication theory of identity'. In S. Littlejohn & K. Foss (Eds), *Encyclopedia of communication theory*. Los Angeles, CA: Sage (pp. 139–141).

Hecht, M. L., Warren, J., Jung, J. & Krieger, J. (2004). 'Communication theory of identity'. In W. B. Gudykunst (Ed.), *Theorizing about intercultural communication*. Newbury Park, CA: Sage (pp. 257–278).

Heppell, S. (2011). 'A new renaissance in learning'. In J. Holden, J. Kieffer & S. Wright (Eds), *Creativity, money, love: Learning for the 21st century*. London: Creative and Cultural Skills (pp. 44–56).

Holmes, D. (2005). *Communication theory: Media, technology and society*. London: Sage.

hooks, b. (1995). *Art on my mind: Visual politics*. New York: New Press.

hooks, b. (2003). *Teaching community: A pedagogy of hope*. London: Routledge.

Hughes, T. (1970). *Amulet*. In R. McGough (Ed.), *100 best poems for children*. London: Puffin Poetry.

Ihde, D. (1995). *Postphenomenology: Essays in the postmodern context*. Evanston, IL: Northwestern University Press.

Illeris, K. (2009). *Contemporary theories of learning: Learning theorists . . . in their own words*. London: Routledge.

Isaksen, S. G., Lauer, K. J. & Ekvall, G. (1999). 'Situational outlook questionnaire: A measure of the climate for creativity and change'. *Psychological Reports*, *85*(2), 665–674.

Janis, I. (1972). *Victims of group think: A psychological study of foreign-policy decisions and fiascos*. Boston, MA: Houghton Mifflin.

Jefferson, M. (2015). 'The power of drama pedagogy and research to open doors: Dwelling in the house of possibility'. In M. Anderson & C. Roche (Eds), *The state of the art: Teaching drama in the 21st century*. Sydney: Sydney University Press (pp. 1–23).

Jeffrey, B. & Craft, A. (2001). 'The universalization of creativity'. In A. Craft, B. Jeffrey & M. Leibling (Eds), *Creativity in education*. London: Continuum (pp. 17–34).

John-Steiner, V. (2000). *Creative collaboration*. New York: Oxford University Press.

Kasckak, M. P, Jones, J. L, Carnanza, J. & Foz, M. R (2014). 'Embodiment and language comprehension'. In L. Sharpiro (Ed.), *The Routledge handbook of embodied cognition*. London and New York: Routledge (pp. 118–126).

Keating, J. (2009). *A new federalism in Australian education: A proposal for a National Reform Agenda at a glance*. Education Foundation.

Kekes, J. (1995). *Moral wisdom and good lives*. New York and London: Cornell University Press.

Kettley, N. (2010). *Theory building in educational research*. London: Bloomsbury.

Kincheloe, J. (2007). 'Critical pedagogy in the twenty-first century: Evolution for survival'. In P. McLaren & J. Kincheloe (Eds), *Critical pedagogy: Where are we now?* New York: Peter Lang (pp. 147–183).

King, A. (1993). 'From sage on the stage to guide on the side'. *College Teaching*, *41*(1), 30–35.

Klenowski, V. & Wyatt-Smith, C. (2012). 'The impact of high stakes testing: The Australian story'. *Assessment in Education: Principles, Policy & Practice*, *19*(1), 65–79.

Koopman, M., Den Brok, P., Beijaard, D. & Teune, P. (2011). 'Learning processes of students in pre-vocational secondary education: Relations between goal orientations, information processing strategies and development of conceptual knowledge'. *Learning and Individual Differences*, *21*(4), 426–431.

Kristeva, J. (1980). *Desire in language: A semiotic approach to literature and art*. Oxford: Blackwell.

Langer, E. (1997). *The power of mindful learning*. Cambridge, MA: Perseus Books.

Lave, J. & Wenger, E. (1991). *Situated learning: Legitimate peripheral participation*. Cambridge: Cambridge University Press.

Leach, J. & Moon, B. (2007). *The power of pedagogy*. London: Sage.

Leeds-Hurwitz, W. (1993). *Semiotics and communication: Signs, codes, cultures*. Hillsdale, NJ: Lawrence Erlbaum.

Leeds-Hurwitz, W. (2009). 'Semiotics and semiology'. In S. Littlejohn & K. Foss (Eds), *Encyclopedia of Communication Theory* (vol 2). Thousand Oaks, CA: Sage (pp. 874–876).

Levi-Strauss, C. (1962/1966). *The savage mind*. Trans from French by George Weidenfield & Nicholson. Chicago, IL: University of Chicago Press.

Lieberman, P. (1991). *Uniquely human: The evolution of speech, thought, and selfless behaviour*. Cambridge, MA: Harvard University Press.

LIGO Hanford Press. (2016). *Gravitational waves detected 100 years after Einstein's prediction*. Retrieved 5 March 2016 from https://www.ligo.caltech.edu/system/media_files/binaries/310/original/LHONewsRelease-11Feb16-Final.pdf?1455201669

Lombardi, M. (2007). *Authentic learning for the 21st century: An overview*. Retrieved 25 February 2016 from https://net.educause.edu/ir/library/pdf/eli3009.pdf

Mahn, H. & John-Steiner, V. (2002). 'The gift of confidence. A Vygotskian view of emotions'. In G. Wells & G. Claxton (Eds), *Learning for life in the 21st century: Sociocultural perspectives on the future of education*. Cambridge, MA: Blackwell (pp. 46–58).

Manjoo, F. (2011). *True enough: Learning to live in a post-fact society*. Hoboken, NJ: John Wiley & Sons.

Marshall, B. K. & Picou, J. S. (2008). 'Post-normal science, precautionary principle and worst cases: The challenge of twenty-first century catastrophes'. *Sociological Inquiry*, *78*, 230–247.

Martin, A. J. (2009). 'Motivation and engagement across the academic life span: A developmental construct validity study of elementary school, high school, and university/ college students'. *Educational and psychological measurement*, *69*(5), 794–824.

Martin, A., Anderson, M., Gibson, R., Sudmalis, D., Liem, G., Fleming, J., Mansour, M. & Munday, C. (2013). *The role of arts education in academic motivation, engagement and achievement*. Report to the Australia Council for the Arts.

Mayer, R. E. (2004). 'Should there be a three-strikes rule against pure discovery learning? The case for guided methods of instruction'. *American Psychologist*, *59*, 14–19.

Mayer, R. E. (2010). *Applying the science of learning*. Upper Saddle River, NJ: Pearson.

McBurney, S. (2008). *A disappearing number*. London: Oberon Books.

McBurney, S. (2012). *A disappearing number resource pack*. London: Oberon Books.

McLaren, P. (2015). *Life in schools: An introduction to critical pedagogy in the foundations of education*. New York: Paradigm.

McNeal, Jr, R. B. (2014). 'Parent involvement, academic achievement and the role of student attitudes and behaviors as mediators'. *Universal Journal of Educational Research*, *2*(8), 564–576.

Meier, B., Schnall, S., Schwarz, N. & Bargh, J. A. (2012). 'Embodiment in social psychology'. *Topics in Cognitive Science*, *4*, 705–716.

Mezirow, J. (1990). 'How critical reflection triggers transformative learning'. In J. Mezirow (Ed.), *Fostering critical reflection in adulthood*. San Francisco, CA: Jossey-Bass (pp. 1–20).

Mezirow, J. (1997). *Transformative learning: Theory to practice*. San Francisco, CA: John Wiley and Sons.

Mezirow, J. (2009). *Transformative learning in practice: Insights from community, workplace and education*. San Francisco, CA: Jossey-Bass.

Mintzberg, H. (2005). *What do we mean by "Critical?"*. An oral presentation at the Academy of Management Meeting: Hawaii.

Moran, S. & John-Steiner, V. (2003). 'Creativity in the making: Vygotsky's contemporary contribution to the dialectic of development and creativity'. In R. K. Sawyer, V. John-Steiner, S. Moran, R. J. Sternberg, D. H. Felman, J. Nakamura et al. (Eds), *Creativity and development*. New York: Oxford University Press (pp. 71–90).

Moran, S. & John-Steiner, V. (2004). 'How collaboration in creative work impacts identity and motivation'. In D. Miell & K. Littleton (Eds), *Collaborative creativity: Contemporary perspectives*. London: Free Association Books (pp. 11–25).

Moreno, R. & Mayer, R. (2007). 'Interactive multimodal learning environments special issue on interactive learning environments: Contemporary issues and trends'. *Educational Psychology Review*, *19*, 309–326.

Morreale, S. P. & Pearson, J. C. (2008). 'Why communication education is important: The centrality of the discipline in the 21st century'. *Communication Education*, *57*(2), 224–240.

NACCCE (National Advisory Committee on Creative and Cultural Education Report). (1999). *All our futures: Creativity, Culture and Education – Sir Ken Robinson*. Australia.

Nakhid, C. (2014). *Twelve thousand hours – Education and poverty in Aotearoa New Zealand* [Book Review].

Narev, I. (2015). In M. Drummond, *Why Commonwealth Bank Chief Ian Narev wants you to stare at blank walls*. AFR Weekend. Retrieved 26 February 2016 from http://www.afr.com/lifestyle/arts-and-entertainment/why-commonwealth-bank-chief-ian-narev-wants-you-to-stare-at-blank-walls-20150626-ghyadr

Neelands, J. (2009). 'Acting together: ensemble as a democratic process in art and life'. *RiDE: The Journal of Applied Theatre and Performance, 14*(2), 173–189.

Nemeth, C. J. & Nemeth-Brown, B. (2003). *Better than individuals? The potential benefits of dissent and diversity for group creativity*. Oxford: Oxford University Press.

Obama, B. H. (2009). 'Inaugural Address: Presidential Inaugural'. Capitol Building, Washington, D.C., 20 January 2009.

O'Toole, J. (2006). *Doing drama research*. Melbourne: Drama Australia.

O'Toole, J. & Stinson, M. (2013). 'Drama, speaking and listening: The treasure of oracy'. In J. Dunn & M. Anderson (Eds), *How drama activates learning – Contemporary research and practice*. London: Bloomsbury (pp. 159–177).

Pashler, H., Cepeda, N. J., Wixted, J. T. & Rohrer, D. (2005). 'When does feedback facilitate learning of words?' *Journal of Experimental Psychology: Learning, Memory, and Cognition, 31*, 3–8.

Paulus, P. (2000). 'Groups, teams, and creativity: The creative potential of idea generating groups'. *Applied Psychology, 49*(2), 237–262.

Paulus, P. B. & Nijstad, B. A. (2003). *Group creativity: Innovation through collaboration*. New York: Oxford University Press.

Pellegrino, J. & Hilton, M. (2012). *Education for life and work: Developing transferable knowledge and skills in the 21st century*. Washington, DC: The National Academies Press.

Pierse, L. (1995). *Theatresports down under: A guide for coaches and players*. Kensington, NSW: Improcorp Australia.

Pintrich, P. R. (2003/2005). 'The role of goal orientation in self and regulated learning'. In M. Boekaerts, M. Zeidner & P. Pintrich (Eds), *Handbook of self-regulation*. Burlington, MA: Elsevier Academic Press (pp. 451–502).

Pintrich, P. (2004). 'A conceptual framework for assessing motivation and self & regulated learning in college students'. *Educational Psychology Review, 16*, 385–407.

Plumer, B. (2013). *Nine facts about terrorism in the United States since 9/11. The Washington Post*. Retrieved from https://www.washingtonpost.com/news/wonk/wp/2013/09/11/nine-facts-about-terrorism-in-the-united-states-since-911/ (Date accessed 20 September 2015).

Podlozny, A. (2000). 'Strengthening verbal skills through the use of classroom drama: A clear link'. *Journal of Aesthetic Education, 34*(3–4), 239–275.

Pulkkinen, L. & Kokko, K. (2000). 'Identity development in adulthood: A longitudinal study'. *Journal of Research in Personality, 34*, 445–470.

Reid, C. (2015). 'Public diversity; private disadvantage: Schooling and ethnicity'. In H. Proctor, P. Brownlee & P. Freebody (Eds), *Controversies in education*. New York: Springer (pp. 91–104).

Rice, C. (2002). 'Interview with Condoleeza Rice; Pataki talks about 9-11; Graham, Shelby discusses War on Terrorism'. *CNN Late Edition with Wolf Blitzer*. Aired 8 September 2002.

Rice, S., Volkoff, V. & Dulfer, N. (2015). 'Teach for/teach first candidates: What conclusions do they draw from their time in teaching?' *Teachers and Teaching, 21*(5), 497–513.

Ringland, G. (2010). 'Frameworks for coping with post-normal times: A response to Ziauddin Sardar'. *Futures, 42*(6), 633–639.

Roberts, B. W., Walton, K. E. & Viechtbauer, W. (2006). 'Patterns of mean-level change in personality traits across the life course: A meta-analysis of longitudinal studies'. *Psychological Bulletin, 132*, 3–27.

Robinson, K. (2001). 'Mind the gap: The creative conundrum'. *Critical Quarterly, 43*(1), 41–45.

Rodgers, C. R. & Scott, K. H. (2008). 'The development of the personal self and professional identity in learning to teach'. In M. Cochran-Smith, S. Feiman-Nemser, D. J. McIntyre & K. E. Demers (Eds), *Handbook of research on teacher education*. New York and London: Routledge (pp. 732–755).

Sahlberg, P. (2014). *Finnish lessons 2.0: What can the world learn from educational change in Finland?* Williston: Teachers College Press.

Salazar, A. J. (2002). 'Self-organizing and complexity perspectives of group creativity: Implications for group communication'. In L. R. Frey (Ed.), *New directions in group communication*. Thousand Oaks, CA: Sage (pp. 179–199).

Salazar, A. (2009). 'Creativity in groups'. In S. Littlejohn & K. Foss (Eds), *Encyclopedia of communication theory*. Los Angeles, CA and London: Sage (pp. 210–213).

Sardar, Z. (2010). 'Welcome to postnormal times'. *Futures*, *42*(5), 435–444.

Sawyer, K. (1997). *Pretend play as improvisation: Conversation in the preschool classroom*. Mahwah, NJ: Lawrence Erlbaum.

Sawyer, K. (2003). *Group creativity: Music, theater, collaboration*. Mahwah, NJ: Lawrence Erlbaum.

Sawyer, K. (2007). *Group genius: The creative power of collaboration*. New York: Basic Books.

Sawyer, K. (2015). 'A call to action: The challenges of creative teaching and learning'. *Teachers College Record*, *117*(10), 1–34.

Sawyer, R. K. (2011). 'What makes good teachers great? The artful balance of structure and improvisation'. In R. K. Sawyer (Ed.), *Structure and improvisation in creative teaching*. Cambridge: Cambridge University Press (pp. 1–24).

Saxton, J. & Miller, C. (2013). 'Drama, creating and imagining: Rendering the world newly strange'. In M. Anderson & J. Dunn (Eds), *How drama activates learning: Contemporary research and practice*. London: Bloomsbury.

Schön, D. A. (1983). *The reflective practitioner: How professionals think in action* (vol. 5126). London: Basic books.

Scorolli, C. (2014). 'Embodiment and language'. In L. Sharpiro (Ed.), *The Routledge handbook of embodied cognition*. London and New York: Routledge (pp. 127–138).

Scriven, M. & Paul, R. (1987). 'Critical thinking as defined by the National Council for Excellence in Critical Thinking'. In *8th Annual International Conference on Critical Thinking and Education Reform, Rohnert Park, CA*.

Sharpiro, L. (2011). *Embodied cognition: New problems of philosophy*. London and New York: Routledge.

Sharpiro, L. (Ed.) (2014). *The Routledge handbook of embodied cognition*. London and New York: Routledge.

Shaull, S., Foreword in Freire, P. (1970). *Pedagogy of the oppressed (MB Ramos, Trans.)*. New York: Continuum.

Shute, V. J. (2008). 'Focus on formative feedback'. *Review of Educational Research*, *78*(1), 153–189.

Slavin, R. E. (2011). 'Instruction based on cooperative learning'. In R. Mayer & P. Alexander (Eds), *Handbook of research on learning and instruction*. London: Routledge (pp. 344–360).

Smith, D. (2013). *An independent report for the Welsh Government into Arts in Education in the Schools of Wales*. Retrieved 5 March 2016 from http://gov.wales/docs/dcells/publications/130920-arts-in-education-en.pdf

Sternberg, R. J. (2003). *Wisdom, intelligence, and creativity, synthesized*. New York: Cambridge University Press.

Stoppard, T. (1967). *Rosencrantz and Guildenstern are dead*. London: Faber and Faber.

Storey, H. & Joubert, M. (2004). 'The emotional dance of creative collaboration'. In D. Miell & K. Littleton (Eds), *Collaborative creativity: Contemporary perspectives*. London: Free Association Books (pp. 40–51).

Swift, J. (1726/2000). *Gulliver's travels*. London: Penguin Classics.

Tan, S. (2001). *The red tree*. Australia: Lothian Books.

Taylor, M. (1986). 'Learning for self-direction in the classroom: The pattern of a transition process'. *Studies in Higher Education, 11*(1), 55–72.

Teese, R. (2006). 'Condemned to innovate'. *Griffith Review, 11*, 113–125. Retrieved 8 February 2016 from https://griffithreview.com/articles/condemned-to-innovate/

Thomson, P. & Hall, C. (2008). 'Opportunities missed and/or thwarted? Funds of knowledge meet the English national curriculum'. *The Curriculum Journal, 19*(2), 87–103.

Thomson, P., Lingard, B. & Wrigley, T. (2012). 'Reimagining school change'. In T. Wrigley, P. Thomson & B. Lingard (Eds), *Changing schools: Alternative ways to make a world of difference*. London: Routledge (pp. 1–14).

Trueman, M. (2013). *Interview: The founders of Complicité*. Retrieved 5 March 2016 from http://www.ft.com/cms/s/2/6afbab60-c14c-11e2-9767-00144feab7de.html

Vance, A. (2015). *Tesla, SpaceX, and the quest for a fantastic future*. South Africa: Ecco.

Victorian Department of Education and Early Childhood Development. (2014). 'Unlocking the potential: A digital learning strategy for Victorian learning and development settings 2014–2017'. Author.

Vygotsky, L. S. (1931/1998). 'Imagination and creativity in the adolescent'. In R. W. Rieber (Ed.), *The collected works of L. S. Vygotsky, vol 5*. New York: Plenum Press (pp. 151–166).

Vygotsky, L. S. (1934/1966) quoted from Hanfmann, A. & Vakar, G. (1966). *Thought and language*. Cambridge, MA: MIT Press.

Vygotsky, L. S. (1960/1997b). *The collected works of L.S. Vygotsky, vol 4* (R.W. Rieber, Ed.). New York: Plenum Press.

Vygotsky, L. S. (1978). *Mind in society: The development of higher psychological processes* (M. Cole, V. John-Steiner, S. Scribner & E. Souberman, Eds). Cambridge, MA: Harvard University Press.

Vygotsky, L. (1983/1997a). 'Interaction between learning and development'. From: *Mind and society*. Cambridge, MA: Harvard University Press. Reprinted in M. Gauvain & M. Cole (Eds), *Readings on the development of children*. New York: Worth Publishers (pp. 79–91).

Vygotsky, L. (1984/1999). *The collected works of L. S. Vygotsky, vol 6* (R. W. Rieber, Ed.). New York: Kluwer Academic/Plenum Publishers (pp. 1–68).

Wagner, B. J. (1998). *Educational drama and language arts: What research shows*. Portsmouth, NH: Heinemann.

Ward, S. (2004). *Baby talk*. London: Arrow Books.

Waring, M. & Evans, C. (2015). *Understanding pedagogy: Developing a critical approach to teaching and learning*. Abingdon, Oxford: Routledge.

Warren, J. (2009). 'Critical communication pedagogy'. In S. Littlejohn & K. Foss (Eds), *Encyclopedia of communication theory*. Los Angeles, CA and London: Sage (pp. 213–216).

Webb, N. M. (2013). 'Information processing approaches to collaborative learning'. In C. Hmelo-Silver, C. Chinn, C. Chan & A. O'Donnell (Eds), *The international handbook of collaborative learning*. New York: Routledge (pp. 19–40).

Wentzel, K. R. & Wigfield, A. (2009). *Handbook of motivation at school*. New York: Taylor & Francis.

Wilde, O. (2007). *The complete works of Oscar Wilde: Volume IV, Criticism: historical criticism, intentions, the soul of man under socialism*, J. M. Guy (Ed.). Oxford: Oxford University Press.

Winkielman, P., Niedenthal, P., Wielgosz, J., Eelen, J. & Kavanagh, L. C. (2015). 'Embodiment of cognition and emotion'. In M. Mikulincer, P. R. Shaver, E. Borgida & J. A. Bargh (Eds), *APA handbook of personality and social psychology, Vol. 1. Attitudes and social cognition*. Washington, DC: APA (pp. 151–175).

Wittrock, M. C. (1974). 'Learning as a generative process'. *Educational Psychologist, 11*, 87–95.

Wood, D. J., Bruner, J. S. & Ross, G. (1976). 'The role of tutoring in problem solving'. *Journal of Child Psychiatry and Psychology*, *17*(2), 89–100.

Wray-Lake, L., Flanagan, C. A. & Osgood, D. W. (2010). 'Examining trends in adolescent environmental attitudes, beliefs, and behaviors across three decades'. *Environment and Behavior*, *42*(1), 61–85.

Wyn, J. (2015). 'Schools not fit for purpose: New approaches for the times'. In H. Proctor, P. Brownlee & P. Freebody (Eds), *Controversies in education: Orthodoxy and heresy in policy and practice*. New York: Springer (pp. 13–26).

Yates, L. (2004). *What does good education research look like? Situating a field and its practices*. London: McGraw-Hill Education.

Yeager, D. & Walton, S. (2011). 'Social-psychological interventions in education: They're not magic'. *Review of Educational Research*, *81*(2), 267–301.

Yingling, J. (2004). *A lifetime of communication: Transformations through relational dialogue*s. Mahwah, NJ: Lawrence Erlbaum.

Yu, C. (2014). 'Linking words to world. An embodiment perspective'. In L. Sharpiro (Ed.), *The Routledge handbook of embodied cognition*. London and New York: Routledge (pp. 139–149).

Zusak, M. (2008). *Interview with Sarah Kinson*. Retrieved 3 March 2016 from http://www.theguardian.com/books/2008/mar/28/whyiwrite

Index